To Suzy & Steve
Love

Users' Guide to

COMPUTER CRIME

Users' Guide to COMPUTER CRIME

Its Commission, Detection & Prevention

Stephen W. Leibholz & Louis D. Wilson

CHILTON BOOK COMPANY
Radnor, Pennsylvania

Published in Radnor, Pa., by Chilton Book Company
and simultaneously in Ontario, Canada
by Thomas Nelson & Sons, Ltd.
Designed by William E. Lickfield
Manufactured in the United States of America

Library of Congress Cataloging in Publication Data

Leibholz, Stephen W.
Users' guide to computer crime.

1. Electronic data processing departments—Security measures. 2. White collar crimes—United States.
I. Wilson, Louis D., joint author. II. Title.
HF5548.2.L393 364.1'62 74-10662
ISBN 0-8019-6095-9

Foreword

FAMILIARITY breeds contempt, but of a special kind. Not the nostril-dilating contempt of a Grade C Western, but the nonchalant assumption that everybody shares your knowledge and concerns. Perhaps this is why—in addition to a normal instinct for preserving the panache of infallibility—the subject of computer crime has not received adequate exposure.

The idea of writing this book for the businessman—and potential victim of computer malfeasance—germinated during an investigation of the security of a new $50,000,000 on-line central data processing facility housing all the vital records of one of the nation's largest insurance companies. This facility was designed to tie computer consoles located around the country to the central computer files, so that many employees in any major city could add, subtract, read, and change vital policy information on-line. (As will be shown later in the book, a minimally secure system of this type might as well have a sign hung on every console: "Cheat Me.") Aside from routine physical security, the expenditure for design concerned with electronic data security amounted to $5,000, or one-hundredth of one percent of the system cost—far less than the expected loss due to one major computer error or one embezzlement.

Our resolve to write this book was crystalized when we were interviewed by Martin J. Sikora of the Philadelphia *Inquirer*. Stories we gave him—cases, opportunities for theft, and crime histories—data we thought common knowledge—turned out to be revelations. The ideology of the Infallible Computer seemed as firmly entrenched as Motherhood. So, being computerniks ourselves, we decided to do something about it. This book is the result.

Preface Warning and Disclaimer

THIS book is about theft, fraud, sabotage, and espionage conducted via computer. It tells how to commit them, how to detect them, and how to stop them. Every trick described in this book has been committed, and—here's the warning—found out. In some cases details and *dramatis personae* have been modified.

Since all the methods of committing computer crime detailed in this book have been detected and stopped (a necessary precaution) a reader might conclude that no difficult problem exists in computer security. The contrary is the truth.

Many cases of computer crime do not appear on these pages for reasons of legal and moral discretion. The authors do not intend to convey any judgment or cause any embarrassment to those who might recognize themselves or their organizations herein. We have striven for objectivity and accuracy, limited our case citation to the public record, and felt duty-bound to expose the reality.

Acknowledgments

THE principal authors, Stephen W. Leibholz and Louis D. Wilson of Analytics, would like to express their deepest appreciation to the following contributing authors:

Lois L. Cohn, a partner in the international accounting firm of Laventhol, Krekstein, Horwath & Horwath, for her excellent assistance regarding auditing implications of computer systems and for her direct contribution of Chapter 11, "Auditing and Internal Controls."

Margaret Eisen, a Philadelphia newspaper reporter, for her research of the Equity Funding case and for writing Chapter 3, "Equity Funding and Other Diversions."

Stephen J. Harmelin and J. Taylor DeWeese, members of the Pennsylvania Bar, for their guidance and advice on legal matters and for their contribution of Chapter 12, "Legal Implications: Crimes and Torts."

Fred W. Mumma of Analytics for his work as principal working compiler and for contributing several technical sections.

Many additional people have contributed to this book, some overtly and some unwittingly. In addition to the contributing authors, we would like to commend: Fred Blum and Sandy Epstein who, among others, contributed ideas and criticism and Mary Ellen Floria and Sylvia Heit—all of the Analytics Staff—for their typing of drafts and masterful revisions. And finally, the principal authors' wives, Ellie Wilson and Ann Leibholz, who advised, consented—and forbore. This book is for them.

Contents

Introduction

In *The Prince,* Machiavelli describes deception as an essential element in the making of a fortune or the winning of a political or military campaign. Unfortunately for his reputation modern readers rarely separate his cold-blooded appraisals from the ethical difficulties that cling to them, and thus he has become undeservedly immortalized as the archetypal political cynic.

To this day, men have recognized the validity of Machiavelli's insights. On the day the earliest caveman began trading hand-hewn tools for food and furs, others began attempting to steal his goods, methods and customers.

As methods of manufacturing and commerce have evolved, methods of criminal attacks on such operations have also become more sophisticated. Most recently computers have become a tool for businessmen. They assist in record keeping of all kinds and in developing his general business strategies at all levels, and they even contribute directly in some manufacturing processes. *Unfortunately, computers also further remove the businessman from day-to-day supervision.*

As can be expected, individuals possessing the Machiavellian philosophy and modified personal ethics have been at work devising methods to use the computer to obtain their own ends. This book shows, through documented case histories, that money, physical assets, information, plans and virtually every other aspect of business entrusted to a computer have been stolen or otherwise criminally violated, and this is happening today.

Our purpose in this book is to document and analyze crimes and other losses that can occur via computer. We also suggest steps that can be taken to minimize risks and losses. It is not possible to eliminate either risks and losses or the possibility of criminal violation of a computer system, and we make no claim to that effect.

We attempt in all cases to show steps that can and should be taken to minimize risks. As in all aspects of business, economics must prevail. One must carefully evaluate the cost of protective measures versus the loss value in the event that loss occurs. In general, however, the cost of protective measures is relatively low whereas the value of a loss can be very significant.

We have organized the presentation of material into four sections. Chapters 1 through 4 present the basic problems as they exist today. Case histories of known events have been used to illustrate the many facets of computer-related losses, particularly computer crime.

Ways of attaining a reasonable degree of protection from such losses are then discussed in Chapters 5 through 10. We have provided specific measures that can be taken, as well as general operating principles that should be practiced in order to achieve protection.

Chapters 11 and 12 present methods of detecting criminal activities as well as the auditing and legal implications of computer use. Here we discuss not only how to detect criminal activity and the prosecution possibilities of same but also the responsibilities of a computer system user.

In Chapters 13 and 14 we present programs of action required by computer users and programs in the accounting and legislative areas that are required for the reasonable future development of computer data security.

Appendix A presents a checklist of items to be accounted for and acted upon in establishing proper security of the data processing operations. Appendix B is a reprint of the first of 105 counts in the Equity Funding indictment. Appendix C presents a brief survey of programmer ethics. Finally, Appendix D is a reprint of the Fair Credit Reporting Act.

This book is a businessman's guide to security relative to computer operations. Having studied this material, the businessman will become enlightened to the risks represented by his computer operations, aware of the threats against which he must take protective measures, and knowledgeable of some primary protective measures available to him for limiting losses or eliminating threats.

Part I
THE PROBLEMS

Chapter 1
How to Lose a Bundle
The Anatomy of Computer Crime

JERRY NEAL SCHNEIDER never worked for the Pacific Telephone and Telegraph Company, but that didn't prevent him from parlaying an ingenious mind, boyish enthusiasm and a flexible sense of morality into a major competitive business furnishing Pacific Telephone Company equipment to industries along the West Coast. He did it all with his little touch-tone phone, by "breaking the code" used by Pacific Telephone to order spare parts from suppliers for its warehouses. It wasn't a hard code to break; all that was required was a secondhand teletype machine and an orderly mind. He ordered what he needed on-line as if he were a Pacific Telephone maintenance shop and stole the equipment from a warehouse after delivery but before inventory could be taken. All told, Schneider pyramided a shoestring into a million-dollar business. He might have gone undetected for years, had he not been turned in by an employee. Jerry was found guilty of grand theft and was sentenced to 60 days in jail and 3 years probation.

Computer fraud is big business in the United States. Arlen Specter, former D.A. of Philadelphia, has called it "the new sophisticated crime wave." The take is enormous—it is known to be more than $15 million per year, with $27 million exposed in the first half of 1973 alone. The total probably comes to many times this amount.

Computer fraud has rarely been detected by auditing or conventional means. Discovery has usually been by sheer accident, and since it is impossible to say how many accidents have not yet happened, no one knows how high the annual take really is. Further, many cases discovered are never openly disclosed because of the embarrassment such a disclosure might bring to the victim.

Using computers, people both inside and outside a company have stolen information, clients, merchandise, and money. The offenders may be new employees challenged to exploit their computeristic genius, old employees out to collect what they feel is their due, or total strangers who never even set foot on the premises. Computer systems in many automated banks across the country are wide open to anyone possessing a pair of wire clips and a touch-tone telephone. Automated order entry and inventory control systems are easy prey for anyone having access to one of the 200,000-odd teletypes in the country. Computer fraud requires about as much education and expertise as a typical scientifically inclined high school student might possess and appears to offer an excellent reward/risk ratio to the enterprising thief. A recent survey reported in *Computer Abuse** showed that in 64 recent cases of non-computer-related white-collar crime, the average take was $100,000 per incident. In the same period (calendar 1970) only 12 cases of computer-related embezzlement came to light, but for these the average take was *$1 million* per incident.

Plain Old Crime and Computer Crime

Since the Book of Genesis (25:31), and probably before, fraud has been a concomitant of civilization. Whenever a structure exists whereby contracts can be made, credit extended, or promises made and fulfilled, the implied trust and conventions can be broken for unfair advantage. Yet computer crime, a profession less than 15 years old, represents a qualitative change and a quantum step in business crime. Why is this so?

First, the computer is a faceless medium. There is a perverse challenge in "beating the machine," and such crime seems somehow less odious than face-to-face deception.

Second, the vast accumulation of data in a typical computer system boggles the mind, particularly the mind of the executive and auditor faced with inspecting it.

Third, files can be removed and changed without leaving a trace. Data can be altered and the tracks covered in milliseconds.

Fourth, computer printouts, knee-deep boxes of rows and columns of numbers, themselves exert a hypnotic effect on the reader. "It's all there; you just have to find it."

Fifth, audit trails through a computer process are generally lacking.

Sixth, on-line data systems and remote-entry processing create the option of exploitation via phone-tapping by total outsiders.

Seventh, it is possible to steal one's way to fortune, using a computer by extracting nickles and dimes from each of many accounts, the differences being unnoticeable to the individuals affected.

Eighth, a clever programmer can introduce into a coded procedure subtle changes that lie hidden and dormant, perhaps for months;

*A study prepared for the National Science Foundation by Donn B. Parker, Susan Nycum and S. Stephan Oüra of Stanford Research Institute; November, 1973.

these changes are then triggered by an external event, such as the disappearance of the programmer's name from the payroll. Pow!

Ninth, and perhaps most important, is the computer mystique. More about this later.

Here is the mysterious monster spewing out miles and miles of paper, computing anything in sight, determining the future of businesses and nations to the last penny, attacking problems hitherto incomprehensible to the human mind, and doing so at blinding speed to a symphony of psychedelic light and sound. The danger grows in direct proportion to the efficiency with which the computer system helps one's operation and the reliability and smoothness with which it lulls him into a conviction of its omniscience.

Some computer frauds are not computer frauds *per se* but conventional theft hiding itself in a miasma of paper work cunningly designed to cloud the mind of any reasonable auditor. Witness the Equity Funding scandal (see Chapter 3). Here was a theft whose essence consisted of creating nonexistent insurance policies and nonexistent clients, then wholesaling these policies intermingled with legitimate policies to reinsurers—most of whom apparently placed their entire trust in the miles of computer printout and the neat little sums at the bottom of the folded sheets.

Other computer fraud is sometimes wholly indigenous to the computer operation.

Cynthia Crooks had a boyfriend who worked for a service bureau that serviced a brokerage firm. As is typically the case, the programs used for this account were developed and owned by the service bureau, not the customer. The boyfriend was a computer operator and thus had access to a copy of the programs used by the brokerage, which Cynthia managed to obtain. When she called the president of the firm and arranged to sell him the programs, he notified the Fort Wayne, Indiana, police. Cynthia was arrested when she tried to pass the programs to the brokerage firm president. She was found guilty of attempting to sell the programs and given a one-year suspended sentence.

Assuming that a crime is discovered, management of the business must decide whether to admit the loss at the cost of some loss of face. It is often easier to take the less embarrassing solution and keep the loss secret; we know of several discovered crimes that have never become public record. A large firm of private detectives was recently the victim of a computerized-payroll scheme that cost them an estimated $50,000 per year. Considering the potential effect of public exposure on their detective business, they chose not to prosecute. This reaction is all too ubiquitous.

It is certain that many computer crimes exist undetected today. There are probably a number of Equity Fundings waiting to be discovered —perhaps by a wrecking crew probing the ruins of a Chapter 10 bankruptcy proceeding.

The Computer Mystique

The first step toward reestablishing parity between management and computer operation is to disenfranchise the computer mystique—the notion that possession of an expensive electronic wonder serviced by an expensive crew of incomprehensible programmers is equivalent to possessing the fountain of knowledge.

The computer mystique works something like this:

1. Computers are created by geniuses; therefore they are geniuses.
2. Computers generate tidy reports; therefore they are correct.
3. Computers are supposed to save labor costs; therefore they are cheap.
4. Computers can be programmed to answer any question decisively; therefore they answer correctly.
5. The EDP manager earns twice as much as the chief accountant; therefore he must be twice as smart.

This reminds us of the famous after-dinner story about the woman who sued for divorce after ten years of wedded bliss on the grounds of nonconsummation of the marriage. Asked to explain this situation she replied, "You see, your Honor, my husband is a computer salesman. Every night he holds my hand and tells me how great it's going to be."

Joe Rodman and his brother operated Food Center Wholesale Grocers, Inc., a supplier to supermarkets in Boston. In their 200,000-square-foot warehouse they had their share of inventory control and distribution problems. In 1962 they decided that the solution to their problem was a computer.

After obtaining the appropriate assurances from the salesman, they leased a RAMAC 305 from IBM.* The salesman assured them that not only would their principal problems disappear, but that they would also be able to cut back their clerical staff.

Installation went smoothly and the day of salvation arrived. With appropriate pomp and ceremony, the system was dedicated and the start button pushed. Alas, nothing happened.

After weeks of probing, the technicians finally got the computer to do

**Our apologies to IBM, but these are the facts; no computer company can control its salesmen completely.*

something. It went on a spree, ordering and shipping from ten to a hundred times the desired quantities and then forgetting the details of the transaction. When asked how much of a certain item was on hand, it would say "none" and reorder the item. Usually there was a carload or so in storage. If the computer said there was some on hand, it usually forgot where the goods were stored. When workers were lucky enough to find the goods, they had difficulty making deliveries because the computer fouled up delivery schedules.

Once shipments were made, the computer had difficulty remembering the transactions. It often refused altogether to bill a customer and when it did send a bill, it frequently charged ten times the actual price of the goods. Once a $3.90 item was billed at $39.00, and another time a $13.00 item was billed at $200.00.

It took more than six months to iron out the troubles and the Rodmans refused to pay the rental on the computer during this time. The Rodmans sued for damages; IBM sued to collect the back rent. After lengthy litigation, Food Center Wholesale Grocers was awarded more than $53,000 in damages, but IBM was awarded $26,000 for back rent.

Once burnt, twice shy? Not in this case! Soon afterward, Joe Rodman, with a little help from his friendly salesman, decided the real answer to his problem was a bigger computer. He ordered a new, bigger system from—you guessed it—IBM.

Computers had obviously caught Joe Rodman's fancy, as they have that of many another businessman. Computer salesmen play on this predisposition, promising the world but seldom warning of risks and potential problems.

Besides the ways of computer salesmen several other factors have been instrumental in fostering the computer mystique. The computer system is a non-income-producing function. Businessmen generally don't understand computers and have thus been afraid of them. Salesmen and computer managers have deliberately kept upper management away from their bailiwick. The knowledgeable computer manager usually is not responsible for the system, but reports to another executive who has this responsibility but little computer knowledge.

The Associated Press wire recently carried the story of Frank B. Haderer, an $18,000-a-year vice president of Walston & Co., Inc., who allegedly stole $270,000 from the company over an eight-year period. Because of the five-year statute of limitations New York District Attorney Frank S. Hogan's office said the charge had to be limited to only $170,000. Haderer admitted everything and explained in detail how he managed to take more than a quarter of a million dollars at the rate of $2,000 to $3,000 per month to support his yen for the good life.

As a vice president of the firm, Frank had easy access to the premises. Sundays or after hours he would alter punched cards used to record margin account interest payments from clients. He first punched the cards to show a smaller amount of interest than they should and then punched the amount of the difference on other cards, crediting the amounts to his or his wife's account. Their personal accounts were used to purchase stock which was then sold for cash. The cash was used to pay for trips to Las Vegas and visits to New York nightclubs.

No money belonging to clients was involved, the firm said, and the losses were covered by insurance. Haderer was discharged and the surety company that covered the losses brought charges. Walston accidentally discovered the thefts while auditing the stock exchange accounts of its employees, a regulatory requirement not related to the computer operation.

Compare a fleet of delivery trucks with a computer installation. Both are non-income-producing support operations that cannot be evaluated on a straight cost-effectiveness basis. Neither in itself saves money or personnel. Like delivery trucks, computers come in many shapes and sizes serving different basic objectives. The businessman, not the truck salesman, has determined the needs. When the truck salesman starts extolling the virtues of his biggest rig, particularly its impressive performance on cross-country hauls, the businessman of course stops him cold if his needs are short-haul local deliveries. He is looking for economy, ease of loading, and ease of handling in traffic. Similarly, if he needs a computer for accounting, why should he buy one that will also handle his inventory and distribution? Is he being sold more computer than he needs?

When it comes to replacing clerks (or any other staff member) with a computer, it is advisable to carefully determine what the individual is being replaced with. Computers gulp down and spit out lots of data. Somebody has to collect the data and prepare it for the computer, then someone must do something with the results. Somebody has to operate the computer and somebody has to tend the tape library (or its equivalent). This all assumes that the system initially does not require programming support to adapt it to changing requirements, a highly unlikely situation. With luck, the head count will perhaps not increase with conversion to computer processing, but a lot of the heads may be more expensive than they were before.

The average businessman does not understand how computers work, why they cost more than the initial estimates, and why he didn't experience the savings expected. When he discusses his problems with the experts, it is carefully explained that the input loop introvated the recursive frummis and a bigger computer is needed. Since computers are beyond mortal comprehension he did not really expect to understand at the outset.

Now the businessman has a computer that he fears, managed by a staff he doesn't trust, all because he doesn't understand either one. But he has them and they must be responsibly managed. So he puts his comptroller in charge. Here is a man he understands and trusts, albeit a man who doesn't really have the knowledge to run the computer operations either—but the computer is performing primarily accounting services. Therefore, the businessman hopes that the comptroller will develop enough interest in the system to learn what it's really all about and how to manage it and its people.

Needless to say, this does not always happen, so the businessman grabs another straw, the computer mystique—he cannot live with the thought that his system cannot be properly managed, but he can live with the myth that the computer is infallible and impregnable and does not really require this management. Thus he needn't worry if the system is not receiving proper control.

In comparison, how well does the average businessman understand his new delivery truck or the new materials-handling equipment in his warehouse? How easily is he convinced that "he" got the wrong model or that this year's model is so much better that "he" simply must have one? Generally, he understands what this equipment is for and he sees it doing meaningful work. He understands that the warehouse manager, not "he," needed the new equipment and the warehouse manager is responsible for decisions, actions, and effective utilization of the new equipment. But the businessman really need not understand much more about the equipment.

As with trucks, the businessman must understand why a computer system is needed, what the system is supposed to do and how its results are supposed to be used to help him obtain more profits. He must understand the risks involved in using the equipment just as he understands the risks with other equipment. Finally, he must determine whom the system is supposed to serve and see to it that the appropriate manager or managers accept the responsibility for effective system utilization and correct system selection. But at no time is it really necessary for the businessman to understand how a computer works.

The computer mystique is gradually being overcome, and the attitude that computer-processed data must perforce be correct has nearly disappeared. In fact, the publicity given to computer errors has generated a great public distrust of computers, but the attitude that computer-processed data must be wrong is as unjustified and incorrect as the initial attitude that such data must be right.

The computer is a tool. It is really no more complex than a fleet of delivery trucks. It can be understood and used wisely to great advantage. If misunderstood or allowed to maintain an aloof air of myth and mystery it will become a club used against the user.

How Vulnerable Is Your System?

There are four basic types of computer installations with virtually all graduations in between: batch processing, remote batch processing, direct-access remote processing, and dial-up remote processing. Each type has its own type of security risk; generally as the number of users increases and data communications are employed in a system, the risks increase dramatically.

The batch-processing installation is the most common, the classic "shiny blue computer." Basically it is a closed-door computing facility reporting to a specific department, such as accounting, and processing data on a demand basis as a corporate staff function. Data input is presented in a batch, either in paper form, such as time cards or invoices, requiring conversion to computer-readable media or already in computer-readable form. Processing is performed strictly on a scheduled basis. Usually, only one program is run at a time, although in recent years multiprocessing systems have been introduced that enable two or more programs to be run simultaneously. In these systems the need for an executive program or operating system plus the demands of data security may easily outweigh the savings anticipated through apparent increased efficiency.

Remote batch processing is similar to batch processing except in its geographic relationships. Generally there are consoles located adjacent to the principal in-house users (such as production, sales, subsidiaries) which are tied to the main computer facility through the courtesy of Ma Bell (or equivalent), although sometimes the mails or couriers are used. In this case, however, the data communications facilities are not "on-line"—they do not communicate directly with the main computer or its programs. Rather, they gain access to bulk storage media that hold the data until the scheduled run time. Remote batch systems generally employ multiprocessing techniques.

Direct-access remote processing always requires data communications. These communications facilities are dedicated to the computing system and may or may not be part of the general office telephone network. Such systems are developed to service large organizations housed in sprawling facilities. In general, these systems enable data preparation and storage on-line, but runs are performed on a batch basis.

Dial-up remote processing is similar to direct-access remote processing, but it utilizes public telephone facilities. These may be direct-dial toll services, TELEX, WATS or other services; this type of system provides significant interactive processing capabilities in addition to on-line data preparation. Dial-up remote processing is the typical service offered by time-sharing companies and used by national or international corporations with widely dispersed offices.

Figure 1-1 illustrates the relative risks of these types of system when no security measures are taken and gives an estimate of the extent to which risks can be reduced when good security measures are implemented effectively. Risk level zero indicates no possibility of loss and is not obtainable. Increasing risk levels represent decreases in the amount of effort required to effect a crime against the system. Risk level ten indicates little protection against criminal intrusion.

Athough in terms of modern business practices, the batch-processing system is often least efficient in support of timely business operation, it does provide maximum inherent security. Such security is attained with a dedicated batch-processing system, isolated with controlled access, thorough program and program-change control and validation, and minimal maintenance requirements. In such a system, only operations and maintenance personnel have physical access to the computer room. They are few in number and their movements can easily be controlled. Only one job and its associated files are on the system at any one time, so file security is impossible to breach on a planned or regular basis without the cooperation of several individuals.

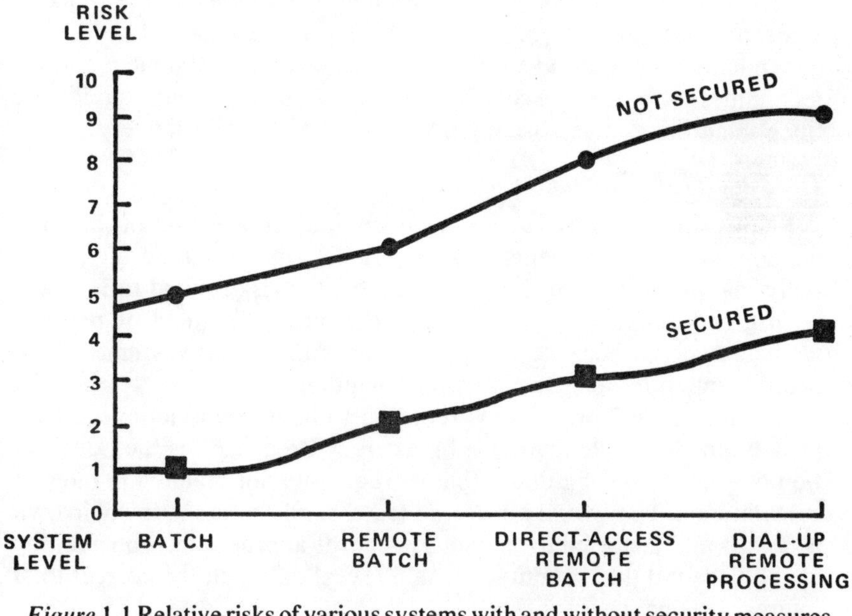

Figure 1.1 Relative risks of various systems with and without security measures

If all inputs and run requests are processed through a central control point and all outputs are delivered to the control point for distribution, the system security officer can be in charge of the control point and thus have discretionary control over total system operations. He can verify the right of the requestor to obtain a run and the right of recipients to receive the outputs.

Of course, accidents still happen and no system is completely safe from penetration by a clever, competent felon. Further, absolute completeness and accuracy of input data cannot be checked or assured by the system. But by reducing the number of individuals with opportunities for foul play and imposing reasonable control over all personnel, risks can be minimized.

The maximum challenge to security is posed by dial-up remote access systems serving multiple users simultaneously. These systems impose the least direct control over users, systems access, and general system usage. Because system access is via dial-up communications lines, it is easily breached; and because many files are on-line, they are more generally available than less widely used systems to anyone wishing to breach them. Finally the international standard computer data code in almost universal use is about as secret as the Morse code. In dial-up remote access systems, the operations personnel generally rely on the security provisions of the operational system. If a request for mounting a file is given to the operator, he assumes that the appropriate clearances have been obtained and seldom questions the validity of the request. Thus, access to the system, use of programs, and access to data files are dependent upon user identifications, passwords and similar control techniques subject to discovery and use by unauthorized individuals. Such unauthorized use usually involves little risk of discovery.

The Role of the Computer in Crime

Many crimes or losses attributed to computers have also occurred in noncomputer environments. But computer crime differs in the potentially massive nature of the loss. Further, the risk/reward ratios have been greatly changed. Crimes that were once infrequent or petty in manual systems because the payoff per transaction was small have become much more attractive with computers.

A major New York bank is reported to have been victimized by a programmed swindle involving breakage. "Breakage" is the odd fraction of a penny or of a dollar that is frequently not credited in interest calculations. The programmers added the odd amount to their own accounts and distorted the summary records appropriately; an auditing check "around the computer" would reveal only that the correct total interest was paid.

This type of theft is particularly hard to detect. Any check values calculated would prove out because the thief took only what was legitimate interest to be paid. If a customer did calculate his interest and note a discrepancy, he probably didn't figure it worth the fuss. On the other hand, if he did report it, he probably received a polite brush-off on the premise that he had calculated incorrectly. After all, the computer calculated the interest! Such fraud is generally discovered accidentally when a system failure or a change in the system forces manual processing or where parallel processing is performed to check out a newly acquired system. Sometimes it is not clear that a fraud involved computer operations.

Two areas of computer-related crime pose little difficulty: theft of the computer system itself, and when advertisement falsely proclaiming use of computers which are not, in fact, being used. The latter was true in a number of instances in which companies claimed to be computer dating companies but in fact did not utilize a computer to generate dating references. In both cases the crimes are conventional.

A third area poses a slight philosophical problem. In this case the criminal uses the computer as a tool to help him plan a crime or select victims. These crimes are generally conventional crimes, such as burglary, espionage, or embezzlement. In one reported case the criminal used credit reference files to select burglary victims of means. In another, the criminal used a computer, setting up a gaming model of his company to determine how and how much he could embezzle with the least likelihood of detection.

Finally, the computer system creates an environment within which the criminal functions. It is in this area that the greatest question arises regarding whether a crime is a computer crime.

Probably the most significant role is the accumulation of massive quantities of data in a central location and in relatively compact form. A single reel of magnetic tape may contain as much information as ten four-drawer filing cabinets. And a reel of magnetic tape is easily lost, whereas ten filing cabinets are not. The data maintained in a tape library the size of an executive office would usually be widely dispersed throughout a company in paper form. In the event of fire or natural disaster only a portion of the paper records would be lost while the entire tape library would probably be lost.

In this sea of data fictitious or faulty information may easily become buried. Leverage is significantly increased over manual systems, since frauds such as the interest breakage case become attractive only when a large number of accounts can be accessed. Further, all accounts are processed by the same computer, thus differences in the way different people handle accounts do not arise.

The crimes committed are not new. The methods, however, have changed. The question of whether a crime is a computer-related crime generally revolves around the question of whether the crime could have been carried out to the same extent if the computer had not been involved.

Chapter 2
Opportunities and Scenarios
The Computer Criminal's M.O.

A PROGRAMMER recently was caught manipulating federal withholding taxes in a major manufacturing concern. Each payroll was processed on the computer, which properly calculated gross pay and withholding. Quarterly, a tax report was made and the withheld taxes forwarded to the government. The programmer had written the program to retrieve the appropriate employee information including the total tax withheld and print the information including the total tax withheld on the appropriate reporting forms. However, the programmer had also included a calculation that reduced each employee's quarterly tax-withheld total by about 25 cents. He accumulated these differences, added them to his reported tax withholdings and adjusted the total retained in the company files.

Since the total reported taxes withheld matched the total of the weekly total taxes withheld and the year-to-date totals of the individual accounts matched the year-to-date weekly totals, no one became suspicious. *After all, the program only printed forms.* None of the employees noticed the dollar or so difference in withholding as reported on their W-2 forms. But, alas, when a system malfunction forced manual processing of the payroll, one of the employees involved decided to verify his account "just for practice" and discovered a difference.

There are three basic classes of loss in information systems: loss of services, loss of assets, and loss of information. Prevention of loss requires both an understanding of the causes of loss and an implementation of measures calculated to eliminate these causes. A loss must be detected if it is to be minimized and repetitions eliminated.

Loss of the services of the data processing center occurs if: the equipment is not operating; the software is not available or has been stolen; the master data files are missing or unusable. The most catastrophic loss of services occurs when all three elements occur simultaneously. A major time-sharing company was recently nearly put out of business by the theft of its services. In another case a mischievous student, besides stealing programs and services through the telephone lines, would occasionally deposit in other people's files the phrase "F . . . you, signed the Phantom."

Fire, natural disaster, vandalism, and sabotage are the most common causes of simultaneous loss of equipment, programs, and data files. In fact, fire and natural disaster are currently the leading causes of catastrophic loss of all kinds. The destruction of the University of Wisconsin computer center in 1970 caused a loss of two lives, an estimated $1.5 million in physical losses, and untold data losses.

Power failure, equipment failure and spilled food are the leading causes of system shutdown and temporary loss of primary service. Abuse of a system through improper handling and operation of equipment—deliberate or accidental—can also cause a serious system shutdown.

The deliberate or accidental destruction of storage media will cause the loss of programs and data files stored on the media, but backup copies of such data should be available. Such a loss happened recently at one of the world's largest insurance companies, coincidentally with a strike.

Program bugs, errors in input data and procedural errors are all the more serious since resorting to backup versions of the information will not help. Until corrected, such losses deprive the users of computing services and can be more disruptive, if not more expensive, than the loss of equipment services.

Loss of assets is the most common loss. It includes loss of funds, inventory, and capital goods. Generally these are of value to the thief or finder either directly, as in the case of funds, or after resale, as in the case of inventory items. Loss of assets also includes acts of sabotage in which the company experiences a loss which does not result in any commensurate direct financial gain to the perpetrator. Sometimes, the company's suppliers or employees are responsible for the loss of assets.

Loss of information is different from loss of data files. Here, loss of information means information diverted to unintended recipients and does not imply any loss of the use of the data by its owner. Such loss can occur through the improper handling of waste, a mixup in the delivery of printouts, the deliberate making of extra copies of printouts or the theft of copies of master files or printouts. Wiretapping, misdirection of calls, and deliberate or accidental misidentification of terminals can all lead to loss of information in systems using data communications.

In 1970, a reference book publisher brought suit against several of his computer operators. In the suit it was alleged that the operators had made a copy of three million names and addresses from the company's preferred customer list. The names and addresses were then sold for one dollar each to other mail-order firms.

The Ways Losses Occur

Losses can occur through criminal acts, malfunctions, and natural disasters. Fraud, espionage, and sabotage are all entirely people-instigated criminal acts. The people may be employees, suppliers, customers, or total strangers. Their intent may be personal gain or harm to the company. They may be interested in obtaining assets or information to establish or improve a competitive business, or they may simply wish to attract attention to themselves or a cause with which they are deeply involved. Finally, they may attempt to blackmail management by threats to perform such criminal acts.

What are the objects of computer crime? What attracts the criminal? Deliberate crimes against a company are always perpetrated for one or a combination of three reasons: financial gain, competitive advantage or harm to the company.

The first type of crime is *fraud*. Fraud is deceit, trickery, or breach of confidence used to gain some unfair or dishonest advantage. By far, the largest number of deliberate acts against a company and its computing system fall into this category. In general, fraud is perpetrated more for personal gain than as a means of harming the company. Indeed, many perpetrators have the attitude that "the company can afford it" or "the company will never miss it." The targets are money, property (such as the computer itself and the companies' products), services (such as computer time), and information (such as financial or personnel records and marketing strategy or new product introduction plans). Computer time, computer programs, and physical inventory are the most common commodities attacked. Financial records are attacked to gain money or marketable information or to manipulate the "value" of the company—particularly the value of marketable securities.

Although some of the individuals perpetrating such crimes are in fact criminals who have planned their career development or manipulated their work assignments to be placed in opportune positions, many just happened to be in the right place at the right time. Most of the latter are simply unethical individuals who feel that they have discovered a means for personal gain with no risk of being caught. Others rationalize that the company owes them something, and they are thus only taking what was due them anyway.

Crimes whose purpose is to gain competitive advantage are known as *industrial espionage*. Here, the "gain" is the growth or increased profitability of the instigator's own company. Espionage is the practice of spying to obtain data or other information to gain unfair or dishonest advantage. In general, it is necessary to put these data to some use in order to gain the advantage. The perpetrator and the instigator of such acts are usually different people with different objectives. The perpetrator is paid for his efforts and is out for direct personal gain. The instigator is frequently looking for subtler or indirect satisfaction, such as recognition of success in business or an improvement in his employment position. The financial gains are not unappreciated, however, since they are further evidence of success.

Sabotage, the third class of crime, is the deliberate interference with a company's operation. Individuals perpetrating such crimes are usually looking for personal satisfaction, such as settling a grudge against the company, rather than financial gain. Unions or activist groups may use sabotage to intimidate or blackmail management for concessions not otherwise obtainable. Other activist groups may simply desire to draw public attention to a company whose activities are considered objectionable, unethical, or illegal by the activists.

Malfunction includes accidents, mistakes and failures to which nature and people contribute both separately and collectively. Unlike criminal acts, malfunctions generally occur through acts of omission rather than acts of commission. Nature's contributions are aging and dirt, while man's contribution is failure to exercise due caution or to take appropriate precautionary measures.

Food spills and maintenance neglect are the primary causes of person-oriented equipment malfunctions. General carelessness, laziness or their equivalents are major contributors that combine with natural influences to create problems. Incompetent and ill-trained personnel are generally at the heart of the problem in installations suffering persistent losses due to malfunctions.

Natural disasters include floods, earthquakes, hurricanes, and lightning. All of these are relatively unpredictable, uncontrollable, and unavoidable. Thus, efforts against losses to natural disasters are directed toward limiting loss rather than preventing the event causing the loss. Primary steps that can be taken with reasonable expectation of successfully lessening the impact of natural disasters are good site selection and internal measures to minimize loss when the event occurs.

Areas Vulnerable to Criminal Attack

Losses resulting from criminal acts, particularly fraud, are by far the least understood and to date the least protected against. Since it is relevant here to consider these crimes from the view of prevention and detection, we will examine the various areas of computer operation and explain the most vulnerable aspects of each. We will also look at certain industrial groups and special risks related to these groups.

COMPUTER TIME

One of the most obvious assets that data processing personnel can steal from an employer is computer time, a highly salable commodity. Programmers and operators are keenly aware of the value of this commodity and are in the best position to steal it. Even in a well-controlled operation, some manipulation is possible. In a loosely controlled installation, the sky is the limit.

As an example of the sort of exploitation possible, a welfare agency in a large eastern city discovered that a number of its employees were running a commercial data processing business using the facilities of the agency—actually selling the services of the agency's computer center. Because of the looseness of controls, it was impossible to accurately determine just how much time they had diverted to their business. But that was not all. The employees were also selling their own services as programmers and system designers. Whether they worked on their own time (moonlighting) or on the city's time is difficult to determine, but the value of the services they sold was estimated to be in the mid-five figures.

It is even easier to steal computer time from systems using remote terminals. An unscrupulous outsider with a computer terminal or teletype unit—and scores of thousands of these are in use today—can obtain (by accident, bribery, or the cooperation of an insider) the system's telephone number, a customer identification, and the necessary passwords. A clever user can even manipulate his way past the passwords of others. For example, on one popular system the user need only print out the password file—its own "password" being highly standardized. In another system in use today an outsider can establish remote communications with another console—unbeknown to the latter—and listen in for passwords and procedures. Or, like Jerry Neal Schneider, he may find what he needs in the outside trash bins.

With this information, the thief has full access to the resources of the system and can tap them from his remote terminal. This terminal, in his home or office, becomes a siphon on the system's resources which he can use at will.

In many remote-access systems, detecting such freeloaders is extremely difficult. The telephone company will rarely cooperate without a court order. Safeguards can be provided, but very few systems have gone to the trouble of installing them. This, even though the theft of computer time is one of the most obvious and easiest types of computer fraud. The reason for such laxity is probably that this type of loss is one of the least likely to endanger the operations of the company as a whole. Further, a certain amount of time must be scheduled for hardware and software maintenance. This time is generally not tightly controlled and, if not utilized, becomes a temptation. Idle operators may start to play with the system or offer the unused time to others.

COMPUTER PROGRAMS

As any concerned executive realizes, a company deeply involved in data processing spends huge amounts of money to develop computer programs. Sometimes this "software" is so specialized that it is of questionable value to an outsider, but often it is sufficiently general that it can be used by anyone after only minor alterations.

In one widely publicized case, an employee of the University Computing Company (UCC) Palo Alto, California (a computer service bureau) allegedly stole a program from another service bureau, Information Systems Design, Inc. (ISD) Oakland, in the hope of using that program to entice a valued client from the competitor. Both companies use Univac computers with remote processing terminals. The theft involved the use of a remote terminal and telephone lines; no physical entry was necessary. This case reached the courts when ISD charged the employee with grand theft. The charge of grand theft was dropped when the employee pleaded guilty to stealing a trade secret. According to the Oakland Police Department, the theft was accidentally discovered only because the thief made mistakes which revealed his crime outside the computer loop.

This is one case in which the theft was detected and redress was possible. In many such cases well known to people in the business, programs have been stolen and used successfully in direct competition with the victim company. New consulting companies have been built with stolen programs as their original stock in trade. One company was founded on the basis of programs for pricing trucking rates which were stolen by a group of employees of a large express company.

While stolen programs may be used in competition with the defrauded company, they may also be used in areas which in no way impinge upon that company's business. In such cases, the victim company may be totally unaware of the theft, merely losing potential income. The thief generally proceeds with no significant risk of discovery because the victim is neither aware of the loss of the program nor aware of the loss of potential income.

PAYROLL

Most sizable companies using computers for any reason also generate paychecks with the computer. Generally, the information necessary to compute a payroll is stored in permanent computer files. This exposes the company in three ways: these files can be sabotaged (the files can be extremely costly to reconstruct, and when a payroll must be met, a delay generally cannot be tolerated even for a short time); money can be stolen by manipulating the payroll; or payroll information may be stolen and used to the detriment of the company.

Generally, tampering with payroll files can be made to appear accidental. If the offender is discovered, he can plead accidental error and merely return the funds. Properly executed, the risk of prosecution in this type of theft is minimal.

The fraudulent manipulation of payroll files appears to be widespread. It includes creating fictitious personnel, revising base-pay information, and adjusting deductions. For example, in May of 1972 the borough of Brooklyn reported a fraud in the payroll of its Board of Education. The District Attorney charged that a ring of swindlers had submitted to the computer center fraudulent payroll reports that included hours worked by teachers no longer employed by the city. The computer system processed the reports in a normal manner, apparently because the system was not programmed to note employee severance. Reportedly, discovery of the manipulation occurred when the computer rejected a card because the name on it was misspelled. When the correct spelling was being checked, it was found that the teacher was no longer employed by the Board of Education.

The manipulation was probably executed in the following manner: city, state, and federal education authorities at various locations throughout the city submitted their payrolls to the data processing center by means of a separate payroll report for each employee. The larcenous employee simply inserted extra payroll reports into the system and retrieved them after they had been processed. Checks were mailed to the nonexistent employees at a post office box from which the thief retrieved them.

In another case, the Human Resources Administration of New York City claims to have lost about $2 million during the first nine months of 1968 due to fraudulent Youth Corps payroll checks. It is estimated that they issued a hundred erroneous checks a week. Here again, the fraud was discovered by accident when a policeman found a batch of the checks while investigating an illegally parked car.

ACCOUNTS RECEIVABLE

The accounts receivable file can very well be the lifeblood of a company. It provides a reasonably complete listing of the company's customers, particularly the biggest ones, and so would certainly be of interest to competitors. Such files have been stolen and used in a variety of ways. But most important, in many companies, the only record of monies owed lies in the receivables file. If this file suddenly disappeared how could it be regenerated? Would the company be able to establish who owed it what? If bills could not be sent for a month or two and much of the monies owed were suddenly removed from the cash flow pipeline, could the company survive? The cost of such a loss could be fatal, and this in fact occurred in at least one case. The company was thrown on the mercy of its customers. Some customers paid; some didn't. Bankruptcy was the result.

ACCOUNTS PAYABLE

In a conversation with one of the authors, the assistant comptroller of a large utility pointed to a two-inch-thick book lying on his desk. Each page listed a vendor from whom he purchased materials. Although his organization spot-checked entries, he considered it entirely possible that the book contained many nonexistent vendors who were paid for nonexistent services.

Over a period of four years, the manager of the data processing center for a large stockbroker embezzled over $80,000 from the firm by having computer-generated checks made payable to fictitious payees. He then cashed the checks and obtained the money himself. The theft was discovered when a check was returned to the company because it had been accidentally mailed to the wrong address.

An operations manager for one nationally known industrial firm had been systematically defrauding the company for a number of years and was formally charged with issuing forged checks with the help of a computer. He was apparently detected because he carelessly went on vacation before one of his false checks had come back from the bank.

The fraud involved an ordinary four-part form, the first part of which was a company check. In the design of the system, it was assumed that all parts of the form would be created simultaneously so that the second, third and fourth copies would be identical to the first. The clearing process did not include a verification that the check was actually made out to the same payee named on the remaining parts or recorded in the computer files, and the system was fooled quite simply. The first part, which was the check itself, was removed before automatic equipment printed the form. The latter parts showed the name of a *bona fide* contractor (from a table stored in the computer), but the check was really made out to a coconspirator. Only the payee name was changed.

The company's home office bank microfilmed the face of all checks received but recorded on computer tape only the check number and amount. It did not record the payee's name. Using the tape provided by the bank, the firm's computer noted that the check had been paid in the proper amount but could not catch the fact that it had been paid to the wrong payee. The culprit intercepted the canceled checks and destroyed them before they went to the records group. He then filled out the necessary forms to indicate that the checks had been sent to another branch for storage. Naturally, these forms reached only the local records group, who were thus satisfied. Having no reason to report the checks missing and no opportunity to verify the payee, they never thought to double-check with the other records storage group.

Since the amounts involved never exceeded a thousand dollars per account and the checks appeared to be made out to approved contractors, the controls in the company computer system assumed that any imbalances would eventually work themselves out. Therefore, when contractors reported open balances not shown in the system, an inadvertent error was assumed and the amount reentered as due the contractor. No record of how often this happened was kept.

The firm has since requested that the bank record the payee's name with the check number and amount and has modified its programs to verify payee as well as amount.

OPERATIONS INFORMATION

The marketing and sales files stored in a computer usually contain customer lists and sales records as well as information pertaining to compensation of sales personnel. They could provide full customer information and also reveal the salesmen who are most effective and the nature of their compensation plan. All these pieces of information would be of great interest to competitors.

Additional targets for industrial espionage are new product development, new design methods, and new manufacturing techniques. The use of the computer in the analysis of new techniques and the design of new products could expose valuable proprietary information to competitors. Extremely detailed product analysis and fabrication data may be available on computer tape or in other computer-readable files.

The management information stored in a computer can also reveal many aspects of long-range operational planning. There is increased use of gaming techniques to predict the effectiveness of various long-range options. The results of these planning studies often include a detailed performance analysis of various departments or divisions of the company. Such planning and gaming (using operations research and statistical analysis) could be invaluable information to a competitor or supplier.

Management files may also include personnel records carrying rather detailed information about every employee. There are many possible illegal applications of such information. The computer may also be handling such sensitive information as financial planning, including planning for corporate cash needs. Foreknowledge of these needs could be abused by a competitor in a variety of ways. Growth or expansion plans could be accurately assessed, for example. Such information would also be of use to investors.

In general, this type of sensitive information is carefully guarded by corporate management, particularly when it is in their possession. But it is often much less carefully guarded by those who generate the supporting statistical or financial reports.

The computer is also often used in marketing and sales gaming to help develop manufacturing and sales statistics. Such computer-based information generally includes lists of customers and prospects, both of which would be of great value to competition. Although it does not often reach the press, instances of such industrial espionage are many. In some industries, the practice of bribing competitors is not at all unusual.

SABOTAGE

Besides being susceptible to exploitation for fraudulent gain, a data processing system is also susceptible to malicious damage, manipulation, or destruction. The perpetrator may be an individual who feels he has not been given a fair deal by a company, or a labor union embroiled in negotiations with management or on strike. The intent is to disrupt company operations or blackmail the company by threatening such destruction.

Damage to expensive computer systems is also very much an objective of various action groups who seek to win support for their cause. They may wish to call attention to companies which they feel are not conducting business in a manner consistent with their ideals and objectives. Not long ago, one such group published a manual giving specific techniques for sabotaging a computer system.

Dow Chemical Company, at one time a target of action groups opposing the Vietnamese War, had its computing center invaded and seriously damaged. Obviously the attackers had been thoroughly briefed; they understood the major points of vulnerability and proceeded to effectively attack them. The cost to Dow was estimated at more than $1 million dollars.

One of the nation's largest insurers suffered indeterminate damage during a period of labor-management strife when someone caused its remote input terminals to transmit their branch-office data at times when the central computer was not prepared.

A U.S. Government organization introducing real-time computers to its day-to-day operations has been plagued by mysterious system breakdowns that can only occur when specific operator errors are fed into the system.

Special Risks

Each industrial computer application has its own special risks and vulnerabilities. Certain of these are examined here.

MANUFACTURING AND RETAIL

Inventory of all types tends to be the prime target for thefts in manufacturing and retailing organizations. Although financial accounts are expected to balance to the penny, for some reason inventory shrinkage (the difference between what goes into inventory and what ultimately is sold or used) of three to five percent is usually accepted as normal. If shrinkage can be directed, or if a theft elsewhere in the accounting chain (such as credit billing) can be disguised as shrinkage, voila! That is what happened to a large mail-order house when an employee purchased many high-priced items, tagged them for special pricing, and later drastically reduced the price.

A small percentage take is not enough to raise suspicion or be investigated very vigorously. Consequently, covering up the theft is easy and the risk of discovery is low as long as the thief is not too greedy. But even a half percent of a $20,000,000 inventory is not a bad haul.

Shrinkage generally stems from three major causes: theft by outsiders (such as shoplifters); theft by employees; and inventory errors. Inventories managed by a computer are extremely vulnerable. After all, what is the (observable) difference between an accidental inventory error and a "guided" error?

Theft by employees occurs in retail, wholesale, warehousing, and manufacturing. Pilferage is a constant problem with all levels of employees. It may center around minor items, such as stationery and office supplies, but it can be much more extensive and broader-based, involving all kinds of tools, supplies, equipment and finished products. The most obvious cover is to falsify records, and the dishonest employee with access to computer-stored files has numerous opportunities to manipulate them to his benefit.

Thefts from inventory can be accomplished in many ways. Any given purchase for inventory may be shipped to several warehouses. Revised shipping instructions may be generated that are not properly attached to the originals and for which there is no appropriate auditing trail. Seizing his opportunity, a thief could direct the computer to create revised shipping instructions calling for a drop anywhere he finds convenient. When the shipments received reports are processed, since the extra drop does not appear, it is ignored and the quantity received redistributed according to the original shipping instructions. Since the computer generated all the paper work and all the warehouses are experiencing about the same inventory shrinkage problems, no one's suspicion is aroused.

On the sale side, the thief may establish a seemingly legitimate account which he has marked for special pricing or discount. By receiving goods on an extremely favorable price basis, he can resell them at a profit. Or he can simply alter point-of-sale computer input—which nobody takes the trouble to verify because of its high volume and because "the computer doesn't make mistakes." Or he can simply take advantage of the impossibility of balancing out every single retail transaction and change a sales invoice for $1950 to $19.50 on the sales punch card. Carefully executed, this will look like an inventory loss from the affected department.

Another significant risk in manufacturing and retail is the creation of fictitious accounts payable, fictitious employees or false overtime as discussed earlier. Businesses of this type generally experience seasonal or cyclic variations in business level. Order quantities, suppliers and labor force fluctuate, and during periods of increased business all activities pick up, including inventory shrinkage. Help is generally not available to perform extra checking. During these periods fictitious temporary suppliers and employees are especially easy to introduce and are significantly less likely to be detected. This type of crime is becoming more prevalent because of the malfunction of audits of computerized payroll and accounts payable—it is so easy to trust the computer.

BANKS AND FINANCIAL INSTITUTIONS

As the interest breakage case shows, banks and financial institutions frequently must protect their customers as well as themselves. A small miscalculation of interest or service charge is generally not noticed by the customer. Multiplied by a large number of accounts, this small miscalculation can provide the felon with a handsome annual bonus. Further, since the interest paid or service charges collected were proper from the institution's standpoint, this type of embezzlement seldom raises suspicion unless enough customers object.

Misappropriation of funds, stocks, or other assets on a "borrowed" basis is another common form of fraud. With inadequately monitored computer operations to assist them, the borrower can appear to return the assets to their proper accounts if a surprise audit is held.

Outright theft of funds in the classic sense of embezzlement is also possible. In some cases this may occur by accident. For instance, take the case of the depositor who requested a two hundred dollar transfer of funds between two of his accounts. When he discovered that two hundred thousand dollars was credited through an error, he immediately withdrew the money, filtered it through various accounts, including securities and travelers checks, and disappeared. By the time the error was discovered, he and the funds were long gone.

Embezzlement has also been accomplished by creating fictitious assets, primarily stocks and certificates of deposit. The Equity Funding case is a well-publicized case in point.

The new automatic tellers pose their own special risks. The coded key cards are easy to copy or forge, and even MICR checks have been forged. The greatest challenge to a thief is obtaining the personal passwords used by depositors. This may be done by wiretapping or by close observation of depositors using the automatic teller. Most frequently a pickpocket or purse snatcher will obtain the password because the depositor wrote it down to remember it. Once the thief has all the necessary tools and information, he can withdraw funds without fear of recognition.

Recently many banks have opened the floodgates to theft of confidential financial information through the information systems designed to give bank tellers real-time access to customer accounts. In many cases, virtually no safeguards have been erected to prevent unauthorized access to these files. Many of these systems use ordinary touch-tone telephones and automatic telephone dial cards provided by the telephone company to gain access to the central files of all depositor accounts. It is not even necessary for the information thief to acquire one of these automatic dialing devices. All he needs is an ordinary touch-tone telephone. The dial codes employed are generally the most obvious and straightforward; anyone watching a bank teller's operation for about ten minutes can learn them. Once they are learned, a simple telephone tap anywhere within the bank's telephone system is all that is needed to read (and in a limited way modify) any account in the bank, to ascertain whether an account is being used or not (for purposes of forgery or kiting), and to gain detailed information as to deposits and withdrawals in that account. All this can be done without ever setting foot in the bank.

AIRLINE RESERVATION AND CAR RENTAL SYSTEMS

Since airline reservation and car rental systems rely heavily upon data communications, wiretapping and similar techniques can be used to obtain the necessary information to compromise the system. A well-conceived terminal connection will then provide access, and once access is achieved services can be obtained after which the bills (computer records) may become "lost" (assigned to fictitious accounts) or fees simply reduced to nominal values.

In the case of a computerized car rental system an entire car's records can be shuffled through the agency until its auditing trail disappears. The entire car can then be made to disappear as well.

In the case of airlines, baggage records are maintained on the main reservation file. Thus, it is possible to create a fictitious piece of baggage, then submit a claim for its loss.

PUBLIC STOCK CORPORATIONS AND INVESTMENT HOUSES

Dealing with information that could affect the value of stock that is publicly held or the stock of public corporations makes the exposure and liability of any organization issuing or dealing in that stock particularly critical. As long as the accounting of these corporations is handled manually under the supervision of accountants whose training and code of ethics have taught them how to handle this information, few problems exist with regard to premature disclosure of earning reports. Now that computers have entered the picture, a typical company that must make regular reports to the SEC suddenly finds itself in a situation where a large number of computer programmers, operators, and outsiders have access to the most critical financial data affecting the company's operations. If the consolidated earnings reports of a large corporation were deliberately or accidentally revealed to outsiders before formal disclosure, *even if this leak did not result in a price movement of the stock,* corporate and personal liability would arise through application of the "insiders rule." This is a serious problem which at least one substantial conglomerate has reported, and special steps are needed to ensure that privileged financial data are kept private until they are formally or publicly disclosed.

An Observation

It might be suggested that fraud of this nature could just as well occur in a completely manual system, that anyone familiar with the system's checks could confound a manual system as well as an automated one. This is undoubtedly true, but manual systems seldom make assumptions about the validity of copies. Further, a human who is verifying check numbers and amounts will notice any discrepancies in payees and report them. A computer will "see" only what it is told to look at and will report only what it has been told to report.

The controls used by auditors to check manual systems (and the manual portions of automated systems) are better understood and implemented than those used in the automated portion of the system. For this reason, and because there is a general lack of understanding regarding the insertion of proper controls in an automated system, computer-based systems are much more susceptible to manipulation. Systems designers and programmers have a detailed knowledge of the methods necessary to circumvent controls, and auditors whether internal or external are more likely to be checking the system for inconsistencies, inaccuracies, or indications of fraud, not for the gimmicks that produce fraud but provide no indication.

Chapter 3
Equity Funding and Other Diversions
A Collection of Tales Out of School

Equity Funding

Computer-related crime on a major scale dates back at least to 1964 when a programmer in Texas stole from his employer $5 million worth of the programs he was maintaining and tried to sell them to one of his employer's customers. He served five years in prison on charges of grand theft.

The Equity Funding scandal that shook the stock market in March, 1973, uncovered a computer fraud of a magnitude that had never been reached before. Yet one observer said that the surprise was not that it happened, but that it had not happened more often. It might well have happened more often, another said, since the only cases made public are the ones that aren't cleverly handled.

The multimillion-dollar fraud perpetrated by the Equity Funding Corporation of America victimized mutual fund customers, stockholders, companies to which Equity Funding had resold insurance policies, and companies from whom it had borrowed. Nineteen employees and former employees of the Beverly Hills firm plus three employees of one of its auditing firms—Wolfson, Weiner, Ratoff & Lapin—have at the time of this writing been indicted on a total of 105 counts by a California grand jury. Further legal aspects will take years to unravel.

In a related legal matter, Equity Funding Life Insurance Company (a subsidiary) filed a class action civil suit against IBM, contending that IBM had failed either to inform its customers about the vulnerability of its products to fraud or to provide sufficient security in its products.

Equity Funding's far-reaching swindle scheme involved creating phony life insurance policies, integrating records of these policies with records of actual policies it had sold, and reselling the mixture to firms who bought the policies with the idea of collecting further premiums.

Equity was said to have created 56,000 insurance policies amounting to some $2 billion out of a total of 91,000 policies reportedly worth $6.5 billion. To prevent discovery, computer personnel had to perpetuate the deceit by manipulating records so as to show changes in the phony policies, such as a reasonable number of lapses, cancellations, and deaths. The computer programs also had to be designed to conceal the fictitious business from auditors and state insurance examiners.

In further efforts to outwit auditors and examiners, the firm installed electronic surveillance equipment in various rooms so that conversations about verification plans could be overheard.

The subsidiary that dealt with the phony policies—Equity Funding Life Insurance Company—used fictitious entries in various types of accounts to conceal its true business operations, as did the parent company, which also gave false information about its entire business picture to the Securities and Exchange Commission and to the entire business community. The parent company also printed counterfeit bonds, formed specious subsidiaries, falsified documents, and performed other acts with a fraudulent intent. The grand jury alleges that Stanley Goldblum, president of the parent firm, gave instructions to have certain figures inflated in annual reports as far back as 1965.

Equity Funding started off modestly enough as an ordinary small firm selling both mutual funds and life insurance. Its spurt of growth started in 1960, when the firm developed the idea of combining mutual funds with life insurance and selling the two as a package called "equity funding." Under a ten-year plan, a customer bought mutual fund shares and used them as collateral for loans to buy life insurance. After ten years, the customer sold enough mutual fund shares to pay off the loans. The hope was that the value of the shares would have gone up so much that the customer would recoup his original investment and have gained ten years of free life insurance besides. The company continued to sell mutual funds and life insurance separately, but the salesmen liked selling the package plan because they gained a double commission.

When sales dropped and quick cash was needed, the firm sold some of its policies to other insurance firms in a procedure called "reinsuring" that is legitimately used in the insurance industry. The reinsurer pays less for the policies than it would cost him for his own firm to sell the policies to the public and gains most of the future premium payments.

The stock market decline in 1970 hit Equity Funding hard because potential customers could not foresee the constant growth in mutual funds earnings that would be needed to pay off the life insurance. It appears that this factor inspired the plan to create and resell bogus insurance policies. The thinking was apparently that it would be a temporary measure, and that future sales would be high enough to cover the additional expense of paying the premiums on the bogus policies.

The swindle continued until a former employee revealed the operation to a stockbroker and to the New York Department of Insurance.

An interesting question and significant factor in the case is, how did the principals expect to get away with it? There were, after all, 22 people named in the indictment, others named but not indicted, and presumably others unnamed who knew about the alleged criminal activities even if they had not participated. Even the mobs have trouble keeping that many people in line without resorting to extraordinary measures.

Apparently, in addition to the fact that they initially intended the criminal activity to be short-lived, they were themselves as much victims of the computer mystique as they envisioned the people they attempted to victimize would be. Considerable effort was expended to maintain all records of illicit activities in the computer and to present policy owner lists and financial information only in computer printout form.

Presumably the perpetrators felt that victims would have confidence in computer-generated reports. Thus they would not question the results too closely. Further, if close inspection were attempted, the fictitious information would, in general, be inside the computer safely out of the way and inaccessible for easy inspection.

The essence of the alleged criminal activities centered around creating fictitious insurance policies and including them with lapsed policies which were made to appear in force. Counterfeit bonds, certificates of deposit, and supporting documents were then generated in order to show an asset value commensurate with the level of business represented by the fictitious policies and to raise funds. These fictitious entities were intermingled with legitimate items of the same type.

A group of individuals was established with responsibility for generating the fictitious names and addresses such that correspondence regarding these policies, bonds, and other items would arrive in friendly hands. The correspondence included auditing confirmations and premium notices. In some cases, such as with larger bonds, where this procedure would be too risky, fictitious foreign companies were established to issue bonds or other financial paper that could appear on the books as assets and were not easily verified. This ensured that responses to such communications could be arranged to maintain the appearance of validity to reinsurers and auditors. It would also appear that programs were created to select policies on a statistical basis for death benefit claims, lapses, beneficiary changes, and other policy-related events to perpetuate the appearance of validity of these policies. Frequently, death benefit claims collected were used to pay premiums on reinsured policies remaining in force.

So in essence, the perpetrators emulated 56,000 policy holders with the aid of the computer, some counterfeit bonds, and other financial papers. These policies and fictitious financial papers were then intermingled with legitimate similar items in computer files in a way supposed to render them undetectable except by their computer and at their command. Safety should thus derive from the anonymity and air of authenticity provided by the computer. Presumably the perpetrators felt that even if they were accused of wrongdoing nothing could be proved.

After the wrongdoing was made public, a team of auditors from Touche Ross & Co. moved into the company's data processing department and records were analyzed to find out what characteristics the bogus policies had in common. It took the auditors six months to identify about 99 percent of the bogus policies.

In many cases, the reinsuring firms relied solely on computer printouts as evidence of the existence of policyholders. One food-processing firm, Anderson, Clayton & Co., whose chief executive was cautious was nevertheless victimized. Ranger National Life, a subsidiary of these Houston food processors, was one of the reinsuring firms. Thomas J. Barlow, president of Anderson, Clayton & Co., sent his own firm's auditors to check Equity Funding's operations when the two companies entered into an agreement in 1969. "We wanted to make sure we were not insuring fenceposts," Barlow said in an interview. But his auditors found nothing, and Barlow added that at the time the fraud was exposed his company was even talking about doing additional business with Equity Funding.

"When we went there at the end of the first year, 1969, there was no bogus business," Barlow said. "And in 1970, I think over 80 percent of their business was good business. Those are better than Las Vegas odds. Besides, the premiums were being paid on the bogus business. It makes it hard when fenceposts are paying premiums."

Barlow said the Equity Funding situation has had far-reaching repercussions that are causing management to take a closer look at internal operations. "We ask, 'Could that happen internally? What are our controls? Let's tell our auditors we want more controls.' We've been more careful from the president on down," Barlow said.

It is hard to say how much the computer mystique influenced the decisions of reinsurers who saw only computer printouts as evidence of the existence of policyholders. The computer mystique could have been very influential, according to Dr. Carl Silver, Professor of Behavioral Sciences at Drexel University, in Philadelphia.

"There are experimental data that tend to show that people —particularly men—are influenced by other individuals whom they feel are higher in prestige. One of the elements that contributes to prestige is the appearance of specialized knowledge or technical superiority. The mere appearance as being on a printout will generate in any but the most experienced skeptical observer a lot more credibility than would the same information in longhand. It's peculiar that this should be so, because in longhand you can ask the guy who did it to vouch for it. People give somewhat more credence to anonymous persons, and to a large extent it's forgotten that what you're getting came from somebody."

Dr. Silver said he considers computer security to be a serious problem. He believes the biggest concern is not unauthorized retrieval, but rather unauthorized input because of the costs of tracking down errors.

"Say you're a major oil or electric company and have accounts for millions of customers. The problem of making sure only authorized personnel have access is not so important because of theft, but because you've got to make your accounts balance out. If changes are made so accounts don't balance out, the amount of money spent to find the errors is large. It's an expensive hobby, not something you can indulge in often.

"Several years ago somebody messed up the payroll of the Philadelphia school system and the teachers went for weeks without pay before that was cleared up. Teachers were crying like mad and the school board had to put people on around the clock to straighten things out.

"In another case, one of my students working on the computer at the University of Pennsylvania decided to write in machine language and he coded something wrong. By coincidence, he hit upon the secret entry codes that get into the executive routine. His instructions were read into the executive routine which, of course, became demented and had to be shut down for a week," Dr. Silver said.

One banking executive who is a strong advocate of caution when it comes to computer security is Edwin J. Poplawski, manager of EDP auditing at First Pennsylvania Corp., a holding company for several large institutions including the First Pennsylvania Bank and Trust Co., Philadelphia's largest. Poplawski, an accountant, said that the more familiar he becomes with computer operations, the more cautious he becomes.

"Fifteen years ago I would have suggested showcasing the computer operations in the bank window the way we used to do vaults, but I wouldn't do so today," he said. "There is too much danger of someone throwing a rock into the window or gaining information he doesn't need to know."

Speaking as a manager, Poplawski says, "My idea is that all people are as pure as the driven snow, but it is the responsibility of management to keep them that way. If they have had a bad day at the track they have to be protected from the temptation to satisfy a crisis."

Poplawski said his organization has some 200 persons in EDP, including 40 programmers, whom he refers to as "40 guys smarter than we are." He blames the programmers if he finds it hard to understand what they are doing, and tells them, "Don't snow me with computer jargon. Tell me in English."

Poplawski said that the Equity Funding situation has caused his company to take another look at its own operations. As a result, one function that had previously been performed by the computer department was switched over to the auditing department. "Nothing alarming occurred, but it prompted us to be doggone sure that the auditing department performs independently with little reliance on the EDP department. If EDP does something for you, you have to realize you're not doing it yourself. You have to satisfy yourself that it does what it purports to be doing."

Working actively toward more security among brokerage houses is John Letson, First Vice President with Bache & Co., a major investment firm based in New York City. In an interview, Letson said that a major problem in data processing is that computer use expanded so rapidly in the 1960's that top management depended to a great extent on "the new computer management" to make sure computers were used properly.

"It seems to me that because many of the senior managers do not have an adequate background in data processing, there is the problem of dependency on newer managers who do," Letson said. "But because their tenure is so short, they are not proven businessmen.

"The growth of data processing is in my mind not going to subside. The security problem that was magnified by Equity Funding should alert senior managements to the need for establishing professional data processing rather than considering it an extension of the previous bookkeeping department. If they're going to buy a $3 million computer, they shouldn't promote the manager of the bookkeeping department from $12,000 to $15,000 a year and say he is now capable of managing the operation."

Letson said he considers shared time one of the biggest security problems. "Security in this area needs attention because the same computer complex might be processing portfolios of security holdings for various banks, for example. If the competition uses the same computer, there has to be more concern.

"A's information could be sold to B," Letson said. "Someone using a service bureau should be asked, 'Is your company bonded against misuse? Do you have business loss insurance to protect against what happens if they sell your information to a competitor? To what extent does the service bureau you are dealing with have procedures for safekeeping your information?'''(An interesting survey of programmer ethics and honesty is presented in Appendix C.)

Other Diversions

Donn B. Parker, 44, is a man who is so concerned about computer ethics that he has become a full-time researcher of computer abuse. Parker, now senior information processing specialist at the Stanford Research Institute in Menlo Park, California, has spent the past three years researching computer abuse on a full-time basis. In studying cases, he said in an interview, he is starting to find a high incidence of collusion in computer abuse. This leads him to the conclusion that the traditional responsibility and dual control in sensitive job tasks are very important.

He has also concluded that more efforts should be put into detection techniques than into prevention. "The computer is the ideal instrument of detection," he said, "because of the detail to which you can program the search for irregular activities."

In his early consideration of the Equity Funding situation, Parker felt that "one of the basic problems in the lack of detection by outside auditors was that they considered computer printouts as documents of record. They did not understand the operations well enough to believe they could be falsified. Auditors are just now barely starting to gain the capability to audit through computer systems," he added.

Under a $30,000 grant from the National Science Foundation, Parker has researched computer fraud cases. His study, "Computer Abuse," was published in November, 1973. Issued by Stanford Research Institute, the study lists 148 cases from the United States, Canada, and Europe. Parker states that the confirmation of the cases has ranged from ones that he has checked out himself to ones that he has read in newspapers all the way to a few that he has heard about that might not have happened at all.

The following are representative cases selected from Parker's list with his identification code. In part we have speculated or edited the M.O.'s employed.

PHONY MICR DEPOSIT SLIPS—WASHINGTON, D.C. (1964)

A depositer exchanged blank deposit slips on the counter in the bank with his own magnetically coded deposit slips, giving his own account number. Normally processed by machine, the deposit slips are not usually verified by the bank as to name and address of the depositor. He accumulated $250,000 in four days from other people's deposits. He then withdrew $100,000, disappeared and has never been caught.

ALTERING BANK RECORDS—MINNEAPOLIS (1966)

A programmer altered the bank's demand-deposit accounting program to ignore overdrafts in his checking account for about six months. He accumulated overdrafts of $1357 before he was caught by manual accounting, only when the computer failed. He made restitution and received a suspended sentence.

EMBEZZLEMENT, CALIFORNIA (1968)

A chief accountant embezzled $1 million from his employer over six years. He used the company's computer to financially model his company. The model gauged which appropriate changes in accounts receivable and payable would remain undetected in auditing, then performed the indicated alterations. For example, if an inventory shrinkage of 5% were common, then phony orders and payments of up to 0.5% of accumulated inventory would not cause alarms to be set off. He was convicted and given a ten-year prison term.

POPULATION REGISTRY DATA THEFT, SWEDEN (1970)

Two employees borrowed tapes of population registry and copied them using another computer. They sold the copies at reduced prices to their employer's customers. Both employees were convicted and given a six-month jail sentence.

CONSPIRED BANK EMBEZZLEMENT, NEW JERSEY (1970)

The computer systems vice president, senior computer operator, and three nonemployees of a bank were charged with transferring money from infrequently used savings accounts to newly opened accounts. They were detected when conversion to a new computer disrupted their work.

LOS ANGELES WELFARE EMBEZZLEMENT, LOS ANGELES (1970)

Eleven employees of the County Department of Social Service used the names of people leaving the welfare rolls for self-enhancement. They extracted lists of terminated state welfare numbers, changed names and addresses, then issued welfare checks to themselves.

TWO-BANK FLOAT EMBEZZLEMENT, JAMAICA, NEW YORK AND QUEENS (1970)

A bank vice president and four others deposited checks designated as "cash deposits," which are recorded for immediate credit. This can be done by bank officials as an accommodation to known clients or when accepting the payroll checks of a local firm. Checks drawn on the account were therefore good until the deposit checks were found not to be covered by another bank. (This requires from 4 to 7 days.) The act was discovered when a bank messenger failed to deliver $440,000 worth of checks to the clearinghouse. The scheme had worked, however, for four years, with a total theft of $900,000.

IRS TAX CREDIT EMBEZZLEMENT, WASHINGTON, D.C. (1970)

An IRS adjustment clerk transferred unclaimed tax credits from one account through a chain of other accounts and finally to a relative's account. The act was discovered when auditors traced a complaint of no refund of a $1,500 tax credit.

COMPUTER SERVICE THEFT, DETROIT (1970)

Two engineers accidentally discovered that a password one digit different than their own happened to belong to the president of the time-sharing firm. The president's password allowed access to privileged customer and accounting data. It thus allowed the engineers to use unlimited amounts of computer time and obtain customer information and proprietary program listing. Discovery was made by computer operators who noticed the password being used at unusual times. The engineers were fired and no other action taken.

PROGRAM THEFT, CALIFORNIA (1971)

A programmer stole a copy of a program from the computer file of his employer's competitor through telephone circuits, using a remote job entry terminal. Criminal charges of theft of a trade secret and a civil suit resulted in conviction and a judgment for $300,000 damages for the plaintiff.

CUSTOMER LIST THEFT, WHITE PLAINS, NEW YORK (1971)

An employee tried to sell listings of new customers to an outside buyer. He was caught when a potential buyer reported the offer to the police. The list was estimated to be worth $37,000 in the address list market. The case was dropped for lack of evidence.

INDUSTRIAL ESPIONAGE, WEST GERMANY (1971)

A secret agent for East Germany is alleged to have copied confidential financial and production data of 3,000 West German firms onto tape and given the tape to the government of East Germany. The outcome of the case is not known.

SALARY ROUND-DOWN, FRANCE (1971)

An employee was authorized to round salaries down to two decimal places, but when he did so he accrued the remainder amounts to his own salary. The total salaries, of course, balanced correctly. The disposition of the case is not known.

OVERSTATED ACCOUNTS PAYABLE (1971)

An account clerk at a catering service used a grocery store owner as an accomplice. He submitted to a computer system false account numbers and invoices for undelivered food. Thefts amounted to $120,000 over eight years. Both conspirators were convicted.

COLLECTION AGENCY REBILLING, TEXAS (1971)

A computerized collection agency sent new bills to people who had paid their bills the previous year. They relied for profit on the reluctance of most people to fight computerized systems.

PENSION FRAUD, CANADA (1971)

An employee in an insurance company changed the account numbers of several deceased insured persons to his own to collect their pensions. He was caught when a staple in a punch card forced manual handling, which revealed several cards with the same number.

PAYROLL FRAUD, WEST GERMANY (1971)

An EDP operator pressed the "repeat" button on the printer to print 200 extra copies of his own paycheck. He was caught when he cashed 37 checks all at the same bank.

SALES COMMISSION FRAUD, ENGLAND (1971)

A programmer in a mail-order company created a sales commission account in the name of Zwana to be the last in order. He adjusted the commission program to collect commission round-downs in the last account. He was discovered after three years when Marketing happened to choose the first and last accounts for a public relations project.

THEFT OF COMPUTER TIME, LOS ANGELES (1972)

The manager of EDP and part of his staff were using the firm's computer to analyze racehorse handicaps, making several thousand dollars each week.

INFORMATION THEFT, CALIFORNIA (1972)

A student copied 500 passwords from the system file by using a text editor program to gain access to the presumably protected file. The password file is now kept in scrambled form; sanctions were privately imposed on the student. It should be noted that a cleverer student could also gain access to the unscrambling program.

THEFT OF PATENTABLE PROCESSES (1972)

Two employees scheduled for layoff took program listings describing secret processes to be patented. One employee was fired, the other died of a heart attack.

PHONY WELFARE GRANTS, CALIFORNIA (1972)

In Los Angeles County, welfare grants are paid from vouchers based on punch cards. Someone put extra cards in the computer to produce unauthorized grants. No suspects were identified.

BANK EMBEZZLEMENT, ENGLAND (1972)

The six employees of a bank mutilated their own paychecks. When rejected by the check reader, they were returned to the perpetrator's department for handling, where they were destroyed and never debited against the check reconciliation file. The perpetrators were convicted of embezzling $8,300, but given suspended sentences.

THEFT OF COMPUTER SERVICES, TEXAS (1972)

A high school student found a privileged password of the computer service's analyst on a listing in a wastebasket. He also obtained detailed specifications of the system—presumably by merely asking for them. He used large amounts of computer time, played computer games and obtained other customers' data. He was discovered when a computer operator noticed scratch tapes being read before being written.* Restitution was made.

THEFT OF COMPUTER SERVICES, CALIFORNIA (1972)

High school students were allowed to use free computer terminal services on one project. The computer system employee involved subsequently left. The students continued to use the services, using new passwords they found. They used $3,000 worth of services before being caught. Now a "poaching bit" is set to alert operators to suspected account activity. Sanctions were imposed privately on the students.

BANK EMBEZZLEMENT, NEW YORK (1973)

A bank teller manipulated hundreds of accounts through his teller terminal into the computer system. The details of manipulation are omitted. He was caught when a raid on a bookie showed large bets placed by the suspect. He was prosecuted for embezzling $1.5 million by the Manhattan District Attorney's Office.

DIVIDENDS FRAUD (1973)

A clerk adjusted a computer program used to prepare dividends, thereby generating dividend checks to former shareholders, but addressed to an accomplice. The program then erased records of the check. The clerk was convicted for embezzling $33,000.

If there is a way your system can be compromised, sooner or later someone is liable to try. It *could* happen to you.

*This is a common ploy. Most computer centers do not bother to "zero" tapes that they release for future use. An astute programmer can learn much by "printing out" any tapes he is given.

Chapter 4

How to Tap, Bug and Spoof a System

The Vulnerability of Data Communications

IN 1971 a major life insurance company was in the throes of a strike. As often occurs during such disagreements, strange incidents occasionally befell various parties to the disagreement. It happens that this life insurance company has one of the largest and most modern computer systems of its kind in the world; each major district office is linked to the central computer via a data communications system that allows insurance policy and other data to be fed in within hours. The advantage of such a system lies in its timeliness. Data files are fully up-to-date each morning; the high risks arising during the underwriting period associated with granting each new policy are minimized by cutting the underwriting time in half; cash flow can be accurately controlled and management visibility optimized.

This life insurance company's information system is of the *dial-up access* variety discussed in Chapter 1. Each district office daily prepares a punched paper tape of its transactions and places them in a reader. Some time later in the day, usually at night, the central computer under program control dials up each office and transmits a coded signal that starts the paper tape moving. The transaction data are then transmitted to the central computer, and each electronic black box bids the other a hearty good evening.

However, things did not go this way on the nights of interest to us. Instead, a group of individuals, having previously invested a few dollars in a teletype machine, placed the data-collection calls a bit earlier. Mimicking the computer, they transmitted "Start Tape" signals to the district office sets, which obediently responded. The data were transmitted to the phony station, and then the next district office was called. When the insurance company's computer dialed up these offices, the tape had already run out, and what the computer received instead appeared to consist of miles and miles of blank tape.

The objective here was probably sabotage, not espionage. The data losses were not discovered for some time, and reconstruction of the data, while possible, required considerable manual effort and paper work. Furthermore, since public long-distance telephone lines were employed, it was difficult to trace the source of the phony calls.

The individuals who played the substitution game were eventually caught and discharged. Now, the law moves slowly, and criminal sanctions regarding computer and communications crimes are not yet fully developed (see Chapter 12). It was therefore necessary to indict them under a law prohibiting—you guessed it—obscene telephone calls.

Data communications represents the single most important new force in the evolution of information processing in the last decade, because it adds a whole new dimension of potential capability. It brings the data base and processor onto the desks of the information source, the query originator, and the information user and allows each element in a widespread organization to enter, find, and obtain data in real time.

Large companies desire to centralize certain data processing functions such as accounting and inventory control. Time-sharing companies provide service to a diversity of users, and retail organizations collect data from many different stores. In general, such applications cover a large geographic area. Two problems arise: getting input data from the point of origin to the computer and getting processed data back to the users. This is of particular importance where real-time considerations are significant. The mails and messenger services have been employed in some cases, but these services are frequently too slow or too costly.

Data communications represented a solution to those problems. Telephones and telegraph have been in common use for years and are readily available. Indeed, telegraph usage had been declining in the states and new users of these facilities were being actively sought. All that was required was a means of connecting the computer to communications facilities and programs to control data transmission.

Tapping Communications

Data communications also opens a wholly new arena of threats to the security of an information system because the system is connected to its components via telephone lines, which generally run outside the owner's physical premises. Here again familiarity breeds contempt, and the average user does not concern himself too deeply with the opportunities open to a thief armed with a little knowledge of how data communications work.

Data security is the area of data communications most generally neglected. First, because the transmitted data are in digital language rather than natural English they are thought to be encoded and relatively safe. Second, although wiretapping is known to occur, it is one of those things that always happens to the other guy. It happens to James Bond, but certainly not to "me." Third, it is often thought that wiretapping is a complicated procedure requiring expensive equipment. Last, and probably most significant, the extent to which communications can be spoofed and the wide range of crimes that can be perpetrated by such acts are not appreciated. For the most part, industrial espionage is the only threat commonly considered.

These are all misconceptions. Computer language is almost as readable to the professional as natural English and machines that aid in translation are readily available. The data codes are international standards (more about this later). Wiretapping is more frequent than most people think, and it is cheap and easy. While a definite risk, industrial espionage is much less a threat than theft or sabotage.

As in the Pacific Telephone case, assets can be stolen by mimicking a legitimate terminal. Computer time *per se* represents a significant potential for loss in such systems. While these losses may be damaging, remote sabotage is even easier to accomplish than theft and, though less common, it can be more damaging.

The fact of the matter is that data communications are easier to tap, bug and spoof than voice communications. Both are orders-of-magnitude easier to violate than the average closed-shop batch-processing computer room (even if security measures there are sloppy).

Types of Systems

There are two primary types of communications link: direct-access, or dedicated-circuit, service (also referred to as tie-line service) and dial-up service. While the ease of access effected by dial-up service is generally realized, few realize that access to tie-line service is nearly as easy, especially if the tie-line utilizes regular Bell System trunks. The major difference is that in dial-up service the telephone companies publish instructions on how to gain access to the system and directories of dialable numbers. For switchboard Bell-furnished tie-line service, the comparable information is not so readily available—especially to those not directly associated with the service—but similar access is possible.

For example, in St. Louis a young engineer fed a computer all the listed telephone numbers in four local exchanges. The computer sorted them and prepared a list of all the combinations that were not published. The engineer then dialed all these numbers to determine which ones hooked him into open long-distance lines leased by corporations. He was then able to dial these numbers to obtain long-distance lines to many cities and he could then dial the desired number within the city on a toll-free basis.

In a dial-up system the initiator dials the number of the desired destination and awaits a tone indicating that a connection has been made. In some cases the computer operator answers the call, and the validity of and transmission coordination with the terminal is established between operators before the computer operator enables connection to the computer. Machine-initiated connections take place in basically the same manner except that validity is established by the transmission of standardized special tones and recognition codes.

A communications link may connect more than one terminal to a computer; so thus, once the physical facilities exist, an electronic connection must be established in order for communications to occur. Generally, connections are initiated at the terminal, but they can also be initiated by the computing system.

In direct-access systems all terminals are essentially—but not physically—connected to the computer at all times. The terminals are not active, though, unless actually in use. When a terminal is ready to transmit data to the computer it transmits an alert signal and awaits permission to transmit data. When the computer transmits data, it precedes the data with a terminal recognition code or address. Only the terminal with that code or address is activated to receive the transmission.

Some terminals have the ability to store data until the data are requested by the computer. When the computer desires the data it establishes a connection and requests transmission. Under this technique, called *out-polling,* the computer periodically initiates connections and requests transmissions from each terminal in the system in a given sequence. Out-polling was the technique used by the insuror. Once the data are transmitted by the terminal, they are erased from the terminal's memory to prevent duplicate transmissions later.

Out-polling techniques are generally very cost-effective, especially if the remote station does not require instant access. In fact, AT&T has established special low-cost tariffs to encourage out-polling data communication from 11 P.M. to 8 A.M. each night.

Ease of Access

Because of the monopolistic utility status of the industry, government control, international agreements, and the necessity for interchangeability of facilities, the communications facilities available today are highly standardized and their characteristics are published and readily available from the telephone company and others (see below). This means that specifications necessary to build equipment to connect to these facilities are easy to obtain and, once a device has been developed, it has a widespread applicability.

In the computer industry, data transmissions standardization has also progressed significantly in order to maintain the flexibility required for interchangeability of terminals and computers. For example, a time-sharing company sells computer time in small increments to a large number of users using many different kinds and brands of terminals. If transmission characteristics were not highly standardized, the selection of terminals suitable for any one system would be limited and adaptation of terminals would be expensive. This would seriously limit the customer base for such companies and would be disadvantageous to the computer industry as a whole.

Bugging Communications

Communications facilities have been bugged from the inception of communications. Bugging may be done in any one of several ways. Three basic ways are: a physical connection, an inductive tap or a "drop-in" transmitter. Physical connection is by far the most common. It requires neither access to the physical location of the unit being tapped nor access to the telephone company's switching equipment.

To show how vulnerable data communications are to interception, sabotage or spoofing, it is worth while to say a few words about how a typical data communications system is organized. Far from being exotic, complex, or secure, the data transmission systems, "codes," and procedures are common knowledge, standardized, and highly spoofable. For an investment of $19.95 or less you can learn far more than you need to know about them.*

Figure 4.1 shows a typical dial-up or direct-access data communications network consisting of three remote entry or console devices connected to a computer or home office terminal. The connection is made through a standard telephone system otherwise devoted to ordinary voice telephone communications; this voice network may either be a private line network, a PBX (private branch exchange) set up by the telephone company for a given industrial concern, or the standard public telephone network complete with dial-up capability identical to that of an ordinary telephone.

Since the data systems utilize the ordinary telephone networks, (less frequently the ordinary TELEX or TWX networks), ordinary dial-up procedures are most frequently used to interconnect a remote console with the home office. These are also quite standard.

There are precisely three dial-up codes used in most of the world for signaling. Two are shown in Table 4.1.

Reference Data for Radio Engineers, (Fifth Edition). New York, Howard W. Sams & Co. Inc., 1972.

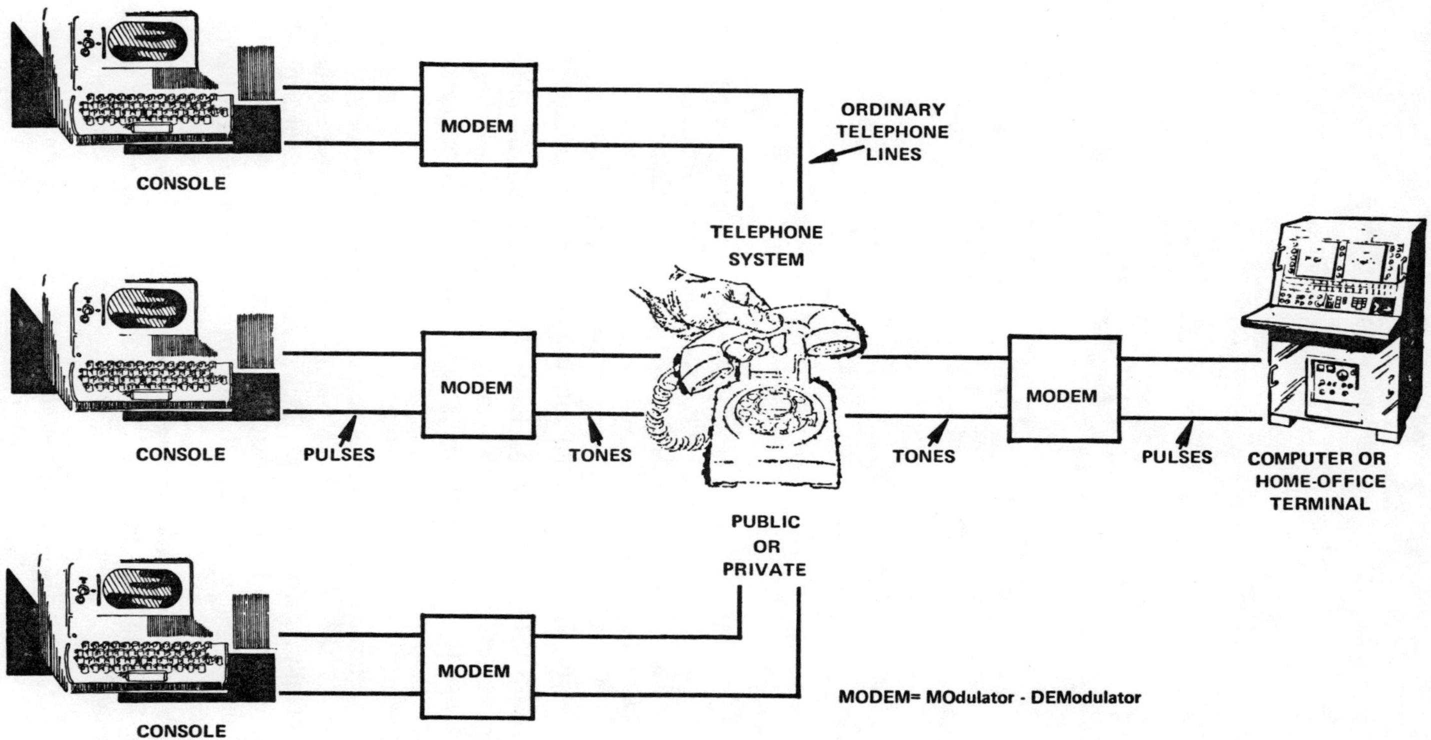

Figure 4.1 Typical data communications network

TABLE 4.1

The Two U.S. Standard Dial-up Codes

	Rotary Dial Phone	*Touch-Tone Phone Audio Frequency Tones, in Hertz or CPS*						
Number	*Number of Pulses*	*697*	*770*	*852*	*941*	*1209*	*1336*	*1477*
1	1	x				x		
2	2	x					x	
3	3	x						x
4	4		x			x		
5	5		x				x	
6	6		x					x
7	7			x		x		
8	8			x			x	
9	9			x				x
0	10				x	x		
*	None				x		x	
#	None				x			x

The rotary dial pulse code is familiar to most telephone users; it interrupts the line briefly a stated number of times as the rotary dial returns to its rest position after being dialed.

The touch-tone code is used for touch-tone telephones. Pushing a button generates two tones, one identifying the row and one identifying the column within which that button lies.

A third dial-signaling system is employed internationally by telephone operators and automatic toll-dialing equipment. This is the "phone freak's code" used to make free phone calls. We mercifully exclude this code.

When a key is pressed on a teletype or computer console this action is usually converted into a series of precisely five, seven, or eight pulses. Table 4.2 shows the three international standard pulse codes, almost universally used to carry data. Each key on the console corresponds to a unique configuration of pulses; the presence of a pulse is called a "one" or "mark" pulse, and the absence of a pulse is called a "zero" or "space" pulse.

The three international standard codes, with minor variations, are used for data transmissions throughout the world and are all easily identified.

The five-pulse (or five-level) Baudot code was originated in 1874 by Emil Baudot, the inventor of the teletype. It is used by most teletypes today (those identified as having three rows of keys on

TABLE 4.2

The Three International Standard Data Codes

(*0* = "Space"; 1 = "Mark")

	Five-Level Code	*Seven-Level Code*	*Eight-Level Code*
0	10110	011 0000	1111 0000
1	10111	011 0001	1111 0001
2	10011	011 0010	1111 0010
3	00001	011 0011	1111 0011
4	01010	011 0100	1111 0100
5	10000	011 0101	1111 0101
6	10101	011 0110	1111 0110
7	00111	011 0111	1111 0111
8	00110	011 1000	1111 1000
9	11000	011 1001	1111 1001
A	00011	100 0001	1100 0001
B	11001	100 0010	1100 0010
C	01110	100 0011	1100 0011
D	01001	100 0100	1100 0100
E	00001	100 0101	1100 0101
F	01101	100 0110	1100 0110
G	11010	100 0111	1100 0111
H	10100	100 1000	1100 1000
I	00110	100 1001	1100 1001
J	01011	100 1010	1101 0001
K	01111	100 1011	1101 0010
L	10010	100 1100	1101 0011
M	11100	100 1101	1101 0100
N	01100	100 1110	1101 0101
O	11000	100 1111	1101 0110
P	10110	101 0000	1101 0111
Q	10111	101 0001	1101 1000
R	01010	101 0010	1101 1001
S	00101	101 0011	1110 0010
T	10000	101 0100	1110 0011
U	00111	101 0101	1110 0100
V	11110	101 0110	1100 0101
W	10011	101 0111	1100 0110
X	11101	101 1000	1100 0111
Y	10101	101 1001	1100 1000
Z	10001	101 1010	1100 1001
Space	00100	010 0000	0100 0000
Car. Ret.	01000	000 1101	0000 1101
Line Feed	00010	000 1010	0010 0101
Fig. Shift	11011	*	*
Letter Shift	11111	*	*
Period	11100	010 1110	0100 1011
Comma	01100	010 1100	0110 1011
Query	11001	011 1111	0110 1111
Slash	11101	010 1111	0110 0001
Bell	01011	000 0111	0110 1111
Blank	00000	000 0000	0000 0000

*Not Applicable or Not Needed

the keyboard). The code sequence (Table 4.2) looks strange. Actually it was designed to minimize wear of the mechanism inside the teletype, assuming 19th century French is being typed. Unfortunately five-level teletype machines practically never wear out, so hundreds of thousands of machines using codes optimized for 19th century French are in use around the world, transmitting business English and computerese very nicely, thank you.

The seven-pulse or seven-level ASCII Code (American Standard Code for Information Interchange) is used by most computer consoles and modern TELEX and TWX machines (those having four rows of keys on the keyboard) and serves as the primary standard for computer interchange. Being a computer-inspired code, the numbers and letters fall into an easily memorized sequence, unlike those of Baudot.

The eight-level EBCDIC Code (Extended Binary Coded Decimal Interchange Code) was championed by IBM and is used exclusively for much of their equipment. The reader may note a similarity between EBCDIC and ASCII in the last four digits of many characters. The differences are significant codewise but not so much in terms of underlying rationale. Why do there exist two such similar codes, one for IBM and one for almost everyone else? Advocates of EBCDIC vigorously deny that this is a clever method of inspiring product loyalty.

The sequence of pulses is then fed to a device called a MODEM, (MOdulator-DEModulator) a conceptually simple black box whose purpose is to convert the pulses to audio-frequency tones which can be carried over the regular telephone network. Typically four tones are employed. Two of these tones serve to identify "one" and "zero" in traveling from the console to the central terminal, and two different tones are used to identify "one" and "zero" traveling from the home office terminal back to the console; a total of four tones. These four tones are:

Going from originator to destination	
Zero or Space	1070 Hertz (CPS)
One or Mark	1270 Hertz (CPS)
Going back to originator	
Zero or Space	2025 Hertz (CPS)
One or Mark	2225 Hertz (CPS)

The pulses of course are transmitted very rapidly, most frequently at around 110 pulses per second, which is far too fast to be read by a human being in the way morse code is read. Therefore, a small investment in machinery is required to decode these pulses. Anyone can buy a console which can read one of the three codes in new condition for about one to two thousand dollars—used or surplus they cost less than five hundred dollars—from between ten to twenty stores in any city. Many of these consoles come complete with a built-in MODEM. Those that don't require the addition of a MODEM at a cost of anywhere from fifty to two hundred dollars; again this can be purchased at a surplus electronic store.

Having made these investments one is now in a position to tap the overwhelming majority of data communication systems, read the data, change the data, throw the timing of the system out of kilter and thereby destroy the data, and engage in other forms of self-enrichment or amusement.

If one insisted on being sophisticated, for the cost of some line amplifiers which any high school student can build in his basement, or for the five or ten dollars they cost in an electronics parts house he can "isolate" his spurious data communications set from the telephone line in such a way as to render it undetectable to most "debugging experts."

But what about the highly touted password system? The average data communication system is designed so that the passwords must be transmitted between the console and the home office computer at the time that communication is initiated, and these of course can be picked up by the intercepting console at the same time that they are detected by the central terminal. Unless these codes are changed with *every single transmission,* they can then be used for spurious entry at the convenience of the thief.

How is tapping effected? In essence, an extension unit is inserted into the circuit being tapped in much the same way as extension telephones are installed in homes and businesses. The ring signal that causes the destination telephone to ring also activates recording equipment at the tap site. A physical tap can be installed anywhere between the headset of the user and the telephone company's central switching center of that user.

Inductive taps work on the principle that current flowing through a coil sets up a magnetic field. Another coil in the magnetic field can pick up the magnetic field variations and convert these into an electric current. Thus the data from one coil is induced into the other. Since inductive taps do not require physical connections, they are more difficult to detect than physical taps, but they do require access to receiving or retransmitting equipment that contains the required inductive coils.

The "drop-in" transmitter is a small radio transmitter that is inserted into a telephone headset. When the telephone is in use the "drop-in" transmitter picks up the conversation and broadcasts it to a nearby receiver. This type of bug is virtually useless for tapping data, but it is particularly helpful in determining user identifications and passwords where voice is used in establishing a connection. Especially where data cryptographic equipment is used, this type of tap may yield considerable information because of the coordination achieved through operator-to-operator voice communications. Planting the bug requires physical access to the telephone equipment in the location being bugged, which of course is a drawback.

Spoofing Communications

Spoofing occurs when one legitimate user or the computer itself is contacted by an unauthorized user posing as an authorized user. The object may be to steal information, interfere with legitimate communications or introduce erroneous information into the system.

To spoof a data communications system, access to the system is necessary. The methods and required hardware were discussed above. Generally, access is accomplished in a direct manner. On dial-up systems it is done simply by dialing the number of the computer or terminal with which contact is desired. In tie-line or direct-access systems it is necessary first to dial a code number to establish contact with the circuit and then to dial an extension representing the destination desired.

Once the connection is established, it is necessary to mimic a legitimate unit. This means that validation procedures as well as identification codes, passwords and cryptographic techniques (if any) must be known. During the interchange of information, these measures must be effectively applied in order to successfully accomplish the spoofing objective.

Bugging is a passive activity in which the offender must await user communications and can only steal what the users transmit. Spoofing is an active endeavor in which the offender induces the system to provide the desired information. Generally, industrial espionage and the discovery of identification codes, passwords and cryptographic use and techniques can be accomplished by bugging. Theft and sabotage use spoofing.

Protective Measures

Three protective measures can be applied against bugging and spoofing: detectors for taps and bugs, masks or other encoding methods to make data unintelligible to unauthorized recipients, and "locks" to make spoofing difficult. Unfortunately, these measures are only effective against the accidental loss of information and amateur offenders; they are only a minor nuisance to the serious criminal.

Communication facilities are electrical systems. A physical tap of such a system puts an additional load on the circuits which though not sufficient to affect operations is detectable. Detection, however, only indicates the possible existence of a tap. A visual search is required to locate and deactivate a tap.

Inductive taps and drop-in transmitters are more difficult to detect than physical taps. In general, visual inspection of facilities is the most effective means of detecting these offenses.

Preventing taps and bugs of any type is primarily a matter of preventing access to communications facilities. This means closely restricting access to all telephone facilities by employees of the host company and by employees of the company providing the communications facilities. Obviously this is virtually impossible to accomplish effectively. New equipment is added, old equipment removed, existing extensions changed and maintenance performed. All of these functions provide an opportunity for system compromise.

Telephone connection and switching equipment is frequently located in some out-of-the-way closet or other corner of the plant or office. As such, it is often relatively exposed. Because the telephone company installs and maintains this equipment and host company personnel seldom if ever have reason to work with it, management tends to consider it as telephone company equipment and give it little regard. Actually, this equipment is being rented just as the computing equipment and physical facilities may be. If the company is at all concerned about communications tapes and bugs they must accept greater responsibility and afford it the protection it deserves—protection consistent with that afforded the computer installation and general physical plant.

While taps and bugs can be discouraged they cannot be completely prevented; to assume they cannot happen in your facility is to bury your head in the sand. As we have seen, a loss of information can occur in many ways. Thus, it is desirable to consider methods of disguising or masking data. By whatever method this is accomplished, the technique is called cryptography.

Commercially available cryptographic equipment can be purchased for encoding and decoding data, and computer programs have been developed that accomplish the same effect. In general, this equipment performs a simple transposition of the alphabet. For each original letter of the alphabet another letter is substituted the same way that cryptograms that appear in newspapers are coded.

Decoding encrypted messages requires only the discovery of which original letter is represented by each letter of the code. In most cases a message of as few as twenty letters is sufficient for a simple transposition code to be broken. The popularity of cryptograms as a pasttime is a revealing testament to the slight protection these codes offer.

The Codebreakers by David Kahn (New York: Macmillan, 1967) provides an extensive discussion of all types of codes and cyphers. It also demonstrates in an interesting, readable manner how codes and cyphers have been and can be broken.

User identification codes and passwords function as locks on the system to prevent unauthorized intrusion. As with standard door locks these techniques hamper or prevent casual attempts at intrusion but do not prevent criminal invasion.

We have already discussed the discovery of user identification codes and passwords through wiretapping and bugging. Much can also be discovered about these items through strategic investigation and manipulation once physical (or electronic) access to the system has been achieved. User identifications frequently consist of key user-related items, such as social security number, federal employer tax number, postal address, cable address, stock ticker codes or other acronyms. These are all well-publicized items of information readily available. Once one or two user identifications have been discovered the installation's code assignment strategy can be applied to other users and a wide variety of user identifications developed for clandestine use.

User-generated passwords follow similar patterns. As with combination locks, the user generally selects a code that relates to himself in some way so that he will readily remember it. In this case, the data name, identification, purpose or other similar characteristics make possible a pseudoscientific search for passwords with a reasonable expectation of success.

Two considerations contribute to the decodability of user identifications and passwords. First, each must be unique so that no two users have the same identification and for each user no two files of different security consideration have the same password. Second, the user must be able to remember his identification and password without resort to written memos that may be lost, copied or obtained by unauthorized personnel. These considerations all yield assignment strategies that can too easily be broken.

Part II
THE SOLUTIONS

Chapter 5
The Strategy of Security
Resources, Concepts

In the first chapters we have tried to lay out, primarily via cases and examples, the breadth and magnitude of the problems facing a responsible executive of a computer-supported business operation. We have delved into the history and histrionics; the kinds of assets which may be affected; the ways in which computer theft, fraud and sabotage can be accomplished; and the particularly sensitive subject of data communications. By now we hope the reader has an appreciation of the problem. To our knowledge there is no little green pill, black box, supersoftware that provides, in and of itself, a computer system with a meaningful degree of protection against any but the most obtuse attack.

Most frequently those who are concerned with computer system security think first of physical protection: locks, alarms, guards, surveillance devices, fire extinguishers. These are all important, expensive and easy to understand because they form a part of physical security which has been routine in American business plant design since the first flintlock factory posted a minuteman at the front. Physical security is also easy to understand because any investment represents tangible assets which have a depreciable value and can be inventoried. Such is not the case with many other aspects of security.

The strategy of protection evolves into three parts.

1. Preparation for disasters, including prevention planning and back-up.
2. Controls and audits to assure that things are going well.
3. Mechanisms and procedures to minimize the loss, recovery operations and catch miscreants if 1) and 2) don't work.

Coupled with this is the need for a more skillful mixture of overt and not-so-overt devices and procedures designed to raise and maintain the security consciousness of the staff, discourage venal thoughts, and yet not appear so onerous as to demoralize or invade the privacy of the people who have to work with the system. Finally, an important objective of protection strategy is to leave a clear implication that the managers have a few tricks remaining up their sleeves.

We have discussed how the strategy of protection divides into three levels of timeliness: preparation, auditing and recovery. There is another way of dividing the problem in terms of the kinds of skills and devices which can be brought to bear on the whole problem. These are:

1. Physical plant and people protection (Chapter 6)
2. System hardware protection (Chapter 7)
3. Software security (Chapter 8)
4. Personnel management security (Chapter 9)

It requires a skillful mixture of all four security subsystems to achieve a given level of protection. In the judgment of the authors, no partial approach: plant, people, hardware, software or management suffices to solve the problem.

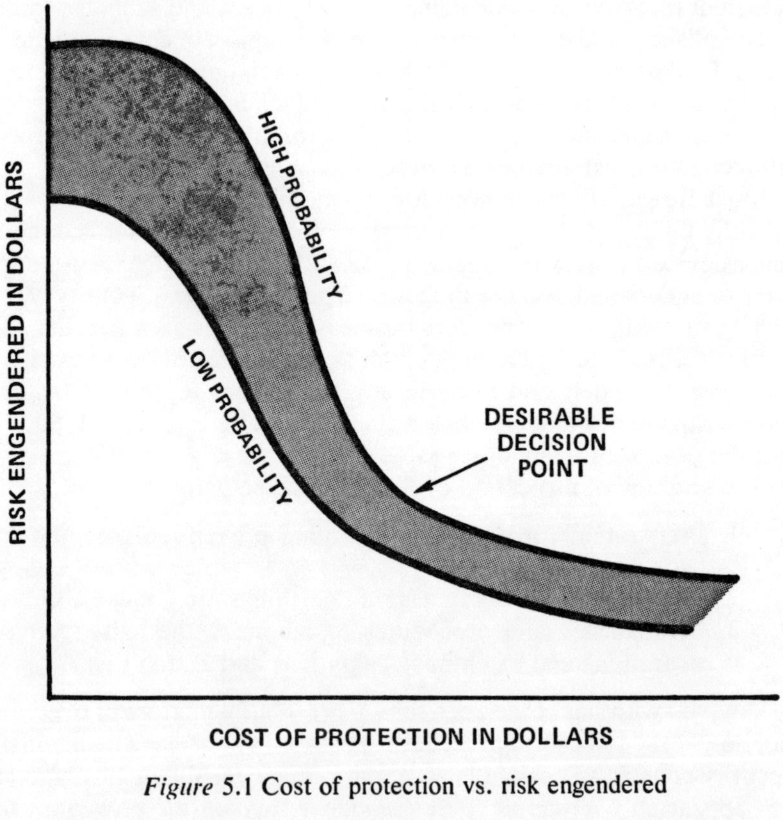

Figure 5.1 Cost of protection vs. risk engendered

A major uncertainty under cost-benefit analysis of computer security relates to the probability that a given event (e.g., a major payroll fraud) can occur. One cannot really assign firm probabilities to events generated by people, especially crafty people. However, an analysis can be done parametrically, as shown in Figure 5.1.

Looking at each possible source of compromise one can usually guess high or low values defining the range of occurrence to each one of these events based upon industry history. Each of these probabilities (high or low), is then multiplied by the dollar exposure, and the products added together. The result is a graph such as shown in Figure 5.1, which instead of having a single curve has a grey area of uncertainty. The businessman's risk decision can be made by inspecting the graph to decide upon the investment appropriate to computer security.

Needless to say, intangible costs and benefits cannot be so neatly evaluated. However, the authors' experience is that the analysis of this type will generally yield a conservative decision, i.e., one whose benefits relative to cost have a solid floor under them. Unfortunately, it is rarely possible to actually test the dollar savings unless scientific controls are set up using two smaller companies, one protected and one unprotected. Not many businessmen would be willing to submit to such an experiment.

Cost-benefit thinking must come into play with laying out security for an existing and planned system. In general, a small investment buys a small degree of protection and a moderate investment buys a great deal of protection. There is, however, a point of diminishing return in which the risk and exposure don't merit the cost of protection. Therefore, a system security plan has to be developed from a cost-benefit analysis. This must include at least the following factors:

1. *On the cost side:*
    a) investment in depreciable assets,
    b) amortization on expendable front-end costs,
    c) operating costs,
    d) audit and review costs,
    e) intangible costs for system or personnel performance by the security function, either physical or moralwise.
2. *On the benefit side:*
    a) subjectable likelihood of each type of natural or deliberate loss event,
    b) the cost of the business if that event occurs,
    c) the intangible effects of negative or positive publicity,
    d) the intangible risk reduction if people are made to believe that the system is indeed secure.

In other words, the planner must be ready to evaluate and accept the risks warranted or unwarranted in each decision to acquire or reject a given element in the total security package. Now, this sounds like fairly obvious preaching. It is, however, critical in the case of system security to perform numerical or rational cost-benefit analyses because

Each of the possible events usually involves low probability and large losses, adding up to high risk.

The benefit-cost leverage is generally very large, up to a point.

The investment of from 2 to 5 percent of the total system cost in security is a generally warranted cost benefit, yet is rarely made.

Chapter 6
Physical Security
The First Line of Defense

FOR the first 15 years A.C. (After the Computer), the Big Machine was a showpiece for its proud possessor. Better than a cross between a PhD from the Harvard Business School and a year-round Christmas Tree. Mere ownership of a computer was considered a fact worthy of advertising and display. To some degree, this was correct. Computer facilities were installed in plush quarters, glass-enclosed and readily accessible to public view. The marvel of modern science was displayed to the world at a considerable expense. Much less was expended to protect it from the world. There was no need, for unless you were an Institute, the machine was not useful to you.

The aura of mystery and science fiction that once surrounded computers has faded somewhat. Today every company of significance has one or more computers; the computer center has become the nerve center of the management function. As such, it is a vulnerable spot in the corporate structure, an ideal striking point for theft, sabotage and vandalism by groups wishing to attract attention or to interfere with company operations.

The showplace setting of early installations left them vulnerable to all types of violation. For this reason, there has been a concerted move away from the glass-front showplace and into the unexposed innards of corporate buildings or into separate computer centers well guarded against intrusion, fire and other possible catastrophes.

In addition to planned attacks on systems, natural disasters and other catastrophes have befallen numerous installations. Fires and floods have all but wiped out some installations. In some installations, a momentary power outage or electrical surge can decimate tapes and scribble up files. Because of the significant role the computer plays in many operations, the massive quantities of data stored in computer files and the sensitivity of the electronics, such events have given rise to losses out of all proportion with previous experience.

Although a computer can do the work of hundreds of employees, the hundreds of employees would be physically distributed over a wide area while the computer is not. Generally, a disaster would not significantly incapacitate many of the people and damage to records can be confined to a small portion of the total. A fire or other disaster in the computer room many inhibit the entire computer "work force" from access to its data.

In this chapter we will discuss some of the measures that can be taken to reduce loss potential. We look first at the physical facilities and some basic considerations in site selection and preparation and then at the various threats to plant and people.

Site Selection

When a new computer facility is being established it is desirable to place it in a position of low vulnerability to any forces that might interfere with its operation. These include outside intrusion, fire, water, storm or other natural calamity, failure due to power problems, or problems with the building's environmental systems. It is also desirable to minimize the exposure of the computer center to accidents, vandalism or attempted sabotage. Warnings and alarms to indicate potential trouble are also necessary.

Ideally a computer facility should be in a location that is neither too congested nor too remote to be accessible in bad weather. Its building should be fireproof, on ground high enough not be threatened by flood damage. Operating power should be stable and adequate and available from at least two sources. That is, power from a local power company should preferably be supplied from at least two generating facilities with automatic switchover so that in the event of a failure by one, the other picks up the load without interruption.

Site Improvement

Unfortunately many installations were established without proper regard for protection problems. Economic factors often limited site-selection precautions to levels that are less than ideal. Fortunately, most of the steps needed to improve protection can be applied to existing sites. While retrofitting may be more costly than initial inclusion, it is nevertheless possible.

The primary area of precautions not easily adjusted after original installation is exposure to natural elements. If the installation was made in a facility subject to flooding, mud slide or other natural calamities, costly measures must be taken to achieve reasonable safeguards. Sometimes it may even be economically desirable to relocate the computer site within the building or to a new less-exposed building. This option is particularly attractive if new computers are being installed at the same time.

Outside Intrusion

The control of access to the data processing facility is extremely important. Controls are of two general types: locks to keep people out and alarms to indicate a violation of control measures. The threats protected against are man-made, consisting of theft and violent attack.

Access to the computer room should be controlled by a locked door. This lock can be a conventional cylinder lock, but in many respects various electronically operated locks are superior. The combination or code to an electronically operated lock can easily be changed in such a way as to no longer accept the key, card or number of a discharged employee. Changing the "code" for a conventional pin-tumbler cylinder lock is much more difficult.

Access to the computer room should be directly available only to authorized operators, data processing managers having a need to enter and the security force.

Access to the computer room by the computer manufacturer's maintenance personnel should be positively controlled by security or the computer room manager and work should be done only under the supervision of the manager or a member of his staff. Access by maintenance people for cleaning should be similarly controlled, and cleaning should be done under the surveillance of security.

If an unknown maintenance man, complete with I.D. card, appears at your installation—whether or not a previous appointment had been made—check him out via a call to your representative. It is very easy for anyone to call in. "This is XYZ Computers. We're sending Mr. Jones over to do a monthly refabulation of the coordination blivets."

Entrance to the computer facility should be through a single door, although additional emergency exits should be provided.

No computer programmer should have unescorted access to the computer and no programmer should be permitted to operate the computer. An exception might be made for one carefully screened and bonded hardware and systems programmer per shift to assist the operators if a breakdown occurs. All runs for program testing and debugging should be made by computer operators. The reasons for this restriction lie in both machine operating efficiency and security. The programmer will tend to do his debugging from the computer console, tying up the whole equipment. His need for "hands-on" access can usually be precluded by his thinking a little bit more about his work beforehand—his protestations not withstanding.

Programmer access to the computer implies a freedom of action that is wholly inconsistent with reasonable security. This is, in a sense, the equivalent of allowing a professional locksmith free and undisturbed private access to a bank vault. It is just unreasonable to allow people with all the needed knowledge and tools free opportunity to manipulate the system.

The movement of tapes, disks, card decks and printouts should also be tightly controlled. All flow of this material into and out of the computing facility should pass through a central control desk that is under the direct control of the computer operations security officer. Where these procedures are not followed the risk of theft of files or programs is high and critical master files can easily be "lost." (Further discussion on this aspect of operations appears in Chapter 9.)

Access to the exterior of the building should also be controlled. First, for the safety of center personnel and their possessions in parking areas and around the building; and second, to minimize the possibility of unauthorized access to the building. The nature of the control depends on the location and type of surroundings. In crowded urban areas it is probably necessary to have guards on duty whenever this building is in use.

Depending on the configuration of the parking facilities and the nature of contiguous areas, it may be necessary to supplement the guard with closed-circuit television. In general, access to the parking lot should be by permit only, with a permit sticker on the bumper or the forward surface of the rear view mirror to identify authorized vehicles.

Finally, it almost goes without saying that all doors not used as normal (controlled) entrances should be kept locked at all times with alarmed panic bar locks designed so that exit is possible and entrance is not.

Fire Hazards

As has become increasingly clear with the occurrence of numerous fires in modern high-rise office buildings hitherto considered fireproof, fire remains a hazard regardless of building construction. While the basic structure may be fireproof it is impossible to exclude all flammable materials in the contents of the building. All buildings contain wiring with insulation which is always somewhat flammable, plus flammable partitions, magnetic tape, carpets, upholstery, furnishings, draperies, books and papers.

Defective electrical wiring, defective heating systems, careless disposal of smoking materials, failure of electrically operated equipment such as computing equipment, typewriters, adding machines, calculators, recorders and dictating equipment can all cause fire. Therefore, to protect both the people and the data processing function, we must consider systems to detect and control fire as well as procedures for handling fire emergencies.

The building housing a computer should be protected by a general alarm system using both heat and smoke sensors to trigger alarms and a basic water sprinkler system to control fire. (But no water on the computer, please.) The protection of the computer facility itself must be considered separately. Those portions of the computer facility which house personnel only, for example programmers' offices, should be handled in the same way as the balance of the building. The alarm and control system should be designed primarily to safeguard the people and the building structure itself, and normal good housekeeping procedures in handling flammable materials such as paper, forms, punch cards and tapes should be followed.

In the computer room itself, much more extensive alarm systems and controls are highly desirable. There should be an alarm system using both ionization-type smoke detectors and temperature sensors. In a typical computer room with a false floor to provide wiring space, detection equipment should be used beneath the floor as well as within the room itself.

It is also highly desirable that there be a master switch in the computer room near the door which can be used in emergency to cut off all electrical power to equipment.

To control a fire in the computer room, consideration should be given to dry pipe sprinkler systems, Halon-type fluoride gaseous control systems for area flooding, and local hand-held extinguishers using carbon dioxide. Experts disagree on the choice between dry pipe sprinklers and fluoride gas systems, but all agree that CO_2 extinguishers are a must. Neither dry pipe sprinklers nor Halon-type systems are inexpensive. Recharging a gas system, so that a rekindled fire not fully extinguished will not find the system exhausted, takes time. However, Halon is less likely to damage equipment and in the concentration required to extinguish fire it will not injure personnel.

Area flooding systems using carbon dioxide are dangerous. Although they will extinguish the fire, people trapped when the system releases its gas are likely to be killed if outside help doesn't reach them immediately.

The tape and disk library should be separately protected. The library should be of fire resistant construction with an automatic temperature-activated door mechanism so that in the event of fire it will be isolated quickly. The library should be protected with its own alarm and extinguishing system and the desirable extinguishing system in this case is Halon, since it will effectively limit fire damage in the library but will not seriously harm personnel temporarily trapped inside. Here the detection system should also use both temperature and smoke sensors. If the tape library cannot be isolated and protected, a fireproof safe should be considered for tape and disk pack storage. Additionally, storage of these items in a safe can afford protection from falling debris.

It is impossible to overemphasize the importance of good housekeeping in preventing disastrous fires. A recent fire did over a million dollars in damage to the office of the Insurance Company of North America. Some of their data processing operations were interrupted as a result of damage to the building, although the fire was not in the data processing area. The fire in this case was apparently caused by an electric typewriter which was plugged into an "octopus" and carelessly left turned on over a weekend.

The lesson from this is clear. Wiring in accordance with underwriters' accepted practices is an absolute must. If extra electrical equipment is required, additional proper wiring must be installed. The use of underrated extension cords with multiple outlet terminations is dangerous and should not be permitted. It is equally clear that all equipment not in use should be turned off at all times, particularly when the facility is unoccupied.

The minimum requirements for fire alarm and fire control systems are generally covered by local ordinances; these should be checked carefully. In most cases it will be desirable to provide protection beyond that required by ordinance.

Water Hazards

Probably the greatest single hazard in a computer installation is water. Water can completely ruin a computer installation. Cleanup can be very expensive and there is no guarantee it will be completely effective. Threats of water damage are widespread, consisting of natural floods, fire-fighting efforts, breakage of water pipes, steam-heating pipes and leakage through the roof.

The computer center should not be located in the basement, since water damage problems are more likely there. If possible, the facility should be located where no major water or drainage lines run directly overhead.

Where natural flooding is a threat, the base floor level should be at least five feet above the established high-water mark. This practice not only minimizes the danger of natural flooding but also provides a large escape area relieving the risk of any water intrusion.

Plastic covers should also be available and utilized. It is desirable to place these coverings over equipment over weekends and any other periods of system shutdown that lasts a few days or more. The use of these covers will also protect equipment against dust and dirt that can damage the equipment.

Wherever pipes, wire conduits, and air conditioning or heating ducts lead to higher parts of the building, water seals or traps should be employed to prevent water from following these paths into the computer room. The protective coverings should be used to prevent water from getting into the hardware if perchance it does get into the computer room.

It is also desirable to see that drains are installed in the area under the false floor to insure the drainage of any water leaked into that area to prevent the wetting and shorting of interconnecting cable.

Storms and Natural Calamities

Protection from hurricanes, tornados and earthquakes is primarily a matter of careful site selection and appropriate construction. Unless there is structural damage to the building, there is little threat to the computer installation. If structural damage is extensive, avoiding damage to the computer installation will be a matter of luck.

Wind is the primary threat in such risks and a number of defensive steps can be taken. First, window areas should be minimized and equipment should be located away from windows. Second, damage to the roof from wind (or weight of ice and snow) can pose a threat. It is desirable to locate equipment one floor below the top level, but the top level would be preferable to the bottom level where such a choice must be made.

Power Problems

There are basically two threats related to power, both of which have been discussed earlier: loss of power and power-related fire. The electric power used to run the computing equipment should be obtained from a stable, reliable source. Preferably it should feed from at least two generating facilities with automatic switchover capabilities. Where a quality supply of power is not available or where the risk of power loss due to natural calamity, such as ice storms, is high, backup power facilities must be considered. These can range from batteries that have a life of several hours to diesel generators that operate so long as fuel is available.

The installation of adequate service by professional electricians is the best protection against electrically originated fire. Second-best protection is to refrain from abusing power capabilities by overloading the circuits.

If it is necessary, computer systems can be selected and programmed to provide orderly shutdown in the event of a power failure. The few milliseconds of "flywheel action" available after power quits and before the equipment power supply capacitors run down is sufficient to protect the files and core memory, allowing a restart with minimum manual confusion. However, such *power interrupt protection* only works if the necessary line sensors, protection hardware and—most critical—power interrupt protection software are installed.

Another level or quality of protection is called *no-break power*. With this type of supply system, an electronic or motor-generated backup power source is always operative and synchronized with the line. In the event of a power failure, the backup source switches on within 1/10 to 1/60 second to provide uninterrupted power. No-break power is probably unnecessary for most installations not using extensive and continuous on-line remote console operation.

Problems with Building Environmental Systems

Heating, air conditioning and humidity control are all generally utilized even if not necessary parts of a computer installation. All require equipment subject to malfunction or failure. Heat and water pose major threats to such systems.

We have already discussed the water risks. One additional water risk is the possibility of condensation due to high humidity or a rapid temperature change. Such risks are low, and if the system is shut down as soon as it is realized that a threat exists, damage will be minimal. Again, protective covers can be of significant value. By limiting exposure to air currents, covers can reduce the equipment's rate of heat loss and provide a temporary covering of stale air with lower moisture content.

Heat in the quantities generated by a runaway heating system or by failures in the air conditioning system may be extremely uncomfortable for operations personnel but will generally not harm the computing system. In fact, in all likelihood the computer will be shut down due to the inability of the staff to continue to function before any real danger of damage to the system arises. Under these circumstances the system should be shut down rather than left to operate unattended.

Heat generated by a failure of air conditioning directed to the machines, by a failure of blowers within the system or by leaving cabinets open can ruin equipment and files. (Yes, leaving cabinets open can cause the formation of hot spots due to improper air flow.) The facility must include temperature-rise warning alarms to alert against these possibilities.

Humidity control in the range of from 20 to 60 percent is critical to the proper operation of circuits and to the preservation of magnetic tapes. Most environmental control systems tend to lower relative humidity, and this must be raised to an acceptable level.

Warning and Control

Unfortunately, no foolproof risk-prevention methods have been invented, and after all appropriate measures have been taken against intrusion, fire, flood and other catastrophes, they will still occur. Alarms are therefore still needed. The obvious intent of alarms is to limit the extent of the losses.

In the previous discussions we presented measures that can be taken and equipment that can be provided to limit loss if it occurs. In the following discussion we will discuss additional steps to be taken when a threat materializes and an actual loss appears imminent.

ALARMS

Access to the building by extraordinary means should always trigger an alarm. That is, all doors normally used for exit only should be wired to operate an alarm. The alarm in general should be simply a light at a guard's desk or security headquarters during normal working hours. During nonworking hours the alarm should be audible as well as a light to indicate which door has been opened. All emergency exit doors from the computer room should operate an alarm at all times.

Some of the more sophisticated electronic key systems used for the computer room entrance door can be set to indicate the attempted use of a key which is no longer valid. Those that operate by use of a combination can also be set to give alarm if the wrong combination is attempted. While anyone can make a mistake, the repeated use of the wrong combination generally indicates that someone is manipulating or attempting to manipulate the lock.

The tape and disk library should be protected so that an alarm is given if any attempt is made to open the door during nonworking hours. At the very least, the parking areas should be checked by periodic patrol by security force. In high crime urban areas closed-circuit TV covering parking areas is probably desirable. The use of sensing systems to guard the building periphery may be desirable in high-crime areas. Systems available for this purpose include closed-circuit TV, infrared beams systems and pressure or magnetically operated buried cable systems. The advantages of each should be examined for a given installation.

MAGNETS—A CANARD

Although some news stories describe magnets as a threat to tape files, the need for protection to prevent the use of magnets to destroy computer files is highly overrated. A strong permanent magnet wiped along the outside of a tape or disk will create errors that processing may or may not correct. However, a miscreant can do as much or more damage by switching tape labels or nicking the edge of the wound-up tape with a fingernail file.

Magnets at long range don't work. Even a powerful 10-pound magnet with a pulling force of, say, 200 pounds has to be brought within one inch or so of a magnetic tape or disk to create any effect.

EMERGENCY PROCEDURES

It has been well established through experience that it is extremely desirable to have a well-defined emergency procedure with clearly assigned responsibilities. Every section of the organization should have designated leaders and a carefully prepared, written list of procedures to be followed in an emergency. These procedures must be impressed on all personnel by the use of regular drills at reasonable intervals without prior warning.

The drill procedure should cover all aspects of getting personnel out of the danger area, alerting security forces and local fire departments. Reasonable steps should be taken to fight the fire where it is within the capabilities of the local group, since the first steps taken to protect data and equipment can be the most significant. It must be remembered that equipment can be severely damaged by water used to fight fires. If possible, water resistant covers should be placed over equipment. The emergency procedures must clearly define the functions of the internal security force and assign responsibility for contact with the local fire department in order to insure the fire department's and the local staff's proper preparedness.

Clearly, procedures should be maintained for all anticipated situations and should make use of the building or facility security force as well as local police. The nature of the procedures depends upon the type of situation and the size and availability of the local security force. Procedures should be established to handle the triggering of access alarms at any time, including the actual invasion of the building by unauthorized personnel or threats to the building by unruly crowds or mobs. The procedures should also include the handling of bomb threats.

Miscellaneous Emergency Control

Hopefully, the proper choice of a location will help to minimize the possibility of damage from storm or flood, but in unusual circumstances even this may not be adequate. Should flood threaten, the first step must be to cut power and the next to transfer tape and disk files and, if possible, backup documentation to a safe location. Beyond that whatever steps can be taken to protect equipment and facilities from water damage will depend on the circumstances and the availability of emergency equipment and personnel.

In the event of a power failure, shutdown procedures should be defined to minimize the possibility of damage to tape or disk files that are on the machine at the time. Procedures should also provide for restart and recovery. Power failure problems can be limited by proper power installation, and one should consider the cost of various levels of power backup in light of the cost of lost capability. It may well be that in a given installation it makes sense to simply accept the fact that power will be lost from time to time and trust that such losses will not be long enough to significantly interfere with operations.

On the other end of the spectrum, highly critical on-line real-time systems may require complete power backup including emergency generating equipment. The range between includes such facilities as dual feeds from different power plants, short-term emergency power to allow the system to be shut down without loss of data or the creation of undue confusion. Power-regulating equipment may also be necessary if the stability of the power source is poor. In any case, a cost-effectiveness analysis is desirable to determine the amount of money that can and should be spent at any given installation.

The air conditioning system for a computer room should preferably be designed to use two smaller units rather than one large unit. This provides the advantage that in the event of a failure the remaining single unit can handle the load in all but the hottest weather.

Loss of heat is not likely to cause damage to equipment or data. It is much more likely to cause only discomfort to personnel unless heat is lost for a protracted period and in very cold weather. In such a case freezing may rupture the pipes and cause leaks.

Chapter 7

System and Hardware Security

A Comment on Infallibility

In this chapter we will look first at the security implications of various types of computer equipment and at the important security considerations affecting equipment selection. The contribution of redundancy within the system will then be discussed, showing both the positive contribution and the added security requirements it can impose. We will then examine the effect of the power source upon security. Two final considerations concern system failure. First, what security measures are appropriate for processing capabilities when the main system is not operational. Second, how do you implement effective maintenance without compromising security?

Selecting Equipment

Equipment has a significant bearing upon the extent to which you can protect on-line data. But effective methods and procedures play an important role, too. Since the configuration (mix) of equipment affects the accessibility of programs and data files, it dictates the security measures required for reasonable data protection.

For example, a medium-sized system composed primarily of magnetic tape units will limit the amount of on-line data and centralize security problems to proper tape library procedures. However, the volume of work relative to the tape library may itself pose a problem that could compromise security. On the other hand, a greater utilization of disk packs, while probably increasing the on-line data exposure, should reduce the library's proper work. Since the disk packs would be stored in the library, they would be afforded the same basic protection while stored as the tapes.

Further, a medium-sized system composed primarily of magnetic tapes could probably be replaced by two smaller systems. This type of configuration can simplify many aspects of security. While the medium-sized system must probably run more than one job at a time to be effectively utilized, the smaller systems may be as efficient while running only one job at a time. Additionally, the two-processor configuration will provide at least a partial backup in the event of a system failure.

What makes these trade-offs, which were previously uneconomic, possible in the 1970's is the growth of the minicomputer to adulthood. In recent years it has become possible and economically feasible to acquire a small yet powerful computer system to handle a collection of well-defined, repetitive tasks such as payables-payroll-disbursement-inventory-reordering, for as little as $1500 per month. These minicomputer systems are very fast, but they have only limited reprogramming and multiprogramming capability relative to larger machines.

Trade-off possibilities must be considered. How important is data security? What is the cost of securing one particular mix of equipment versus another? If data security is necessary, would it be most effectively achieved with an equipment mix that concentrates security in one given area? A clear and precise statement of management's goals in the data security area greatly aids system analysts to make the best possible trade-off evaluations.

CENTRAL PROCESSOR AND MAIN MEMORY

The central processing unit and associated main memory form the heart of any computer installation. The primary security-related features of these units are the memory-protect and privileged-instruction capabilities.

"Memory protect" refers to the partitioning of memory into working units. User programs can then be confined to certain regions within the whole of memory. A "privileged instruction" can be executed only within a designated area of core or only if a "privileged enable" indicator is set. Both features are required for an effective operating system.

Memory protection is generally implemented through minimum and maximum checks on the effective address of each instruction executed. This facility operates only on a high-order portion of the address, thus dividing memory into large units. For instance, if a five-digit address is used to gain access to memory but only the high-order two digits are checked, memory must be allocated in thousand-word units to ensure effective protection. If an address violates the established bounds, an "interrupt" alerts the operating system and prevents the execution of the instruction. The reaction of the operating system to this situation is a key to good security. The job should be automatically aborted.

The privileged instruction set generally handles input-output and interrupt functions. The key hardware facility is required to achieve any substantial degree of on-line data security, preventing users from gaining access to data files or records before their right to do so is verified. Software provisions (such as password control) can be easily bypassed by a knowledgeable user and the protection they offer is thus marginal.

Unfortunately many of the memory-protect subsystems in use today rely principally or totally on software for their operation. This means that a clever programmer can bypass such "soft" protection, even from outside the facility.

The best of such systems utilize a combination of hardware and software to effect memory protection, segmenting and data password control. Sometimes the best-known commercially available equipments need to be augmented with additional memory-protective devices—both hardware and software.

DATA COMMUNICATIONS

Chapter 4 treats the primary causes of security leaks in data communications. A few operational and equipment-related precautions are desirable in this area to assure relative data security. Two main hardware features are generally available: one is a built-in terminal recognition system, the other is the data scrambler (cryptographic equipment). In the first case, each terminal connected to the system is given a unique recognition code to enable access when it wants to transfer data to the system. Restrictions are generally placed upon the types of data that can be transmitted to and from each terminal—this is somewhat similar to password protection—but at the terminal end of the line. In effect, each terminal is assigned a security level consistent with its vulnerability. Data scramblers serve a similar function and tend to enhance terminal security. They force a "pirate" not only to fake terminal recognition, but also to be able to unscramble transmitted data. Thus an accidental security breach is less likely.

MAGNETIC TAPE DRIVES

Magnetic tape provides the greatest opportunity for theft of data files within the on-line system. It is fairly easy to "borrow" a tape and take it off the premises, even while observing established security procedures. This is particularly true of a program development effort that requires program checkout on an off-site backup system. For instance, the master file tape could be registered with its label altered as a scratch tape in use for program checkout, and its data may be easily retrieved once the tape is beyond the direct observation of the system's administration. This is the electronic equivalent of going through the discarded scratch paper in a wastebasket.

On the other hand, one advantage of magnetic tape files is that they are not readily available on-line without a record of their use being generated. The fact that they must be obtained from a library and physically mounted on computer tape drives provides a second line of security control. In systems that utilize magnetic tape as scratch or master files, a good tape library procedure is required. Tapes should be separated according to use so that those used for program debugging or off-premises operation are never used during processing of critical data files.

MAGNETIC DISKS AND DRUMS

Disks and drums are widely used to provide large-volume storage. Since they provide a large on-line file capacity they are subject to all of the security frailties of all on-line files. Removable disks, however, provide a whole new dimension of control problems. A disk pack is an assemblage of disks in a holder which may be removed as easily from a disk drive as changing a recording on a record player.

The disk pack can be used on any disk drive and therefore, like magnetic tape, is a conveniently portable package of information which can be carried away and read, altered or destroyed at leisure off the premises.

PUNCHED CARDS

Punched cards are seldom used in a computing system today except to put in initial data. In some cases, program source language decks are maintained for backup, but this practice is declining. Protection of this medium concerns the actual handling of the cards and is not much affected by the equipment itself.

The only equipment security measure possible here is the use of nonstandard punch codes. In general, this is costly and ineffective. Any such coding scheme is easily cracked, after which it is useless.

AUXILIARY SECURITY HARDWARE

Special counters and clocks are available to measure the frequency and duration of access to the various devices (tape drives, disk files, etc.) in a computer system. These provide data about the amount and time of use of the device but do not indicate the files to which access was gained. They can provide data in direct computer-readable form, which permits internal accounting and reporting of usage with a minimum of overhead. By recording file names read from file labels, the operating system can report access statistics and then relate them to specific files, as well as to the run in progress. That is, it can report the name of the job that used the files, the names of the files used, and the number of times each file was used.

A code scrambler for input-output channels is another security device which serves a useful function in a communications environment but is generally ineffective for data protection within the computer system proper. It can inhibit certain types of accidental loss or petty "borrowing" of file tapes, but cracking the scramble can be easy for the deliberate thief, and once cracked, it is relatively useless as a security measure.

Hardware-implemented password protection is also available. The password is placed in a special register or a device which independently checks authenticity.

When data is written, the password is automatically affixed to the data. Upon reading, the password is automatically checked and removed from the data prior to transmittal to the processing program. Lack of password will cause a stop and an operator alert signal.

This type of equipment capability reduces overhead and provides password protection with a minimum of effort on the part of programmers. It does, however, require the use of password protection whether desired or not. If a "check bypass" capability exists which permits the avoidance of this built-in password check under certain circumstances, special features must be included in the operating system to prevent its abuse. Otherwise a "hole" will exist in the security system.

Various sensory "pulse-taking" devices have been built to independently assure that a computer is operating correctly and has not quietly gone berserk. These are particularly useful in the time-critical applications where operators, switchover devices and/or users must be quickly alerted.

RELIABILITY

Reliability is a significant factor in data security. Error rates, types of errors, error-detection capabilities and reaction to errors are all important factors. A high error rate exposes the system to maintenance requirements which may mask attempts to breach security. Errors on data channels can affect password and similar protection devices. They can be costly and can expose the system to security risks.

General system reliability can be a significant factor in the overall cost of a system and in the effectiveness of data security measures. Only those systems which have proven their reliability should be considered if data security is a significant consideration. Before contracting for any system or related devices (from a reputable, stable manufacturer) current users should be interviewed to determine their experience with the system or device and the support they receive from the manufacturer. User group meetings and computer conferences are excellent places to obtain this type of information.

Redundancy

As the word implies, "redundancy" refers to the protective duplication of equipment and files. Redundancy is employed to minimize the effects of sabotage, error and equipment failure.

Equipment redundancy is generally implemented for types of equipment susceptible to frequent failure or essential for system operation. The trade-off that must be considered is the cost of maintaining redundant equipment versus the costs that might result from a loss of service if failure occurs. (This topic is discussed more fully in the second following section on backup.)

It is a general practice in well-managed computer facilities to maintain three generations of tape files at all times. As a file is updated, both a copy of the file before update—usually called the "father"—and a copy of the file before the previous update—called the "grandfather"—are kept. This procedure provides for three generations of any file to be maintained at all times. Thus, if the new master is lost or for some reason unusable, it may be recreated by a repeat of the update process.

This procedure provides file redundancy and affords good protection against the adverse effects of malfunction while avoiding the expense of making duplicates of the current master to obtain this level of protection. If copies of the grandfather and father files are kept at another safe location, this procedure may also provide protection against sabotage or natural calamity.

If redundancy is required to protect against sabotage, duplicate copies of programs and files should be kept physically separate from the working library. This is also highly desirable for protection against fire or other catastrophic damage and is a common practice. The cost of maintaining the separate library facility, together with the safeguards necessary to ensure appropriate levels of security, must of course be evaluated against the risk and cost loss.

Power

Power is seldom directly related to data security factors. The primary considerations are the system reaction at the time of failure and the loss of services if power failure is lengthy.

In the case of an abrupt power failure, physical damage may occur to disk, drum and tape storage surfaces. If recording is in process, intermittent data errors could compromise password security or introduce errors in the data. In general, none of these directly compromises data security to any significant extent. Simple precautions such as erasing the data in question and rerunning programs in progress at the time of power failure are about the only steps required to prevent data compromise. These are natural follow-ups to a power failure whether data security is involved or not.

Where actual physical damage to the storage media occurs, two factors must be considered. First is the disposition of the physical device and the manner in which it is to be eliminated. If, as in the case of a disk or drum track, the damaged area is to be deactivated but not discarded, care should be taken to erase the data. Otherwise, it could still be retrievable. If the damaged medium is to be discarded, it should be erased and broken, cut or otherwise rendered totally useless.

Second is the reconstruction of data lost to damage. Generally, one would hope that a backup data set exists. If this is not the case, care must be taken to reconstruct this data in a manner which will not compromise security. The best security measure with respect to physical damage is to select hardware that has some built-in protection against such damage.

The loss of power over a long period of time can be a more serious threat to data security. Data processing which must be completed can only be done by manual procedures which expose the data to people directly or by transferring data storage media to alternate facilities for processing. The data security capabilities of alternate facilities should be screened and care taken not to leave unerased scratch files exposed after use.

Generally, the power supply and system capabilities selected (along with backup power sources) are more directly related to economic factors than data security. At a minimum, these should be sufficient to ensure that physical damage will not occur to any equipment.

Backup

The method of providing backup in the event of a malfunction in the primary computing system is critical, particularly if data security is involved. Four basic options are available: a complete backup computing system in-house; an in-house manual system for critical applications; a second-party supplier of computing time, like a service bureau; or an exchange agreement with another user of the same type of equipment. A complete backup computing system in-house provides the same data security as the primary systems. It is both the safest and the most costly type of backup, and it is as susceptible to loss as is the primary system when power fails.

Where computing needs require a relatively simple, small-to-medium scale system, the backup system is an unnecessary extra cost. Any attempts to market the computing capacity of the backup system immediately create additional complications. An obligation is assumed that may be difficult to fulfill in the event of main system failure. The backup system might not be available to serve its intended purpose. And subletting (or the sale of time) provides second parties with access that could endanger data security more than the use of a service bureau.

Often overlooked in the design of a computing facility is the possibility of a system being comprised of two similar, if not identical, systems, both of which are fully utilized. Such an installation provides practical backup. One system is generally available for processing highly sensitive or urgent data, while the less sensitive (or less critical) processing awaits repairs or is handled on an outside system with minimal concern for security.

Reliance upon manual procedures for backup is risky at best. Seldom are there sufficient numbers of adequately trained personnel to perform the job. From the standpoint of data security, maximum risk is involved because clear data is made available to large numbers of untrained or inexperienced people. For those so inclined, the data is relatively easy to obtain; the remainder are given data to talk about, even if they mean no harm.

Reliance upon a service bureau or second-party computer time supplier is a commonly used backup. The identification of potential suppliers should be a part of the basic system selection effort and the data security capabilities of these suppliers should be carefully studied to ensure their adequacy. Then these capabilities should be utilized in the primary system. This precaution ensures that the selected backup systems can be used in time of need. Further, it permits the study of data security measures to expose weaknesses and indicate future precautions for backup systems. Contractual arrangements with backup facility suppliers should clearly define the supplier's responsibilities in the area of system and facility security.

Maintenance

Maintenance and backup considerations go somewhat hand in hand. The quality of maintenance service, its availability and the availability of spare parts will often significantly influence backup considerations.

For most installations a full-time maintenance staff is impractical. Quite apart from the expense, competent people require a challenge. Unless a real "lemon" is involved, the maintenance staff will move on for lack of interest. Further attempts to maintain a staff in such an environment can lead to inferior personnel who are incapable of adequate performance in time of need. Maintenance service should be purchased from either the hardware manufacturer or from a third-party maintenance firm.

The most critical maintenance problems affecting security are those which are not clearly either hardware or software failures and those which involve secure data sets in some way. Most often, these problems arise because of an incomplete hardware or software checkout, but they can also occur as a result of hardware malfunction. These problems are generally caused by a combination of instructions and data characteristics which make them difficult to identify and isolate. This means the live data and processing programs may be required in the maintenance effort to isolate and correct the problem. Programs and data files are thus exposed to possible security risks.

Needless to say, the efforts taken must be proportionate to the seriousness of a security breach. At worst, program or data changes may be necessary to avoid the difficulty and exposure, but this drastic alternative is not usually required. It should be possible to develop a dummy data set and associated programming through a partial isolation of the problem. This permits maintenance with the least exposure of live programs and data.

Disks and drums pose the greatest security problems during simple equipment failure. When failure occurs, the data is exposed to security breach and, though maintenance procedures should permit efficient maintenance without affording access to sensitive data, it is virtually impossible to ensure that such data is not accessed.

The best security can be achieved in this area by:

- Selecting reliable equipment from a reputable manufacturer.
- Demanding extensive preventive maintenance programs that do not involve live user programs or data files.
- Removing sensitive programs and data files from the computer area during maintenance.
- Turning off storage devices which contain sensitive data that cannot be removed.
- Changing passwords and other security mechanisms immediately following possible exposure during maintenance.

Remember, well-trained maintenance personnel know the holes in a system. They are more familiar with the best ways to circumvent security measures than any other individuals who come in contact with the system. Further, they have the greatest opportunity to exploit security breaches if they are so inclined. Maintenance personnel should therefore be selected with great care.

Chapter 8
Software Security
No Panaceas Here Either

What Is Software?

In this chapter we will be concerned with security measures in software. Software is used here in the broad sense to mean all computer programs other than specific applications programs. The degree to which these measures should be implemented must be determined by the importance of the data being protected versus the cost of implementing security safeguards.

Many internal operations which have nothing to do with generating useful output are necessary just to enable modern computer systems to function. These internal function programs are called *system programs* or *software*. They enable the system to process other programs that do produce useful output, such as a payroll. Examples of software instructions might be "read in blocks of information from magnetic tape to working memory" or "write onto magnetic tape the contents of memory registers starting with register m" or "print table X in format Y." Programs that produce useful output are called *applications programs*.

System software includes compilers, programs that translate from human-oriented languages such as the language of mathematics or accounting into a computer's internal instruction code. The program prepared by the programmer in the quasinatural language is generally called a *source* program. The translated output produced by the compiler is called the *object* program.

Another major component of system software is the *operating system*, sometimes called the *executive* or *supervisor*. In a modern ultrafast data processing system, the actual time to run most applications programs may be quite small. In order to use the system efficiently it is necessary to have a succession of jobs lined up and waiting to be run. In simpler systems, the operating system uses job control information supplied with each program to assign peripheral equipment and memory as needed, to initiate processing and to call on stored input-output control programs, compilers or other system software as needed. In more-complex computer systems, the operating system may run two or more jobs in parallel or intermixed to maximize utilization of the system.

An effective operating system is the key to software security. Without adequate and proper security provision in the operating system, no effective on-line security measures can be implemented. In such instances the only security obtainable is that provided for through methods and procedures (see Chapter 10).

No matter how good the security measures provided by the operating system appear to be, additional measures can be provided in the applications program to give backup to the operating system against malfunction or deliberate manipulation.

Procedures for input data validation are also important to security. While proofreading and similar procedures are generally performed manually, it is possible to provide similar automated procedures.

The security provisions of applications programs generally fall into the category of detection rather than prevention, while input data validation procedures provide both prevention and detection.

Equipment and software security features must be combined to provide a security scheme that achieves maximum confidence, but the greatest degree of effectiveness can be gained or lost in the software features. For example, the best memory-protect hardware facilities, which are intended to prevent writing into protected memory areas, are totally ineffective if the operating system does not prevent applications programs from gaining access to and manipulating the controls of the memory-protect facility. Likewise, the best password access-limitation feature can be compromised if application programs are reckless about leaving password information laying around in the memory or accidentally outputting it to users or operators.

The operating system provides security protection and detection features in two primary areas. First, it restricts access to the system, to programs and to data. Second, it provides logging and user information. The first helps prevent unauthorized access while the second provides access records enabling the detection of violations and malfunctions.

Remember, it is virtually impossible to develop a system that is totally secure just as it is virtually impossible to keep a determined burglar out of a house. Therefore, a critical feature of an effective security scheme is the ability to rapidly and positively detect a security breach as soon as it occurs.

System Access Restriction

Limiting access to the system to certain users at certain times is a less common security measure. The system may limit access to a specified group of users with a security rating below a certain threshold, users above a certain threshold or users in a certain security category. This type of access limitation was first developed by the government for use in military installations, but it is also quite useful in large computing systems where data sensitivity varies widely.

Program debugging presents the greatest opportunity for security breach. Most often these activities are carried out during off hours, frequently with less than a full complement of operations personnel present. Restricting the security levels of programs and data files that can be accessed during those periods serves to some extent to compensate for fewer checks by procedures.

The implementation of this type of a scheme requires a multilevel password capability within the operating system. The highest password level must be placed under the control of a security officer. He then assigns security levels to all programs and files, determines the security levels that can be accessed at any point in time and effects the necessary communications with the operating system at the appropriate times.

This type of security system can be used to limit exposure while training new operations personnel, particularly operators, since the risk of accidental security breach is higher than normal at this time. It can also be used to prevent authorized personnel from manipulating data files or obtaining extra runs during off hours when appropriate supervision is not available.

Program Access

Consider the payroll clerk who must have access to the payroll file for weekly processing to produce the payroll checks. It may also be necessary to make him responsible for adding and deleting employees, changing employee tax status and changing pay rates. Thus, he must have access to the file for both processing and changing.

On the other hand, it may not be desirable to have the same clerk produce certain kinds of managerial reports, such as personnel turnover or absentee rate analysis. A way is needed to limit access to certain processing programs by particular people.

Access limitation of this type can be achieved by establishing user-specific program libraries. System programs are of course available to all users, but each user will have his own library of applications programs. If a user requests a program not in his user library he is informed that no such program exists. Each user is assigned a unique identification that is used by the operating system in connection with security measures. Each user must protect his "identification" so that it is not used by anyone else, and management must monitor the programs in each user's library to insure that no unauthorized programs are included. This security facility should be implemented in conjunction with a well monitored program development and change control procedure to insure that a user does not include unauthorized processing in an otherwise authorized program.

Data Access

Data access security generally receives the greatest amount of attention. Data in this sense is any file of information in the system. This, of course, includes program source language and object language files as well as files of data that constitute the productive work for which the system was intended.

Data access security may be implemented at two levels. The first decision is whether to grant a user access to a file; the second, if access is granted, is whether the access should be restricted. Generally the restriction is a matter of whether the user may change the data or be restricted to read-only access.

Where data security is a serious problem, all three categories of access—no access, read-only access, and read-write access—must be implemented. If access limitations are not imposed there is no effective on-line security since all users would have free access to all data files. If only the access/no-access restrictions are imposed, data files are subject to manipulation by many users, and even if not abused, this can lead to coordination and control problems. In a well managed installation only one user will have read-write access to a data file. This restriction enforces a coordination of changes and insures that one change does not interfere with another. It also forces users to coordinate data needs and clear up misconceptions about the information content of a file or data field.

Two schemes are in common use for controlling data access. The first and most prevalent is access by password. A distant second is to establish user-related file directories similar to the program libraries just described. In some instances—generally in time-sharing systems—a combination of the two schemes is used.

The two schemes are implemented similarly. A directory of data file names and their storage locations is maintained by the operating system. Associated with each entry is one or more user identification and/or access passwords. To gain access to a file the user's identification must appear in the list of approved identifications or he must know the password.

Generally the directory is maintained in part in the core memory and in part on the storage media containing the data. The directory in the core memory lists those files that are currently on-line. Each disk and drum has an area reserved for a directory of the files stored on that device, and each magnetic tape begins with a system-generated label that contains user identifications and access passwords.

The internal directory is created by reading the directory information from storage media as they are placed on-line. As new files are generated and access passwords and authorizations are changed the changes are recorded in the directory in the core memory and the device directory is rerecorded on the device for future use.

Good security protection requires protecting the directory information while it is in the core memory and as recorded on the storage media. The memory-protect facilities and inviolability of memory used by the operating system affords protection against direct changes by applications programs. Requiring the use of the operating system at all times and affording the operating system sole access to recorded directory information provides the best protection of recorded directory information.

Of course, it is necessary to change passwords, access limitations and other security information associated with data files. Thus, the operating system must distinguish between authorization to gain access to the file versus authorization to change passwords and access restrictions. Further, where security classifications or levels are used, it is necessary for the operating system to recognize two or more classes of authorization to manipulate security information.

Any hole in system procedures which enables the unauthorized alteration of directory information is sufficient to enable large-scale data abuse. Embezzlement and other forms of fraud as well as sabotage can run unchecked and undetected in such a system.

User identifications and passwords are like locks on doors and the keys must be given only to authorized users. The amount of security they offer is also analogous. The greater the number of people with keys, the greater the risk. To maintain a high level of security the keys must be periodically changed and reissued to the appropriate authorized personnel, thus purging those who have lost authority or who have by other means obtained a key.

User identifications or similar access keys are like limited master keys that provide general access to common facilities. Second-level passwords are like specific office keys that restrict particular access. It is easier to change the lock and key of a specific office than to change all the common facility locks and keys. And so it is with changing passwords on specific files versus changing user identifications providing general system access. This is also why, for the most part, user identifications are used primarily to control access to the system and passwords are used to control access to particular data files.

In addition to file access limitations on a full-file basis, access limitations can be applied to data fields within a file. This type of access limitation is generally restricted to special service programs offered by time-sharing services. The special service programs are a new sophisticated breed of information storage and retrieval programs which are used to obtain all data processing services relative to certain files. The user does not generally provide programs to process these files but instead defines his requirements in the language of the information storage and retrieval system. The system distinguishes, usually by user identification, between the file owner and other file users. The file owner defines and creates the file including data field access restrictions. The file users may read data from the file, or in some cases make certain kinds of changes in data fields, but they may not gain access to nor change the file definition.

The purpose of such a system is to enable the creation and maintenance of a centralized data file that can be on-line at all times. System users can thus obtain information or reports on a real-time basis. If the data were separated into files based upon user access limitations which must be applied on a full-file-only basis, the equipment configuration requirements and file coordination requirements could significantly increase costs or increase processing time beyond that allowable for effective real-time operation.

The OLSIMS (On-Line Information Management System) offered by On-Line Systems Inc. of Pittsburgh, Pennsylvania, is an example of such a system. OLSIMS provides fully interactive data management and information retrieval using a simple English-like language. In addition to the standard levels of security, it provides for protecting selected fields in a file. Each field may optionally be assigned alphabetic read or read-write passwords which must be given by a user before he is allowed access to or the ability to change a field.

A similar data field access restriction facility can be provided in an operating system but seldom is. This facility is expensive to implement, places severe restrictions on the file structures used within the system and is relatively ineffective. Where available, it is relative only to read-only restrictions, where a user is allowed read-only access to the file with the exception of certain data files. This is accomplished by blanking out the restricted field or fields as part of the read operation before allowing the user program access to the input data.

The Role of the Operating System

In all cases of access limitation, a policeman is required. The policeman is the operating system. To be effective, the operating system must have absolute control over all input-output operations and must maintain both a directory of current authorized user identifications and a directory of data files with associated passwords and access restrictions.

At sign-on or job request time, the operating system must check to insure that the user requesting system access is authorized. To minimize experimenting and unauthorized access, the system should log every attempt, whether successful or not, to gain access. The log should show date, time of day, input device, user identification presented and whether access was granted or not. And the log should be distributed to at least two managers for periodic—if not daily—review and analysis.

Once access to the system is granted, the operating system must verify each run request to insure that the user is entitled to run the programs requested. This check should include subroutines called by the primary routine, a check often overlooked.

The usual argument for not including a check on subroutines is that they are combined with the calling routine at some earlier time such as during compilation or program cataloging. While in general this may be true, the loader of the operating system usually includes the capability of loading subroutines individually and establishing the necessary linkages at run time. If the loader does not perform appropriate access checks on each subroutine, program access restrictions will not be effective because users will be able to gain access to unauthorized processing capabilities by invoking otherwise-restricted subroutines.

Having determined that the user is legitimate and that he is entitled to run the programs requested, the operating system must also check file access restrictions. These checks are required at two separate places. First, an "open file" command must be given to the operating system to gain access to an input file or to label an output file. At this time the operating system must check that the user is entitled to read or create the specified file. Second, instructions for file directory maintenance must be issued to the operating system indicating which files are to be saved and which can be deleted. At this time, access restrictions must also be verified. A user with read-only access obviously cannot be allowed to direct that a file be purged after he has used it.

As an additional security safeguard, the operations log provided by the operating system should include all requests for file directory changes, whether or not these requests are honored. It must also include all messages generated by applications programs to the operator. This information will enable management to detect attempts at unauthorized system use and unauthorized copying of data files.

Again we must stress that security measures will enable rapid and positive identification of a security breach or attempted security violation only when enforced by management and backed by effective manual methods and procedures.

System Development

In developing a new system, the specifications of the system must be detailed and the data flow through the system and the processing steps defined. This means that the system analysts and programmers building the system must know all details of its initial operation. Further, to insure proper system maintenance all these details must be documented and available to the program maintenance personnel.

Because of these considerations any thought of maintaining security by keeping processing diversified and details secret is foolish and ineffective. This is not to say that precautions should not be taken nor diligence exercised in this area. It does mean that in general it is more effective to assume that the processing details are generally known and to obtain security through built-in checks and effective management control of system functions and system usage.

Diligence in the area of program development dictates three considerations. Unless undue processing is involved, processing should be separated into discrete steps that can be programmed as subroutines. This is called modularizing a program. Next, check processes can be developed which are implemented in subroutine fashion. Finally, a periodic review of the program system can determine whether any changes in processing or check procedures will tighten security. Sometimes change for the sake of change is a reasonable and appropriate security measure.

Application Programs

Application program development is a function that can lead to significant system abuse or added security protection depending upon how it is managed. In one previously cited case a programmer created an interest-calculating program that truncated the calculated interest and credited all fractions of pennies to his own account. Thus, the correct total interest was shown in proof figures but he profited from the incorrect distribution. Although his take was only about 3 cents per account per year, when multiplied by an average 20,000 accounts in his bank he still made out well.

In another case a payroll tax-reporting program was rigged so that a few cents were deducted from each employee's withholding tax as reported to IRS and added to the programmer's own reported tax. Again the proof figures balanced in that the tax reported and paid was the same as the tax withheld, but the altered distribution among accounts wasn't noticed.

Many more instances can be cited where the applications programmer's ingenuity provided him with a nice income for little effort.

Four basic procedures must be established and adhered to during program development to prevent such abuses:

Rigid programming standards.
Rigid program documentation requirements.
A separate program validation function.
Periodic performance audits.

These procedures and precautions help ensure proper program development only. They must be augmented by similar strict program change controls in order to maintain proper security protection. Suggested methods and procedures that might be implemented to provide the desired safeguards are discussed in Chapter 10; here, we are concerned with facilities that can be included in application programs to aid in loss prevention and detection. For example, in the interest embezzlement case a separate check run could have been included that reversed the interest calculation process and reported any deviations from the approved interest rates. In the tax case year-to-date salary and tax withheld totals were obviously maintained since these are required for reporting purposes. A periodic recalculation of taxes withheld based upon year-to-date salary and compared to year-to-date taxes withheld would have shown up the discrepancies. Safeguards are always possible. It just takes enough managerial concern to get them installed.

There are three basic ways to build checks into applications programs. One is to build the checks directly into the processing. Second is to build check-processing modules within the programs. Third is to develop postprocessing programs separate from the primary program.

Building checks into the basic processing steps is generally the least expensive, least flexible and least effective method of obtaining such checks. It requires that the checks be designed into the initial system and programmed by the same programmer producing the basic processing programs. If the programmer is inclined toward fraud he will have a knowledge of the checks he must circumvent and the opportunity to manipulate the checks so that they do not expose his fraudulent activities. The inflexibility of this type built-in check makes it difficult to change primary processing or check procedures if necessary. It also complicates detecting the fraud that may be installed by a clever programmer. Therefore, this type of built-in check should be considered only for processing which is not likely to require changes in the near future and where excellent program development and validation procedures exist and are competently implemented.

Developing subroutines that provide built-in checks avoids the problems of the first type. It intertwines checks but exposes the programs to easier manipulation after completion. Its primary advantage is that the programming responsibility for primary processing functions and that of check functions can be separated. Fraudulent activity thus requires collaboration. Second, checks of this type can be changed easily. Thus if fraud is suspected, replacement of the check processes will expose the activity readily and positively or show that the suspicions were incorrect. This, of course, assumes that adequate program change and validation procedures exist and that the individual providing the replacement check subroutines is not a party to the fraud if one exists.

Postprocessing or separate programs developed specifically for checking, fully separates the checking process from the primary processing. Neither activity requires any knowledge of the specifics of how the other functions. It also means that legitimate processing changes may require changes to both the primary program and the check program, thus increasing the cost of such changes. But the unauthorized individual with fraudulent intent must also effect simultaneous changes in two independent programs—one of which he cannot gain access to. The primary drawback is that many processes do not lend themselves to postprocessing checks.

A well rounded data protection program will utilize each of these methods of building in checks on processing and processing results.

At this point it is appropriate to discuss briefly the types of checks and check data that can be built into a program or processing system. Obviously we can only suggest types of checks and check data.

Counts, summary totals and similar accumulation data are the most obvious ways of obtaining check information. To be effective this information must be checked against a proof figure arrived at independently of the primary process. For example, in a payroll program the number of paychecks issued can be counted and compared with the number of employees in the company, obtained from the personnel department's independent files. Similar activity counts can be useful in accounts payable and accounts receivable programs.

The interest and tax embezzlement cases cited earlier gave examples of postprocessing checks that can be implemented. Periodic dummy runs with parameter changes can serve a similar function. These are particularly effective where data that violates basic assumptions of the program can be presented. For example, the withholding tax rate is generally never zero. Thus the offender deducting a nominal sum from each account would easily be detected by setting the withholding rate to zero. Any negative withholding amounts that result would expose the improper processing.

The accounting firm that performs company audits is a good source of ideas for built-in checks and checking procedures because their techniques are generally adaptable to program implementation. Further, this firm will have some experience with this type of problem and should have a knowledge of your particular business. They are therefore in a position to tailor their suggestions to your needs.

INPUT DATA VALIDATION

A clear distinction must be made between input preparation and input validation. Input preparation consists of transcribing data into a machine-readable form. The proofreading and verification procedures of this activity are directed toward insuring that the machine-readable data is accurate relative to the original but generally does little to assure that it is the right data in the first place.

Validation, on the other hand, can be performed in part by the computer and in part by people. When reading original input data, the receiving program should check the data to insure that it is appropriate and reasonable. Where suspect data is encountered it should be recorded on an exception log for managerial review, but it should not be rejected. For example, each employee is placed in a particular labor grade and each labor grade has a salary range. A change in salary that would take it outside the range would be suspect but not necessarily wrong, while an alphabetic salary value would be wrong. The objective of this procedure is to insure that the right data is used.

Another example is found in purchasing. Purchasing should be done by requisition or purchase order, which should be recorded. When the goods are received and the invoice rendered, an input must be generated to be checked against the requisition or purchase order. Where units received, unit value or total invoice value differs from purchase order, an exception report should be made.

In these cases, the processing programs cannot determine what data is correct. They can only indicate that a deviation exists or that established procedures have not been followed.

Again we must point out that while system-implemented checks and data validation procedures will generally catch errors and malfunctions, any deliberate attempts at fraud will take these checks into account and require diligently enforced external methods, procedures and audits to detect. However, the program system can provide the data necessary for these external checks and audits and must provide it if such activities are to have a reasonable chance of success.

SUPERVISORY CHECKING OF APPLICATIONS PROGRAMS

Although most technical opportunities for error and malfeasance of computer software occur in the system programs, a greater amount of damage, particularly in an unsecure system, can occur—and historically has occurred—in the applications programs. There are far more applications programmers in a given facility; the applications programmers deal directly with the business data, and in a typical installation it is far easier for outsiders to gain access at the applications programming level.

Therefore certain principles must be followed with regard to any applications programming which is built into the system, particularly in those systems where the decision (conscious or tacit) has been made to live with a low level of security.

1. The applications program must be well documented as to content, procedure, symbology, glossary and detailed code.*
2. Periodic tests must be conducted to ensure that the code indeed represents what the documentation advertises, that no subtle conditional procedures have been imbedded in the machine code and that system changes have not caused changes in the operation.
3. The so-called source code, e.g., COBOL, which the programmer uses must be spot-checked against the object machine code by the use of comparison compiling and running techniques.
4. Audit trails, both for complete audit and spot-checking, must be built into the code and into test procedures separately. This includes data and procedural audits which can flush out any exceptions to the normal processing.
5. The applications code must include provisions for auxiliary data recording to implement, at least, the "single failure principle": *It should not be possible to lose data through any single failure in the system even though that failure occurs during operation and goes undetected for some period of time.*
6. There are certain methods by which the applications program can be used to gain access to unauthorized password data, obtain entry in the system's privileged memory and instruction areas and perform other undesired actions. Since these unconventional applications can be designed so as to be undetectable by system software protection, auditing procedures and checks must be instituted.
7. Special attention must be paid to "experimental programs" or programs used for one-shot calculations or as part of a program development project because it is precisely these experiments which can be used to determine the vulnerability of the system or to purposely or accidentally broach it.
8. Software security must include a high-quality program and data logging system which clearly shows who did what, who used what, when and for how long. A good "monitor" of this type can

*Every one of these words represents a task.

be built having very little overhead and almost no impact upon normal operations.

9. It is possible to institute protection schemes that make it difficult, if not impossible, to steal applications software. The specific procedure depends upon the computer system installed. In general, however, the source code of an applications program is frequently better than 90 percent transferable to machines of the same or other manufacturers, whereas the object code for compiling source code (the object code being what is normally run during production) can be easily made to have essentially 0 compatibility with any machine except one.

Chapter 9
Personnel
The Heart of the Problem

THE only problems with personnel are people. And, in particular, computer fraud is instigated and perpetrated by people. Preventing and detecting such activities internally are by definition primarily personnel-related problems. The precautions recommended here are intended to detect malfunctioning personnel and thus to limit fraud and damage to the system due to dishonesty, carelessness and error. While problems can be caused by equipment failure, even many of these are due to inadequate or improper maintenance or improper operation by people. Personnel control includes hiring the right people, properly training them, inspiring their enthusiasm and cooperation, keeping them challenged and growing in their work, and handling terminations properly so that the morale of the remaining staff remains high.

Donald Cressey, one of the foremost criminologists specializing in white-collar crime, states* his well-tested hypothesis as follows:

> Trusted persons become trust violators when they conceive of themselves as having a financial problem which is nonshareable, are aware that this problem can be secretly resolved by violation of the position of financial trust, and are able to apply to their own conduct in that situation verbalizations which enable them to adjust their conceptions of themselves as trusted persons with their conceptions of themselves as users of the entrusted funds or property.

Screening New Personnel

In screening applicants one attempts to evaluate their technical ability and skills in terms of the job requirements and to assess the individual's character, emotional stability, ability to handle personal affairs, and any other factors that may impair their performance on the job. A check can be done by the internal personnel department or by outside agencies hired for that purpose. Since we are concerned with security rather than

**Other People's Money*. D. Cressey, Belmont, California, Wadsworth, 1971.

with personnel management, we will discuss these factors as they relate to security and recommend some procedures to insure the elimination of high-security-risk individuals.

Character and emotional stability are the key personal factors that effect security. An individual with deceptive or dishonest tendencies is a major security risk. Financial difficulties can make an honest individual susceptible to exploitation by others with dishonest intentions. Lack of adequate ability or skill can be the seat of later emotional problems and unhappiness, not to mention a feeling of mistreatment by the company. Further, the output from unqualified individuals can be so error prone and sufficiently disorganized as to prevent adequate verification, thus masking fraudulent activity.

While much of the information required to make hiring judgments may be derived through interviews with the applicant, reference checks generally prove more productive. Remember that the individual has carefully selected the reference he has given. Therefore, during reference checks it is of paramount importance to obtain the names of others who can be contacted for deeper checking. In contacting such secondary references, be certain to inform them that the applicant had not given their name.

Many organizations fail to thoroughly check references and previous employers. Checks with previous employers should be made by someone experienced and trained in handling personnel matters who is also technically competent so that he can ask the proper questions and assess the answers. Many former employers tend to play down any employee's failures. No one likes to give a person a bad reference, so that any unenthusiastic reference should usually be considered negative.

With regard to security, the personality of the potential employee is probably more important than is his knowledge or capability in his particular field. Performance is often influenced more by psychological factors than by intellectual factors, and evaluating personalities is difficult. Many companies find it worthwhile to use psychological tests or psychological testing services to better appraise the suitability of an individual for the kinds of work and responsibility to which he will be exposed. The unstable individual may be a bad risk in situations requiring him to handle sensitive materials and information. Although testing is usually reserved for higher-level executives, it should be considered for any sensitive position where a problem personality could prove extremely costly.

The general background check should be used far more often than it has been. At the very least, the employer should be aware of the individual's credit rating. A person with financial problems is more likely to be a bad risk, and such problems often indicate that he manages his own affairs poorly and yields to desires he cannot afford. Sometime in the future he may yield to other temptations, to the company's detriment. Local authorities should be contacted to determine if the individual has a police record.

Personnel Training

Too many employers bring in new people and start them working with no indoctrination whatsoever. A new employee should be put through a formal introduction during which time is spent explaining to him the organization's principles, goals, policies and procedures. He should be shown around, introduced to the people he will work with and shown where emergency equipment is located. He should be acquainted with procedures manuals, and should be given samples of all forms he may use in the course of his work. The individual should be imparted a clear statement of his responsibilities and authorities. This takes less time and money than one might expect, and in the long run it is far cheaper than simply showing the individual where his desk and the lavatory are and leaving the rest to chance.

Internal communication is one major factor in good employee/employer relationships. To insure interested, enthusiastic and effective employees, management must take steps to keep them well informed. Employees who are kept informed of the company's goals and made aware of changes in organization and objectives, who learn of good news formally rather than by the grapevine, who are encouraged to participate in making their own operation as effective as possible, who are asked for suggestions, who know that their ideas are seriously considered, and who know that they will be rewarded for useful contributions will be real assets to any company. This will not only boost their efficiency, it will also make security controls more meaningful because the individuals who have the responsibility for doing work will be aware of the possible risks and will be seriously interested in avoiding these risks for the good of the company as a whole. Proper managerial attitudes towards personnel as well as proper internal public relations can have a greater effect in the overall security of your operation than any other single factor.

This type of personal involvement and response to an organization is simply not possible without proper personnel training. Training must begin on the employee's first day of work and continue until his termination.

Performance Reviews

Periodic performance reviews for all personnel are a major contribution to a good relationship between management and employees. They serve several purposes if properly used. First, they provide each supervisor with the opportunity for a thoughtful review of the performance of those within his managerial scope, and thus, his whole operation. Second, they provide the individual worker with a chance to sit down with his supervisor and receive a formal opinion of his performance. Third, they provide the employee with an opportunity to express dissatisfactions on any aspect of his job or working relationships without having to make an issue of them and before serious problems evolve. All of these are highly useful if not indispensable functions in maintaining good security.

From the worker's point of view, the review confirms his understanding of what is expected of him, how well he is doing and what he can expect in the way of progress in both salary and responsibility. It gives him an indication of his own weaknesses needing remedy. All of these things lead to better personnel relationships and happier employees.

Performance reviews should include not only aspects of the individual's technical performance but should also include such things as general attitude, relationships with other people and attitude or personality problems: all of these factors contribute to the ability of an individual to deal with those around him.

Work Assignment Strategy

Even with the best screening and testing techniques, training program and performance review policy, some poor-risk individuals will still be hired and retained. Here we discuss a strategy for personnel use that will also tend to discourage deliberate misdeeds.

One's a monopoly, two's company, three's a crowd, and four or more is a party. How many popular games can you think of, particularly games of skill, that are usually played with three players? Why the dearth of three player games? Perhaps because three rapidly deteriorates into two-against-one. At best the one feels ill treated but if the game continues over an extended period, outright hostility will probably develop.

Where sensitive data are involved, if a single individual has total responsibility, all kinds of crimes can be perpetrated with little fear of exposure. If two are involved, a bargain might be struck that is satisfactory to both parties. While the risk of exposure is greater than if only one were involved, it is still not satisfactory to management. If four or more are involved, be very cautious. While cooperative crimes are infrequent, it may be impossible to show that losses were not the result of coordination or communication problems among the workers.

The magic number is thus three. Wherever possible the division of work responsibilities should be such that exactly three people are required to perpetrate a crime. Of course this is not to imply that only three people work in each department nor that every function require exactly three people. It simply implies that a strategy should be developed, where possible, such that a concept or piece of data must pass through exactly three people from point of origin to final application.

For example, three steps are involved in effective program development: design, implementation and validation. While a number of people may be involved in each stage, any specific process will be handled by a specific individual at each stage. Of course, the designer must be included in the review of the validation process to close the loop and maintain a three-person involvement. In order to perpetrate a crime the designer, programmer and validator must cooperate, if not deliberately, then through failure to perform their jobs in a responsible manner. One of these people is likely to feel ill treated and blow the whistle on any illicit activity.

Handling Terminations

In spite of the best of screening techniques, training and review, there will be employees who prove unsatisfactory, others who find themselves unhappy, and others who leave for better opportunities. There are a number of rules which should be applied in these situations.

As a general policy, an individual being terminated should be treated politely but always as a potential source of problems. He is no longer loyal to the company. If he feels he has been wronged, not fully appreciated or not fully compensated, he may have feelings of hostility. There is always the possibility that he may spread discontent to other staff members or deliberately sabotage a system. Through carelessness caused by no longer caring about the work he is still doing, he may cause all sorts of problems. For these reasons, it is highly advisable to get the department worker off the premises immediately. Whether the severance is the company's action or his own, salary in lieu of notice is the best procedure—particularly if security is involved. Don't wait until a replacement is found.

On the other hand, the departing employee may be a valuable source of information concerning what is going on in your organization. He can frequently provide criticisims that you will not get from people still on the job. The departing employee no longer feels he has a position to protect and he may no longer be concerned with feelings of those about him. If so, he is more likely to be frank and honest in his appraisals of what has gone on about him. You must recognize that his feelings will be severely biased, but there still may be considerable value to his comments. This information is best obtained via the exit interview.

The exit interview should be carefully structured, and preferably conducted by a personnel department employee trained in handling these situations. The interviewer should elicit feelings about the employee's job as he saw it, the problems he has experienced, his feelings on leaving the company, his feelings about the section within which he was working and any suggestions he may have about the work he was doing.

It is equally important to be sure that the individual departs with only those things that are rightfully his. There have been many cases of employees leaving with copies of proprietary information. Ex-employees can use computer programs for their own purposes; programs may be given to a competitor to help secure a job or utilized to start a new competing company. Businesses have been built on the trade secrets stolen by departing employees. Records should be kept so that all sensitive documents that the individual has in his possession will be returned. Materials taken out by the departing individual should be scanned just to "protect" him and the company.

General Observations

Hire carefully, train well, involve each employee in his work and review his progress. If things do not work out, terminate him graciously. Persistent suspicion of employees and frequent surprise audits are poor practice. All of these activities are managerial expressions of a lack of confidence in its people, personnel policies and security measures. Employees may develop the feeling that their work is not appreciated or even recognized.

Such activities by management may lead to a worker attitude that "they" do not trust "us" anyway so why not take advantage of an opportunity to profit dishonestly. "After all, management has virtually said they expect it." "Other people take advantage, so why shouldn't I?"

Ask for honest, responsible actions from employees and make them feel that you truly expect it. Dismiss individuals who do not live up to these expectations, but do not "make an example" in any case.

Chapter 10
Methods and Procedures
Some Necessary Nitty-Gritty

Operating Manuals

The complexity of the data processing function demands a well-structured and well-controlled organization to avoid chaos. Unless all operations are systematically and fully controlled with every step defined, the way is open to confusion, corruption and collapse. The first step toward effective control is the delineation of exact responsibilities for all functions in the operation. These include:

- Data input
- Operating system management
- Data file control
- Program file control
- Program change control
- Computer room operation
- Program development
- Program validation
- Documentation
- Auditing
- General housekeeping
- Maintenance
- Emergency control

The effective assignment of responsibility for these functions requires the development of detailed step-by-step procedures which must be formalized by being fully recorded in a series of manuals. These manuals must both guide and reflect the actual operation. Preparation of procedure manuals is the responsibility of the data processing manager who must use his own resources and draw on existing materials and experience, plus whatever help can be obtained from equipment suppliers, professional societies, periodicals and books, auditing firms and data processing consultants. The purposes of the formalization are to:

1. Provide "road maps" for directing information flow.
2. Provide controls to assure the accuracy and proper utilization of information in accounting, financial and managerial operations.
3. Assure smooth and efficient operation under all circumstances.
4. Prevent abuse, misuse and loss of information.
5. Facilitate the detection of errors, loss or misuse of information and other assets.
6. Provide accountability for the use of company assets.
7. Provide data for audits.

The development and maintenance of manuals is a continuing operation. The manuals should be loose-leaf books kept readily available to the staff and management. They must grow with the operation and be kept current. A good set of manuals for an average-sized data processing operation may run between 300 and 600 pages. This basic documentation both determines and describes the entire operation, and therefore its existence and content is the starting point for any audit. The minimum set of manuals with associated topics should include:

Users' Manual—To provide guidance and operating rules to the users of information when interfacing with each other and with the data processing function.

Procedures Manual—To define and describe in detail all steps for the flow of data required for the operation and management of the business. One portion of this overall manual will be devoted to the operations of the data processing function. In the procedures manual, the following sections are needed:

Computing Operating Section—To define in detail all steps in the operations of the computer room and all controls to be administered by the operations staff.

Programming Standards Section—To define the rules for producing new computer programs and modifying existing programs.

Documentation Standards Section—To define required supporting textual material for all computer programs.

In many companies the method and procedures evolve through trial and error. Formalization tends to lag far behind actual practice. This haphazard approach usually provides totally inadequate control over the operations and is often one of the basic reasons for both poor security and low efficiency.

A good set of procedure manuals is absolutely essential to the control of data processing, but they serve a useful purpose only if used. Good manuals should be clear, concise, complete and should be a direct implementation of company policy. They will be useful not only for their primary purpose of definition but will also serve as training tools. The procedures manual should contain:

Statement of managerial objectives and goals and the intent of the manuals.
Management structure and definition of responsibility.
Detailed operational procedures.
Detailed program development procedures and standards.
Detailed definition of and assignment of responsibility for housekeeping in the Data Processing operation.

The operational procedure section of the manual should detail:

Operators' responsibilities and duties.
Program run instructions.
Equipment Operating log.
Computer room access control.
Job control procedures.
Operating system usage.
Rules for access control.

The Program Development & Standards section should include general rules for development of new programs including:

General security philosophy.
Controls to be built into new systems being programmed.
Program validation techniques to be used.

The section on Documentation should define the content of standard program documentation which should include:

Initial functional specifications.
The Users of the program output.
Statement of change authorization responsibility.
Complete program logic.
Program printout.
Program change record.

The program change control section should define:

Requirements for initiation and authorization of changes.
Change procedures.
Validation requirements.

Program and Data Control Procedures

Control of changes in programs is a critical area of any computer user's problems. Often associated with such changes is a requirement for rewriting the format or making other major alterations to input or output data files. Both of these areas are subject to possible abuse if not properly controlled. In order to adequately understand the nature of the problems involved here, perhaps we had better review the process by which a program is generated.

It must be understood that in the analysis of a data processing operation a systems designer determines the sequence of procedural steps that must be carried out to assure proper processing. He converts these into a flow diagram or flow statement that indicates the logical processing steps that must then be implemented. This, in turn, is converted by a programmer into a series of processing statements in a language which is either directly understandable by a machine or which through the action of a translation program, called a compiler, can be translated into a machine-understandable language.

When a programmer completes a program it invariably has mistakes known in the trade as bugs. The process of successfully eliminating the bugs in a program is commonly called program debugging, and all programs must go through a debugging phase before they are usable. In more-complex programs it is not unusual for a bug in the program to remain undetected for a considerable period of time. Therefore, there is a continuous maintenance process in which a program undergoes continuous change and improvement, which among other things involves correcting bugs that show up during normal program usage.

In addition to this process, there is a continual changing of the program to meet changing conditions. If, for example, we are concerned with a payroll program, there may be changes in local tax laws, internal revenue regulations or in the method by which compensation is calculated. A union negotiation may, for example, change the basis upon which payment for services is to be made. In any of these cases, changes in the program may be necessary. The control of such changes can easily be the Achilles heel of an otherwise reasonably secure system.

Inadequate change control will leave the individual programmer free to modify programs at any time in any way he sees fit. Such modifications could easily change the entire function of the program. The possibilities are limited only by the skill and imagination of the programmer. The list of disastrous possibilities could be endless and only a good system of program change control can limit the opportunity for such unauthorized program modifications. The following are necessary elements in a good program control system:

A change should be initiated only by a written request which must come from the user of the program, the program maintenance section or the program validation group.

The request for change must have the approval of the programming manager and of the user before implementation can begin.

The responsibility for the change must be assigned to a programmer who will implement it.

When the programmer has implemented and debugged the change, it must in turn be reviewed and checked by the program validation group.

The program validation group must report certification that the change is correct to the programming manager, who will then schedule the introduction of the change.

The schedule date will be appropriately documented so that for future reference the status of the program at any given date is known.

No change in the program should be permissible without following all of the steps of the procedure. If errors in implementation are found during the course of program validation, these errors must be corrected and subsequently checked by at least one other member of the validation group or by the programming manager or his delegate. A record of these corrections should be maintained as part of the program's documentation file. This will insure that the documentation file is maintained current so that the description of the program contained therein agrees with the program in use at all times.

The control of the changes in data file must be similar to that over changes in computer programs. Here authority should be centered in the hands of a data manager, who will be responsible to the file users for the correctness of the information in each file. No changes should be made without the data manager's authorization. He in turn should neither initiate nor approve changes without the prior approval of the data file user.

Again, as each change in the file content organization or format is completed, it must be checked by the validation group and by submission of a file printout to the user. Contents of each file must be documented at all times and the documentation file must be maintained current just as in the case of program documentation.

Operating Systems

Modern computers in order to operate with reasonable efficiency operate under the control of an "operating system." The operating system schedules individual jobs and handles the assignment of peripheral devices to tasks and of memory space to particular tasks. Some operating systems handle only one task at a time. In larger, more complex systems, several tasks can be in operation at the same time using different parts of the system and this sharing of the facilities among tasks in order to maximize the effectiveness of the system is an operating system function. The operating system should be under the control of a system software manager.

The operating system is usually supplied by the equipment supplier. From time to time the supplier will issue new versions of the system to correct bugs in the system or to improve its effectiveness.

The system software manager must be responsible for determining the effect of the changes on application programs in the system. He must schedule the changeover of the operating system at a time which permits corresponding application program changes to be scheduled and properly implemented.

The correctness of the system software, applications programs and data files will still not insure the correctness of results produced by the computer unless the input for each run is correct. The preparation of input material in machine-readable form is both one of the major costs of computer operation and one of the major sources of system errors. It is one of the areas most vulnerable to manipulation, both deliberate and accidental.

There are a wide variety of controls available here. The extent of controls must be dictated by an analysis of the cost effectiveness of controls available. The internal and external auditing staffs should contribute to the establishment of the controls on input data. The controls may include the verification of input data by repeating the input with a second operator. This is usually an operation independent of the main system using separate verification equipment. In some systems a number of input devices may be under the control of a separate minicomputer which will compare the results from two separate keyboardings of the data and indicate disagreements requiring manual correction. In some cases the main computer may be used to compare information recorded on two separate tapes. In addition to the verification of critical data, hash totals such as totals of the order numbers in a batch, columnar totals, record counts, cross footings, limit checks and other accounting checking techniques should be used to validate input information. A complete discussion of the detailed techniques is beyond the scope of this work.

Library Procedures

The system's files must be stored in a form readable by the computer system. The media used are punched cards or magnetic tape for original input data and magnetic tape or magnetic disks for reusable master files. Computer program files may appear as card decks or be recorded upon magnetic tape or disks. These files must be stored for future use preferably in a library that has close control of access and established procedures for the removal and replacement of files stored therein. Scratch tapes and disks should also be stored in the library.

The tape and disk library should be managed by a librarian who issues the tapes or disks as needed by the computer operators for processing. Issuing should be in accordance with a previously provided schedule or other authorization and the operator should sign the tape or disk in and out.

The librarian should maintain complete records of the history of each tape reel or disk. This record should describe the contents of the unit, the normal schedule for its updating, a listing of the specific runs for which it is used, the number of times it has been used and complete information for identification of the particular reel or disk.

To illustrate the importance of tight control of this function we need only cite the case of the disgruntled discharged computing center employee who before leaving his job systematically removed the identification from all of the several hundred reels of tape in the company library. The computing center was out of operation for more than a week while the operator used the computer to read and identify each tape. The complete stoppage of all data processing activities for one week caused problems throughout the company. Payroll checks were delayed, accounting operations largely suspended, deliveries to customers were delayed, invoicing was interrupted and as a result payments were late. The results were felt for many months.

The controls on the library files must, like those in a conventional book library, assure that each file goes out only to authorized individuals and is appropriately signed for and returned on schedule. They must also provide for the proper care and maintenance of tape or disk including inspection, cleaning when required, and replacement when the end of useful life is reached.

Even blank tapes and tapes used for intermediate storage in operations, such as sorting, and tapes used in the updating of programs and data files must be carefully controlled.

In one recent case, a computer operator in a commercial data processing service bureau taped a copy of a program and walked out of the center with it. She then took the tape copy to a client of the service bureau who was a steady user of the program on a rental basis and offered it for sale. It happened that the executive offered the stolen program was a member of the board of directors of the service bureau corporation, and he immediately reported the incident to the bureau.

Program files pose at least one additional control problem in that those tapes or disks or card decks must be accessible to the programer for changes, updating and debugging and must be available to programming groups for validation and routine maintenance. When a program file is removed from the library for any purpose which may require changing information on that tape or disk, this must be handled in a manner which will not destroy the information. That is, a routine must be set up which maintains a copy of the program on a backup machine-readable medium (tape or disk), so that an error by the programmer working on that tape does not affect the backup file copy. This is an absolute must since there have been cases too numerous to list where the programmer has made a mistake in a correction which has resulted in the destruction of the original with which he was working or where a computer operator has made an error in transcribing corrections or in testing corrections and has destroyed the program tape through having erased or written over information on that tape.

This control can also help to protect against such deliberate sabotage as happened at a Defense Department data processing center recently when someone left an additional program module buried in the operating system which caused all program tapes to be erased after being run. The resulting mess shut the center down for several days. Fortunately, backup copies of most programs existed, and once the source of the trouble was discovered, business was soon restored to normal.

File Backup

The problem of program and data file backup requires careful planning and just as careful execution to prevent loss of control or loss of irreplaceable information during emergencies. Let us define what we mean by backup.

The tape and disk library houses a variety of files containing data and programs. Should any of those files be stolen, destroyed, damaged, or made unusable for any reason in the course of either normal or abnormal operation, there must be recourse to a second copy of that information in another location.

Now we must recognize that the files stored in this library are not static, they must be continually changing. A file is useful because it records information concerning some aspect of the running of a business. This information must be kept current, that is, it must be updated on a regular basis. In updating, the contents of a file are changed. Understanding this, it is obvious that a problem arises if we are going to store the information in this file in a second place; the two may no longer agree after a run in which the working copy of the file is updated, and is therefore necessary to develop procedures that will provide several generations of the files to be maintained.

A good data-management policy will require that at the end of every day's operation a new tape or disk copy of each file which has been updated that day be placed in the library. This new copy should be made on a blank tape which then replaces the tape already in the library. This precludes possibility of a system failure erasing both the working tape and the tape being prepared for backup. At a somewhat lesser frequency, perhaps weekly, the updated file should be recorded on a tape stored in a separate location for further backup. Thus at any time, the system will provide a backup tape that is no more than a week behind the current status of the file, a second backup tape which is up to one day behind the present status of the file, and the current working copy of the file.

Computer people have gotten into the habit of referring to these as grandfather, father and son tapes, since they represent three generations in the life of the data on the file. Should there be an accident which in some way destroys the information either through physical damage to the storage media or through a system failure which erases or destroys the information on the media, it is possible with current information and the father tape to regenerate a son tape. Should both father and son in some way be destroyed, it is possible, having recourse to the grandfather tape and current information, to regenerate new father and son tapes.

However, one additional factor must be kept in mind. In the course of the operation of any system there will be changes in processing due to changed conditions. For example, a tax rate may have changed. Unless the grandfather is processed by the correct version of the processing program, it may be impossible to develop usable father and son tapes. It is therefore necessary to have adequate records in the library so that both the various generations of the computer program and the generations of data files are maintained. Full information enabling a programmer or operator to relate the generations of data files to the corresponding generations of processing programs and to the corresponding generations of operating systems must also be maintained. Operating systems change with time due to improvements provided by the manufacturer of the equipment and to the correction of errors in the operating systems discovered either locally or by manufacturers.

It is a good practice in the control of the tape library to maintain the father and son tapes or disks in the tape library and the grandfather generation in a separate vault in a separate location, preferably in another building. Many facilities rent space in a bank vault for such storage. In the absence of a suitable bank vault, a carefully fire-protected and access-protected vault in another building of the company facilities will fill this need.

It is almost equally important as further insurance of the ability to use the corresponding generations of data and program files that any documentation describing either the content and format of the files or the functioning of the corresponding program be maintained up to date with proper correspondence between the generations of documentation and generations of data file and program file. This system documentation must be handled with the same type of systematized library that is applied to the handling of the data and program files themselves and must be kept as current. The lack of such current and correct documentation may allow adequate knowledge of the system to disappear, leaving chaos.

While it is true that the programming people can at the cost of time and effort proceed from a program tape to redevelop the flow of function in that tape, this is an expensive, time-consuming process, and in many cases programmers will have used paths of processing which are not obvious so that a full understanding of the purpose of each step becomes somewhat difficult.

Waste Disposal

While punched cards are less often used for file storage on modern systems they still at times perform this function on some smaller systems where control is just as vital. In addition, both the punched cards used for data input and the printouts of files used for human review suffer from an additional security weakness. They are readable without any equipment and are not reusable. When no longer needed they are discarded. Most data processing installations give little thought to controlling the procedure for discarding such disposable media, yet this can be a significant source of information leakage.

A previously cited case of computer-based fraud involved the systematic theft of telephone equipment from a Pacific Telephone and Telegraph Company by Jerry Neal Schneider, who was using the telephone company's computerized system to order the items he needed to steal to meet the inventory needs of his own telephone installation business. Mr. Schneider apparently stole nearly one million dollars worth of equipment. When apprehended he admitted that he had learned how to manipulate the computer by reading user instruction manuals and program printouts found in the telephone company's trash barrels. What vital company secrets are offered to the world in your trash?

Mr. Schneider pleaded guilty to one count of grand theft, spent 40 days in jail and was placed on probation for three years. Although $100,000 worth of equipment was recovered, the Pacific Telephone and Telegraph Company was not able to really determine the extent of its loss.

In another case, a high school student found a privileged password of a services analyst on a listing in a wastebasket. He also obtained detailed specifications of the system. He used this information to steal large amounts of computer time for his own purposes which included playing computer games and obtaining other customers' data.

The procedures of well-managed computer centers and those of well-managed computer users provide for handling computer waste separate from normal wastes. First, computer-related waste must be kept separate from other wastes by provision of separate disposal containers. Managerial enforcement becomes easier under this procedure since visual inspection will expose the use of normal waste containers for computer printouts or card decks.

Second, the collection and disposal of such wastes should be separate from regular clean-up functions and should be performed near the end of each working day—but not after hours. Disposal can be by burning or shredding or other processes that render the information nonrecoverable. Shredded waste can then be placed with regular waste for ultimate disposal.

Part III
CHECKS AND RESPONSIBLILITIES

Chapter 11
Auditing and Internal Controls
The Locks on the System Doors

The Who and Why of Auditing

Despite the preventive controls we have outlined, errors may still occur. Whether deliberate or accidental, the net cost of the errors to the businessman is the same. Early detection will at least minimize the loss.

Losses can best be detected through accounting and auditing. The internal auditor's function is to check on the effectiveness of any controls which assure accuracy of the accounting process. If the controls are functioning properly, they will detect errors from any source including fraud.

Some deliberate attempts to impair or destroy the integrity of computers files may be very difficult to detect. For example, one employee placed in a payroll program the instruction to, in effect, "self-destruct" if the programmer's employee number did not appear on the payroll for 26 consecutive payroll periods, and 26 weeks after the programmer's termination, the master payroll file was erased. Such "future" instructions would be detected only with careful and technical auditing and testing techniques. Fortunately, this type of malicious destruction is less common than deliberate or accidental errors which cause continuing losses.

The external auditor, the internal auditor and the systems consultant can all contribute to error detection.

The External Auditor

When a public accountant examines financial statements, his examination involves a number of auditing procedures, the results of which give him a basis for the expression of an opinion on the company's financial soundness and the results of its operations.

Prior to his examination, the auditor will evaluate the company's internal controls to determine the extent of testing that will be necessary. The evaluation will cover controls over manual procedures as well as those over the data processing function. He will check not only to see what controls exist but also to gauge their effectiveness. Weaknesses in the controls will be brought to the attention of management, and auditing tests will be extended in the areas affected.

The external auditor plays the important role of evaluating and recommending improvements in internal controls. His audit procedures are based on the existence and effectiveness of the controls, so he will be understandably critical of weaknesses. Although the external auditor is constantly aware that fraud or accidental errors may exist, the normal financial auditing procedures are not designed to detect fraud and management should not rely solely on the external audit for such detection.

The Controller or the Internal Auditor

Management's best source for people qualified to detect computer fraud or accidental errors is the internal accounting staff. Due to their continuous involvement in their company's operations, they can gain an intimate knowledge of the computer systems.

Since the controller's staff has the responsibility for daily accounting transactions, a separate internal auditing staff is a valuable supporting arm and the employment of such a staff is highly recommended. However, in smaller firms where the internal auditing function is not economically justified, the controller's duties must be expanded to cover this area.

The size of the organization and its computer involvement will naturally define the limit of the internal auditor's activities. They may include, but are not limited to, the following.

SYSTEMS DESIGN

The internal auditing staff should be active during the design phase of a new computer system or a major revision of an existing system. Computer personnel are generally not accounting oriented and have not gained an appreciation of the need for auditing trails and internal controls in accounting.

The auditing trail is merely a series of references which leads back to the original source document. It is as important to the data processing department as it is to the auditor. Internal controls assure that all data submitted for processing is introduced into the system, that the data is processed by the system in the manner prescribed by management, that the desired reports are printed and that all processes are performed accurately—exceptions being reported on a timely basis; that is, in time to take appropriate action.

When the internal auditor addresses himself to the controls, he must evaluate them in several ways. First, of course, is their existence. Are record counts produced at the end of each processing run? Are batch totals printed and properly identified? Are customer numbers, employee numbers, or account numbers validated before the transactions are accepted for processing? If check digits are employed, does the program provide the necessary calculation to verify the number?

Each application should be reviewed for possible auditing problems arising from a lack of particular controls. For example, if an order-processing system prepares C.O.D. invoices, there should be a control to assure the funds are received upon delivery. If the order is simply processed to accounts receivable with other open account charges, manual auditing procedures should be instituted to determine that collections are made and deposited in a timely manner. Since many C.O.D. shipments are paid for in cash, this happens to be one of the most prevalent areas of defalcation.

Once the existence of controls is confirmed, their effectiveness should be evaulated. Various methods are employed to handle invalid transactions, and the method used must be evaluated in relation to the critical nature of the transaction. Great homage is paid to header labels, but this control is completely ineffective if the error message can be bypassed simply by typing ignore" on the computer console.

Next is the assurance that controls conform to company policy. What happens when a customer's order exceeds his established credit? What action results when a customer's payment is 70 cents short?* How are credit memos applied, and how are they aged in an aged listing of accounts receivable? The list is endless, and it probably includes many policy decisions which were not conveyed to the systems design staff, or were misunderstood. But company policies are set after management's evaluation of risks or losses to be incurred by the various ways of handling daily transactions, and being important to the financial health of the organization, they must come to bear on the internal decisions made by the computer.

PROGRAM TESTING

Programs should not be put into production until they have been tested by the internal auditor to determine if controls planned during systems design were in fact incorporated in the programs and are operating efficiently. His tests should discover extraneous program instructions. His written approval should be part of the system documentation. The same testing and approval should be required for program changes.

Since errors can cause costly reruns or impair the integrity of data

*In one public utility system, a sloppy program combined with a peculiarity in the computer that differentiated between a plus-zero (+0) and minus-zero (−0) resulted in some dunning notices for $0.00.

files, all errors dilute the assets of a company. Whatever cost is incurred by such testing is more than justified in view of the responsibility placed on the controller's office to protect those assets.

DOCUMENTATION

A copy of an improved program should be retained in the internal auditor's files. He should also have copies of other documentation on the program, such as a narrative description of the system and flow charts. Periodic comparison of his copies with those in the computer center may reveal unauthorized changes. The copies will also furnish the information needed for internal auditing.

REPORT DISTRIBUTION

Reports necessarily disclose the type of data contained in files and may illustrate the manner in which the data can be manipulated. A report may treat changes to employee master files, lists of unmatched cash receipts or lists of accounts receivable written off. Because the indiscriminate distribution of these reports can lead to a serious weakness in output controls, the proposed distribution of each report should be formally presented to management for approval, and a copy of the approval should be a part of the system documentation.

The internal auditor should review the report distribution periodically. He should be advised of proposed additions to the lists so he can assist management in evaluating the additions on a "need to know" basis.

TESTING MANUAL CONTROLS

Many computer systems depend on manually prepared input controls, such as a batch total of hours on a group of time cards. However, suppose the total hours worked as submitted by the payroll department is 1200 and the total hours processed as shown on payroll reports is 1300. The control is ineffective if the difference goes unnoticed. The internal auditor should make sure that such input controls are validated and that all differences are accounted for.

The tedious chore of reconciling bank accounts has been computerized by many firms. The computer captures check numbers and the net amount of checks as a byproduct of processing cash disbursements. Cancelled checks are keypunched when returned by the bank, but with check number only. This data is processed against the file of all checks issued, and a list of outstanding checks is produced. The savings in clerical time may be substantial, but what about endorsements? Did the intended payee actually receive the check? Manual testing is the only conclusive way to verify this.

Recall the Westinghouse example where the employees manipulated the check-writing program in such a way that the payee on the actual check differed from the payee on the check copies. The fraudulent checks were later removed from the group of cancelled checks returned by the bank. Since the bank provided the data processing to produce a list of outstanding checks and since this list was used in the reconciliation, the absence of the fraudulent checks was not noticed. A manual reconciliation of the account on a spot-check basis would have disclosed the manipulation.

"Lapping" is a common form of embezzlement. To illustrate, a payment of $200 in cash is received from Account A. The employee receiving the cash diverts it to his own use. Account B pays $300 by check, and the dishonest employee applies $200 to Account A and $100 to Account B. Cash received for Account C is taken, and the next check received is applied in part to Accounts B and C. In a large system with many cash receipts, lapping may be undetected for a long period of time. However, the occasional testing of bank deposits by the internal auditor—on a surprise basis—would reveal the misapplication of receipts.

Unfortunately, the poor reputation which computers have earned with the general public has contributed to the success of such misappropriations. Since many people have been the innocent victims of computer errors, an apology accompanied by a correction to their account usually stops any further complaints.

USE OF COMPUTER-AUDIT PROGRAMS

Computer-audit programs may be used for both internal and external auditing work. These programs are best described as utility programs or report generators which can be used on a variety of data files for limited purposes. They provide the auditor with a means of manipulating computer files with programs prepared independent of the company's data processing personnel. Some of the uses are as follows.

Simulating Computer Runs. The auditor may take copies of files and process them to achieve the same results as the company's computer system. Any differences in results would disclose errors in the company's system.

An illustration would be a simulation of a run to credit interest on savings accounts. In one instance, the interest was calculated to five decimal places, then rounded to two decimal places. The "breakage" was credited to an unauthorized account. By using a computer-audit program, the entire run could be made independently, then compared to the results of the company's run. Since the credit to the "breakage" account would not have occurred under the computer-audit program, the unauthorized credit would have been discovered.

Extracting Unusual Transactions. The theory of exception reporting is that management's attention should be directed to only those items that do not meet an expected norm. Similarly, the auditor is generally interested in transactions of an unusual nature. Computer-audit programs provide him with the capability to read a file of thousands of records or transactions and print out only those that exceed the criteria he specifies.

For example, in an open-item accounts receivable file, he might select accounts with an unusual number of total transactions or accounts with an unusual number of credit transactions. He may select the accounts whose balances exceed the stated credited limit or all accounts with credit balances. From an inventory file, he might select items with an unusually high inventory value or quantity or unit cost. If the file contains historical data, he could select items with a low turnover to test for obsolescence. Additions and deletions from the files could be selected from payroll master files and confirmed by reference to the personnel department records. Rate changes could be similarly tested. This selection capability greatly enhances the internal auditor's opportunity to detect potential problems in the accounting system.

Performing Independent Calculations. Computer-audit programs can perform mathematical calculations for a variety of tasks. The internal auditor could completely rerun a physical inventory valuation and compare the results with the company's totals. At one firm, the physical counts of inventory were keypunched and listed on the computer by batches to compare the totals to the adding machine tapes submitted with the counts. The same inventory item was stored in several different places in the warehouse, thus creating several subcounts on the same product. To save computer time, the punched cards were sorted off-line on a card sorter, then summarized on an old reproducing punch which the company had from their precomputer days. The summarized cards were then used to run the final inventory listing. By duplicating the entire run with a computer-audit program, the internal auditor discovered that the reproducing punch had failed during the summarizing process and that a number of different items were added together under one product number. Since the unit cost of the various items varied considerably, the company's final inventory was greatly understated.

The internal auditor can verify the calculation of depreciation of fixed assets by use of a computer-audit program, the calculation of income on installment sales or the aging of accounts receivable. Again, the possibilities are as endless as they are valuable.

Performing Ratio Analyses. In extracting only unusual transactions, the auditor may want to look at a number of items which by themselves would not warrant particular attention but which as a group might exceed an expected norm. For example, discounts allowed on one particular item would be difficult to analyze on the basis of individual transactions. By combining all sales of that item and the total discount given, calculating a percentage and comparing that percentage to an anticipated ratio, a difference may appear that would be of interest to the auditor. The ratio of purchases to sales, or inventory quantity on hand in relation to sales, could also be of interest.

Were you aware that there is a reliable ratio of gross salaries to income tax withheld typical of each department or similar group? A variation of even ½ of 1% could indicate an accidental or deliberate error in your tax program. One firm worked for months to balance the individual withholding tax per employee records to the total withheld per the payroll reports. Finally, by developing ratios between the gross salaries and withholding tax by department for each payroll during the period when the imbalance occurred, they were able to discover the error. Fortunately, the error did not appear to be deliberate, but it could have been.

Reviewing Transactions in Employee Accounts. Employees involved in unauthorized transactions are usually sophisticated enough to use phony names or addresses or both. However, the use of a computer-audit program to select all entries affecting employee accounts may reveal specific transactions to be investigated. Many companies have allocated a special block of account numbers to employees in their accounts receivable files, and these are easy to check. But if employees are assigned account numbers in the same manner as other customers, they should be selected for review.

The internal auditor may wish to select the payroll records of employees in the computer center for examination or to select the records of terminated employees to see if there has been any activity in their accounts since their termination dates.

EVALUATING COMPUTER-AUDIT PROGRAMS

The computer-audit programs offers the internal auditor a tool that should not be underestimated by management. The independence from the company's own programming and operating personnel is invaluable. Most of the programs include their own operating systems, thereby eliminating the association with any of the company's own computer processing controls. The internal auditing staff should be encouraged to acquire access to such programs where feasible.

Management will have to give their support to the internal auditing staff in relation to their needs for retention of computer data and computer processing time. Resistance may come from the computer personnel concerning tape or disk shortage or available computer time, but proper planning by the internal auditing staff will minimize the inconvenience in both areas. The results of using such programs more then compensate for the inconvenience.

TEST DECKS

Test decks were originally sets of punched cards used to test programs on the mechanical tabulating equipment—the predecessors of electronic computers. Although casette tapes, paper tapes or magnetic tapes as well as cards may be used, the term "test deck" continues to be used for all.

Test decks are used by programming personnel to debug new programs. Each test card or record on tape carries a condition that the program is designed to handle in a certain manner. The test decks are saved and used to test again after every modification to the program.

The test deck lost favor in the auditing community for three reasons: the time consumed to prepare an independent test deck was considerable; the ultimate value of the test deck depended on the imagination of the preparer; and, the greatest factor in its disfavor, there was no way of knowing that the program being tested was, in fact, the program that was used for actual processing.

The test data generator has somewhat overcome the first objection for the internal auditor. These programs take basic information about a particular file and, with the marvelous redundancy found only in computers, generate transaction after transaction expanding, contracting, adding and multiplying the given factors. They also calculate and print out the expected result of the particular test transaction generated.

The third objection is somewhat overcome by the continuing presence of the internal auditor. He may process his test decks periodically on an irregular schedule. A complete surprise basis seems almost impossible due to scheduling demands, but with this familiarity with the planned processing, he could run his tests with short notice and at a minimum of inconvenience to the computer personnel.

Once a test deck has been generated, the internal auditor should use the deck on a recurring basis on regular production programs. Such tests will reveal any unauthorized program changes as well as authorized changes that did not go through the normal procedures.

As with all computer auditing, great care must be taken not to disturb the integrity of the files. Test transactions must not be allowed to become imbedded in the system. They must be reversed out of the live data or master files. Where possible, the tests should be run against a copy of the company's files. After the tests are completed, the copies can be scratched. The main files are unchanged in any way.

INTEGRATED TEST FACILITY

The integrated test facility is a fairly new concept currently employed by some companies. It involves establishing a pseudocompany whose transactions flow through the system along with valid data. The transactions of the pseudocompany are subjected to the same predetermined rules of the programs as are valid data, but they do not affect the company's actual records. The fictitious entity can be established as a separate division, company, branch or department. All transactions are entered for the test facility in the same manner as for the other groups. Since the results of the test transactions are predetermined, the final reports from the system can be reviewed for differences and the differences investigated.

To use an integrated test facility, the auditor needs to establish dummy master records such as accounts receivable, inventory or personnel files. Special programming is not required. Care must be taken that totals from the pseudocompany transactions do not find their way into the company's financial records. All dummy transactions must be accounted for at all times and reversed at the end of the reporting period.

TAGGING AND PICTURE TAKING

Tagging involves marking live input records by entering special codes in the records as identifiers. *Picture taking* means printing on some output device a copy of the tagged records intermittently during the processing cycle. The auditor compares the content of each record as it is processed to determine how the programs have changed the record. For example, when a cost price change is processed against a perpetual inventory record, the expected result would be the new price in the record. A picture of the records before and after processing would disclose actual changes in all data in the record. For example, one company had a substantial number of differences between perpetual inventory quantities and physical count quantities. After much checking, they found that a price change to the perpetual inventory records caused the quantity on hand to go to zero. The cause was a simple programming error that tagging and picture taking could have easily disclosed.

These auditing techniques do require extra programming, and should be planned during the design phase of a system. While they provide the auditor with an excellent tool for auditing internal processing, they have also been found to be very valuable to the data processing personnel when making program changes.

Since programming personnel are involved, there is the possibility that the programs could be fraudulently changed to bypass the tagged records. While this possibility may decrease the reliance on tagging, the auditing technique still deserves serious consideration.

"BREAKING" THE SYSTEM

Whatever auditing techniques the internal auditor employs, his main objective should be to break the system in order to disclose its weaknesses. Only by constantly challenging the system will he be able to find the areas where deliberate or accidental errors could go undetected.

Even though controls in some areas of weakness may not be cost or risk justified, at least the auditor will be aware of the weakness. He can then direct his manual and computer testing to the potential problems on a periodic basis.

In all the activities listed, the internal auditor needs the dedicated support of management. He cannot be effective without it. Management must set the standards for the data processing operation and take action when noncompliance is reported by the auditor. The control function must be exercised by trained competent personnel, not low-salaried clerks with little knowledge of data processing. Management must insist upon the same quality of control for the input-output control function that they have in other quality control areas.

Management must make data processing personnel accountable for their operations. They should be required to produce job cost reports and production reports as in other areas of the company.

Management should hold periodic meetings with data processing personnel, the departmental users of their services, and the internal auditor. Developing a continuing dialog among them is valuable in educating department supervisors and data processing personnel, as well as in resolving problems.

SYSTEMS CONTSULTANTS

The use of outside consultants provides a further deterrent to fraud or unintentional errors. They should be used on a recurring basis, although not necessarily the same consultants each time. There is a definite psychological impact on a department when the personnel are aware that they are going to be reviewed by outsiders. This is particularly true in a computer area when the consultants have a broad knowledge of EDP.

The consultant can evaluate the efficiency and security of an existing system in areas that internal or external auditors may lack the necessary training to review. Computer consultants can study the more technical aspects of data processing and may discover inefficiencies or weaknesses in the security of the system.

An analysis of the work-load in the computer room may disclose that the amount of equipment on hand is not justified. This may lead to the discovery of unauthorized work being done on the computer. There have been many instances of data processing personnel using their employer's equipment and supplies to conduct service bureau activities for themselves.

A study of the programs may reveal inefficient design which is costing the company unnecessary computer time. The inefficiency may be due to lack of programming experience or may be a deliberate attempt to conceal unauthorized program instructions.

Auditing Necessity

Companies using computers must be constantly aware of the possibility of fraud or accidental errors in the system. While the computer offers an even greater opportunity for good control than manual systems, such control doesn't just happen; it must be developed and policed. The policemen must have the backing of management so that their recommendations are acted upon where feasible.

Computer systems are constantly undergoing changes, and each change opens the door for errors. The examination for weaknesses in the system must be continuing, and a company's decision to computerize must be coupled with a dedication to constant evaluation of the system. The necessary auditing expertise should be considered as much a necessary cost as the computer rental. After the company's resources are relegated to the computer, the protection of those resources remain the responsibility of the officers and directors of the company, and the cost of protection must be paid.

Chapter 12

Legal Implications: Crimes and Torts

Your Vulnerability Under the Law

The Watergate of Computing

Were it not for Watergate, "Equity Funding" would be a household word. On November 1, 1973, the Securities and Exchange Commission announced that a Federal grand jury in Los Angeles had returned a 105-count indictment charging 22 individuals on charges arising out of alleged fraudulent activity relating to Equity Funding Corporation of America. With this indictment, a big-time computer fraud came of age. Estimates of the losses exceed two *billion* dollars in Equity Funding alone. To familiarize the reader with the massive nature of the frauds perpetrated and the part which computer manipulation played in this incredible episode, a copy of count one of the 105-count indictment is included as Appendix B.

Only now are courts beginning to address themselves to the computer's potential for both good and evil. In one incredibly long sentence, the presiding judge in the recent *Telex* v. *IBM* case surveyed the phenomenon called the data processing industry.

> This case involves the electronic data processing industry—an industry based upon a concept and system of reckoning (binary) as simple as turning on and off a switch; in which transmissions are timed in billionths of seconds (nanoseconds), storage capacity (memory), measured by millions of combinations of bits of information (megabytes); in which numerous problems involving logic or arithmetic functions are separately but simultaneously worked upon and instantly solved within a single system: in which in their own peculiar language machines communicate with one another (multiprocessing) and then in words understandable by humans may present printouts of results at the rate of as much as 2,000 lines per minute: in which devices facilitate maintenance by the detection and isolation of their own malfunctions or mistakes (diagnostic programs): upon which most other industries of the country and

countless businesses, as well as science and space explorations, vitally depend; in which product and market developments seem almost kaleidoscopic when viewed from the outside; which appears unique in monopoly context by reason of its youth and apparent dynamics but which by the same token in this ultramodern setting may be unprecedented also because of increased inducements for, and vulnerability to, sophisticated submarket control on the one hand, and massive industrial espionage on the other.

The "black-box" mystic of modern electronic data processing has for too long lulled business executives, accountants and attorneys into the false sense of security which invites fraud and embezzlement.

Accountants are also becoming increasingly aware of the potential for liability via the computer. In the May, 1973 *Journal of Accounting*, a contributor complained, "The detective syndrome is, after all, one of the most common public misconceptions about the auditor, and must be discouraged." The accountants invariably refer to Section 110.05 of the *Statements on Auditing Standards* which holds that the independent auditor is responsible for failure to detect fraud "only when such failure clearly results from failure to comply with generally accepted auditing standards." John C. Burton, chief accountant for the Securities & Exchange Commission, acknowledges that sophisticated fraud is difficult to detect but believes that when fraud reaches the magnitude of Equity Funding the accounting profession must develop procedures designed to catch it. Echoing Burton's view, the chairman of the SEC Ray D. Garrett told the American Institute of Certified Public Accountants on October 16, 1973, that, "I think accountants should be willing to assume responsibility for the detection of management fraud in appropriate cases." He went on to say, "If the accounting profession adopts the view that auditors should never be responsible for detecting management fraud, there is little likelihood that truly onerous and unfair burdens on the accounting profession can be prevented." Clearly, the accountants will be asking tougher questions about the quality of input to and output from the company's computer.

Corporate executives are only beginning to recognize that no amount of hardware is an adequate substitute for hard-nosed internal controls. The corporate manager who fails to recognize the serious pitfalls of this new technology may find himself just another victim of electronic embezzlement. Equally important, he may find himself a defendant in law suits initiated either by disgruntled stockholders who have witnessed their company's assets dissipated or by aggrieved citizens whose privacy has been invaded by the unauthorized exposure of their personal data.

Earlier chapters illustrated with detailed case histories the nature and scope of computer fraud. This chapter undertakes to alert management to the substantial risk of personal liability it faces unless adequate precautions against embezzlement and other unauthorized computer manipulations are initiated and continuously maintained.

The legal duties of the computer manager arise in three specific contexts, depending upon how the data processing system is employed within his organization. First, where the computer performs a control or accounting function, the manager has the duty to assure himself that the corporation's assets are not being overstated by fraudulent manipulation and that all of the records being generated fairly reflect the financial condition of the company. Second, where the computer is used to store or process sensitive information, the system's manager has a duty to protect its confidentiality from unauthorized access. Third, where the corporation has expended funds to devise a new program, the computer officer has a duty to protect this investment against its use by others who have made no contribution toward its cost and development.

Each of these related duties will be dealt with separately.

Manipulation Of Accounting Systems

Business firms increasingly use the computer to control inventory, dispatch assets, disburse paychecks and perform general accounting and bookkeeping functions. The opportunity for fraud in these areas is typified by the thief who programmed the firm's computer to report abnormally high inventory losses as merchandise breakage. He thereby enabled accomplices to steal vast amounts of goods from warehouses without the theft being detected. Later this same employee removed the evidence by simply putting the original figure back into the computer.

The dissipation of corporate assets through the criminal manipulation of computer accounting systems may expose the corporate manager to personal liability in two ways. He may be required to answer directly to the corporation for its losses; he may have to answer to the stockholders whose investments suffer as a result. Almost every state's corporation law states that a corporate officer has a statutory duty to exercise the same care in corporate affairs as he would exercise in his personal business dealings. Should the officer fail to exercise due care, he may be compelled to repay personally the corporation for the losses it suffers.

The question of what constitutes "due care" is a subjective matter which does not lend itself to rigid formulas. The answer will turn on the particular facts of each case, and the final determination is often made by a jury of laymen. Many ordinary citizens have developed a considerable distrust for the computer. They have received the wrong bills for the wrong merchandise, followed by the inevitable inability of the computer to correct its errors. Thus, the average juror may not be sympathetic to the manager who relied too heavily on the computer's alleged infallibility.

Furthermore, the exercise of reasonable care will undoubtedly be judged at two points in time: first when the internal control system is established and second when the fraud or embezzlement occurs. Thus, the computer manager is obligated to continually reexamine and revise the elements of his system in the light of experience gained both by himself and others in the field. As more and more incidents of computer fraud are brought to the public's attention, this standard for review is stiffening. A businessman must recognize that the decision to bring suit against a corporate officer does not rest solely with the corporation. Any stockholder may bring a derivative action on behalf of the corporation. Even a stockholder with limited resources will experience no difficulty in financing such an action since the lawyer representing the stockholder may be entitled to take his fee from the recovery.

In addition to the corporate manager's liability for lost or dissipated assets, he may also be held directly accountable to stockholders who are induced to invest based on management deception and as a consequence suffer a loss on their investment. Depressed stock prices obviously would result from the actual loss of corporate assets. Beyond that, however, it may become customary in appropriate instances for accountants to assert that the corporation has failed to establish adequate internal auditing controls, raising a probability of undetected losses and thus rendering a "clean opinion" inappropriate under the circumstances.

The much publicized case of *Escott* v. *Barchris* has alerted corporate officials to the possibility of incurring personal liability to stockholders resulting from false or misleading statements about the corporation's financial position. Under Section 11 of the Securities Act of 1933, a corporate official who signs a Registration Statement warrants that he has made a reasonable investigation of the portions of that document not examined by experts and has a reasonable belief in the truth of the statements included as well as the absence of material omissions which might mislead investors. The point is that the failure to disclose the absence of an internal auditing control system particularly suited for a company heavily dependent upon computers may well be considered a materially misleading omission.

Independent auditors also run significant risks under the Securities Act. The "due diligence" defense may not be available to accountants if a reasonable investigation would have disclosed the absence of appropriate internal controls. It may well be impossible for auditors to conduct a reasonable investigation of a computerized accounting system unless the computer has been programmed with the necessary checks and balances that would detect misappropriated assets. To guard against this possible legal exposure, we believe that prudent accounting firms will begin to qualify their reports and opinions by disclosing the absence of adequate internal accounting controls and thus allude in their opinion to the possibility that an overstatement of profits or assets may exist. Surely the computer officials who have installed sophisticated computer accounting systems but who have failed to adopt an equally sophisticated auditing mechanism will find themselves on the horns of a severe business and legal dilemma. Failure to acknowledge the absence of controls keyed to the computer will expose the corporation and the auditor to legal liability. To disclose the absence of adequate controls would certainly embarrass the corporation and its offices in the business community. At this point, the corporation's independent auditors may insist on a qualifying statement in their reports and opinion which would cast a possibly unwarranted cloud on the financial picture of the entire corporation.

To guard against legal liability and protect the good name of his corporation, the manager of a computerized accounting system should keep three factors in mind. First, certain accounting procedures are required by the Internal Revenue Service, state corporation laws and various state and federal regulatory agencies. In some cases, as with the IRS, their requirements may already make provisions for automated data processing. In others, the computer system may have to be designed with traditional bookkeeping practices in mind.

Second, care must be taken to preserve a clear auditing trail. An accountant may well be unable to certify a company's computer records unless he is able to track typical transactions from their initiation to the final reflection on the balance sheet. In the standard automated system, the initial transaction may be an electronic impulse, with the immediate steps recorded on magnetic tape and erased at the end of the day's calculating. A clear auditing trail must be programmed into the total system.

Third, in planning a computerized accounting system, careful consideration must be given to building a system with both carefully programmed internal checks and balances as well as close managerial supervision.

Finally, the computerization of corporate accounting records may bring new classes of managerial employees within the scope of the federal securities law. For example, Section 16b of the Securities Act discourages officers, directors and principal stockholders from short-swing trading in their company's stock. These people may not sell shares within six months of purchase without incurring liability to the corporation for the profits resulting from such sales. The theory behind this regulation is that these classes of persons have access to inside information not available to the average investor. In the traditional accounting system, many record-keepers work with scattered bits and pieces of data. These facts, figures and statistics are generally only compiled in a meaningful way at the time an annual report or SEC filing is prepared. At that time, the accounting report is brought under the control of the corporation's financial officer who, because of his insider position, is presently subject to Rule 16b. However, if a firm which uses a computerized accounting system, the data processing manager may be in a position to pull together at his discretion, meaningful records indicating the corporation's financial picture. It is therefore quite possible that the data processing and other middle-level managers who work with the computer may ultimately be brought within the scope of Rule 16b and thus be subject to liability if they engage in short-swing stock trading. In addition, if any information they obtain which is deemed material is leaked to a friend or used for personal benefit, liability may also be incurred under Rule 10b-5 of the Securities Exchange Act of 1934.

Unauthorized Disclosure of Confidential Data

Many businesses utilize computers to store confidential, sensitive information. The firm itself may be in the business of collecting such data. Credit bureaus and investigative agencies fall into this category. Other firms collect confidential data such as employment records or mailing lists. The computer service firms comprise a third category. These organizations perform data processing services and provide time-sharing facilities for many different businesses who in turn entrust them with confidential information and programs.

Some firms that collect and store sensitive information have already come under direct statutory regulation. The 1970 Fair Credit Reporting Act limits those persons who are authorized to receive credit information from credit reporting agencies. The Act requires the credit agency to maintain reasonable procedures to restrict access to authorized persons. Willful or negligent dissemination of a person's record exposes the agency to liability for both actual and punitive damages as well as attorney fees. The larger credit agencies maintain files on several hundred thousand individuals. The possibility of class action suits would expose the firm to substantial liability even if the damage to any one individual were relatively small.

In the future, similar regulations will be imposed on other collectors of sensitive data. A bill was recently introduced in the Minnesota legislature which provided that "whoever is injured (by computer error or misuse) . . . shall recover therefore unless the person who caused the injury established that he was not negligent."

While this particular bill was defeated, it foreshadows future developments. A number of courts have already imposed liability on computer users in the absence of a statute. In *Ford Motor Credit Co.* v. *Swarens,* the plaintiff purchased an automobile on credit and made his monthly payments on time. However, because of an error in the computer's records, collection efforts were instituted against him. Over the protests of the plaintiff, Ford, relying on its computer, seized and sold the vehicle. The customer brought suit for compensatory and punitive damages. The Kentucky Court of Appeals upheld a lower court decision favoring the plaintiff and spelled out the obligations imposed on data processing agencies.

> Ford explains that this whole incident occurred because of a mistake by a computer. Men feed data to a computer and men interpret the answer the computer coughs up. In this computerized age, the law must require that men regard those with whom they are dealing as more important than a perforation on a punch card. Trust in the infallibility of a computer is hardly a defense, where the opportunity to avoid the error is apparent and repeated.

The Swarens case specifically addresses the liability that can be incurred by excessive reliance on the accuracy of the computer records. The same reasoning would impose similar liability on the computer user who placed unjustified faith in the computer's invulnerability to unauthorized access or tampering.

Many companies not in the business of data collection acquire confidential information as a sidelight to their normal business activities. Recall the case of the reference book publisher in which several computer operators were accused of copying nearly three million names from its customer list and selling them to a direct mail company. The mailing lists represented a valuable corporate asset with a market value of three million dollars. Any corporate official who negligently allowed this theft to occur because of poor supervision or inadequate checks in the computer could be liable to the corporation and its shareholders for this loss.

The greatest opportunity for misappropriation lies with the computer service firms. These organizations supply data processing services and rent computer time to other businesses. Here, the danger of unauthorized access takes several forms. Failure to provide adequate physical safeguards might enable unscrupulous persons to tap into lines leading from the customer to the service bureau. Such persons might also gain unauthorized and undetected access to the computer itself and produce a printout of the entire contents of the machine's memory.

In the case of a multipurpose computer, failure to effectively segregate operating and programming personnel might enable a talented but dishonest employee to alter or rewrite a program to gain access to unauthorized information. The problem is particularly acute in time-sharing operations where several programs and several files of information belonging to different users are all stored on magnetic tapes in the same location.

Consider the following hypothetical example: Stocks & Bonds, Inc., a small brokerage house, wants to provide a computer switching service whereby it can process customer's orders by relaying messages from its outlying sales offices directly to the stock exchange floor. The company is not financially able to purchase its own computer network. Therefore, it enlists the services of a data processing firm which specializes in systems and time-sharing facilities for the financial community. The data processing firm designs a system using its own computers and common-carrier communication lines which are leased by Stocks & Bonds.

The data processing firm has many other customers who all use the same firm's computer to switch their messages. Clearly, if Stocks & Bond's orders are misdirected to a rival broker or if their customers' portfolio information is released to a competitor, Stocks & Bonds would be seriously damaged. The service bureau would therefore be liable for negligence if it failed to provide adequate safeguards against one user obtaining such information as the trade secrets of another customer.

Remember the Information Systems Design case, where University Computing Co., the Oakland software firm, was fined $300,000 in a civil case brought by ISD who charged a University Computing employee with stealing computer programs by long-distance telephone from their service bureau. The civil trial followed a successful criminal action against the University employee.

In many cases the computer service firm will incur liability for the loss of confidential information even without proof of negligence or proof of actual damages. In any agreement for computer services, the well counseled customer will insist on a contract spelling out the data processing service's duty to provide information security. To avoid the problems of attempting to prove the value of an intangible business asset, the contract will most likely provide for liquidated damages.

To avoid such liability, the agreement between the computer service firm and its customer should contain specific provisions that impose on the service firm the clear duties to protect the confidentiality of his customer's data. An example of such a contractual term is as follows:

> ___________ Corporation will protect the wires over which data are transmitted, in such a manner that said wires cannot be tapped or any data be taken from said wires or in any way be communicated, otherwise than (a) as may have been agreed to in writing between the parties or (b) by use of terminals located in the relaying or computer rooms of either party.

By such provision, the customer has imposed upon the computer service firm the duty to provide for the physical protection of the communication facilities employed. The customer may achieve additional protection by inserting in the agreement the right to oversee the computer service firm's activities.

> At any and all reasonable times any bona fide permanent employee of Contractee shall have access to said transmitting, relaying or computer rooms and also to any test rooms or other rooms from or through which wires used in the transmission of data pass, and the right to examine the presence of __________ Corporation's officials in charge thereof, all appliances, and observe all operations located or carried out therein, but only for the purpose and insofar as necessary to insure compliance by__________Corporation with the covenant contained herein.

And to insure that the computer service firm's handling of the data entrusted to it is restricted to proper uses provided for in the agreement between the parties, the following provision could be included.

> Except as herein provided, no one shall be authorized to have access to any of the data in said transmitting, relaying or computer rooms during business hours, except the officers of __________ Corporation and its employees engaged in transmitting, relaying or processing the data. No part of the data shall be furnished by __________ Corporation or its officers or employees to any person or in any manner, except as provided herein.

Protecting Software Rights

The computer program represents the lifeblood of data processing. Program development costs are great, and the duty of the corporate official to protect his company's proprietary interest in its software is equally great. To establish either criminal or civil liability for the theft or misappropriation of computer programs it is first necessary to establish ownership of the software. The primary methods of establishing ownership are the statutory laws of copyright and patent and the common law of trade secrets, unfair competition and contracts.

PATENT PROTECTION

Patent laws offer the greatest potential protection. The owner of a patent has the sole right, for a limited period, to control the use of his invention. However, the obstacles and uncertainty of patent protection are substantial.

Until the decision by the Court of Customs and Patent Appeals, *in re Prater and Weis,* the Patent Office had refused to grant patents on software developments. Now that office takes the position that a patent can be obtained if the software is "new, useful and unobvious." This is a difficult standard to meet. Constructing a new program by simply applying basic programming techniques to a new problem will not meet the test. There must be a new concept or approach used in the development of the software which would not be obvious to a programmer of ordinary skill. A stroke of genius is not required, but the program must be more than an anticipated advance in the art of computer programming.

If the applicant is able to justify to the Patent Office that the program is new, useful and unobvious, a court test may still remain. In recent years approximately 70 percent of the patents litigated have been overturned by the courts. Moreover, there is continuing uncertainty about whether their patents will be enforced and if enforced what scope of protection they will be given. To enforce a patent, a patent owner must bring an infringement suit in a U.S. District Court. The U.S. District Courts are not bound to follow decisions of the Court of Customs and Patent Appeals which originally sanctioned the patent. Thus, it is entirely possible that the District Courts will take a contrary position.

Also, a patent procedure is relatively expensive and time-consuming. The average patent application, from filing to issue, takes somewhat over three years; the useful life of a program itself is approximately three years. Moreover, once the patent is published, the program will be revealed to all and unauthorized use may be very difficult to detect.

COPYRIGHT PROTECTION

A copyright offers less protection than a patent, but it is considerably easier to obtain and its underlying validity is more certain. The Copyright Office has ruled that computer programs are copyrightable. Numerous computer firms, including IBM, use this relatively quick and inexpensive method to protect their software. IBM was recently awarded over $13,000 in damages and an injunction against the Telex corporation "from copying any IBM copyrighted material," in the case of *Telex* v. *IBM*.

The copyright office has issued a circular that outlines the basic requirements for copyrightability. The two most important requirements are 1) sufficient literary expressions to constitute original authorship and 2) publication with notice. For the corporate manager, the most crucial act in obtaining copyright protection is "publication with notice." "Publication" means a distribution of the material to other than a very limited number of people. A corporate manager's failure to place the required copyright notice on all published copies of a work may totally destroy any copyright protection. Therefore, it is important that the corporate manager adhere closely to the rules of the Copyright Office.

Section 19 of the Copyright Law specifically provides that:

> The notice of copyright shall consist of either the word "copyright," the abbreviation "COPR" or the symbol "C" (with a circle around it) accompanied by the name of copyright proprietor and the date.

To insure that the notice requirement is met, the following procedures should be adopted.

Place a copyright notice on all printed copies of the program.

Incorporate the copyright notice into the computer system so that any printout of the program includes a human-readable copyright notice.

Place a copyright notice on all reels and tape disks which contain the program.

Punch a human-readable notice on all paper tape versions of the program.

All possible precautions should be taken to insure that there is adequate publication. Where the customer receives a program on magnetic tape, the supplier should provide a printed copy of the program with copyright notice to insure that there can be no argument as to whether there has been actual publication. Some authorities argue that a description in machine-readable form is not publication under the copyright law. Moreover, it is not sufficient that merely the general publication includes the proper notice. Subsequent authorized publication without notice will also destroy the copyright protection. Therefore, it is important that the contract between the program supplier and the customer include a provision requiring the customer to insert the appropriate notice on all copies of the program which the customer makes.

The shortcoming of copyright protection lies in the degree of protection it affords. Protection under the copyright statute is less comprehensive than under patent law. Anyone can produce a similar or possibly identical program to the copyright program without being guilty of infringement. Only exact or substantial copying is prohibited.

What constitutes "copying," or more importantly, "substantial copying" is a question of fact in each case. The most difficult situation arises when a party changes or adapts a program so that it is not an exact duplicate of the copyrighted work. Fortunately, when created, computer programs will include a number of errors or "bugs." The correction of these will leave telltale signs, or they may not have been corrected at the time copy occurred. If someone creates a program independently, it is unlikely that the program will contain the exact same errors and correction techniques. Additonally, as an aid in detecting copyright infringement, nonfunctional instructions should be intentionally inserted in the programs to provide the easy and positive identification of infringing copies.

TRADE SECRET PROTECTION

The most comprehensive protection for software is probably afforded by the common law of trade secrets. The advantage of the trade secret approach, if properly employed, is that it does not require the public disclosure required by copyright or patent registration. Thus, the possibility of undetected misappropriation is substantially lessened. Trade secret protection is also available for all data and know-how developed in the course of designing the program.

To gain trade secret status, the company should institute a program establishing the secrecy of the software to be protected. The ease with which a program can be obtained from the holder may furnish a valid defense against a trade secret infringement action. Therefore, the company should restrict physical access to the program; mark the program "confidential" or "for authorized use only"; and, if the program is distributed to third persons such as customers, technicians or service bureaus, maintain a detailed record of disclosure. In addition, all recipients of the program should be required to sign an agreement to keep the data confidential.

It is important to be able to document the value of the program. The greater the value of the program to its owner and the greater the extent of injury from its use by a competitor, the more likely the court will be to protect the program. The best way to establish the program's value is to keep an accurate log—admissable into evidence—of how often the program is run. Additionally, the firm must be prepared to demonstrate that it originated and developed the software and that considerable effort and expense were involved.

Beyond these precautions, the company should require computer employees who develop or handle valuable software to enter into a contract prohibiting its future disclosure. The contract may also limit an employee's right to compete in the same or similar business in a given geographic area during a specific period, prohibit an employee from soliciting his former employer's customers and prevent him from disclosing information that would not normally qualify as a trade secret. Both covenants against competition and disclosure should be signed at the time employment begins so that the employment constitutes adequate consideration.

Two recent U.S. Supreme Court cases have raised doubt as to the ability of a trade secret owner to enforce his rights against a party with whom he has contracted to use the trade secret. Therefore, similar nondisclosure provisions should also be included in sales, leasing and licensing agreements.

Once the existence of a trade secret has been established, the holder does not actually possess a property right. Instead he has the right to prevent others from taking the trade secret from him in an unfair or improper way. For example, if a competitor is able to inspect a rival's printed report of a study and determine what program was used to develop that report, he is free to go ahead and duplicate the program. But he is not entitled to get this information by improperly obtaining the confidential data.

Currently, 18 states including most of the leading technological and industrial states have amended their criminal codes to specifically include trade secrets within their larceny statutes.

An Observation

There exists no separate body of law devoted to data processing. In the foreseeable future it is likely that the legal problems relating to computers will continue to be addressed within the existing legal frameworks of tort, criminal, corporate and contract law. It is always difficult to predict how the general legal principles operative in other areas will be applied to data processing. On the whole, there has been very little litigation involving computers, but it is not too early to identify potential pitfalls, and to plan intelligently to avoid future legal problems.

What we have sought to accomplish here is merely to alert the computer user and manager to areas of concern so that he can recognize circumstances when the guidance of his company's legal counsel can be most useful.

Part IV
NEEDS FOR THE FUTURE

Chapter 13
A Program For Internal Action
Do It Yourself

The Policy Statement Requirement

It is clear that a company may forget security completely and ignore the risks and exposure to loss. In so doing, the costs of security measures can be avoided. At the other extreme, security can be made so tight as to force a company out of business. In this case, the costs to implement security may far exceed the losses that would occur if no measures were taken. Also, the measures might interfere with effective operations so severely as to bring the business to a grinding halt. Clearly there is a happy medium between these extremes.

Like many other aspects of business, data processing security is a game. It pits company management against employees, outsiders and the elements, with the company's assets the prize. Management must thus develop a strategy that optimizes retained assets at all stages of the game.

It must be a matter of management policy to determine through careful examination the needs and costs of security, based upon the levels of sensitivity of information files and of processes within the data processing operation. They must also examine the costs of damage or destruction of information versus the costs of recapturing or regenerating damaged or lost files and the potential cost of having sensitive information fall into the hands of a competitor versus the costs of various security measures. In each case the costs of safeguarding the information must also be determined and a careful appraisal made of cost versus risk to determine the appropriate level of protection.

Developing the strategy and management policy requires three basic processes: risk analysis, cost trade-off analysis and statement of policy. After the strategy has been developed, steps must be taken to implement it. The steps consist of communicating the policies to responsible management who then must establish, communicate and enforce the methods and procedures designed to achieve the desired results.

Risk Analysis

The first step management must take is to make a determination of the types and extent of the threats to which it is exposed. Obviously, an installation in Hawaii need not protect against freeze-up nor does one in Denver need to protect against tidal wave. Both must consider earthquake, although this is of much greater concern in Hawaii than in Denver.

Similarly, a batch processing installation serving a single user has different threat problems than does a remote-access system serving many users. A system supporting engineers in structural design work may need protection against industrial espionage, but one supporting the accounting department must be protected against embezzlement. Therefore, risk analysis must consider location of the plant, location of the systems within the plant, the type of system and the types of applications the system supports.

Risk analysis must also include an evaluation of the value of the system and system elements to others. Clearly no one will perpetrate a crime for profit knowing that the direct cost will exceed the expected benefits. The threat of sabotage by action groups, labor unions and the like is directly proportional to the extent of reaction such groups can expect from their actions. Finally, industrial espionage is related to the competitive nature of the industry, the importance of the company within the industry and the overall maturity of the industry. It is obvious that risk is directly related to the value that an instigator expects to receive.

Cost Trade-Off Analysis

Once risks have been identified and evaluated, the next step is to determine what measures can be taken to prevent or limit loss. Each possible measure must then be evaluated with respect to its anticipated effectiveness and its cost of implementation. The cost trade-off analysis can then begin in earnest.

Obviously, any measure whose cost exceeds its anticipated return in terms of loss prevention is inadvisable. Implementation of such a measure should be considered only if there appears to be a real future need or if it will eliminate a temptation that could lead an unethical employee to attempt bigger thefts simply because he got away with it in this case.

In other cases, measures that may appear to be cost-effective do not offer a satisfactory level of protection. In such cases, more than one measure may be required in order to obtain the desired level of protection. Obviously, a combination of measures will be required to obtain full security protection against all risks.

The risk analysis and cost trade-off analysis should both be undertaken during the feasibility study relative to acquiring a computer system or services. Management must be prepared for the conclusion that since the risks are too great and the prevention measures will be too expensive, the use of computers is at present not feasible.

While performing a trade-off analysis one must have an appreciation for the types of measure that can be implemented to prevent or limit loss. This, in fact, has been the primary content of this book, but one area has not been mentioned—insurance.

In some areas it is certainly reasonable to cover the potential risk by insurance against loss rather than to depend solely upon the use of loss prevention measures. Here again, one must compare insurance cost against security measures. Insurance coverage against almost any loss is available at a price. There is the usual insurance against loss by fire and the usual bonding of employees who handle money or who handle financial operations in such a way that they are particularly susceptible to embezzlement or other fraud. One may insure against the loss of operating income, in fact against almost any eventuality, but the cost of insurance coverage against a particular variety of loss must be evaluated in comparison to the cost of provisions to limit the possibility of that loss and also against the cost of the possible loss itself.

Statement of Policy

One critical aspect of good computer system use and management is a managerial statement of policy with respect to computer system usage and, in particular, data security. A policy statement provides direction to lower level managers and provides a framework within which they can then develop methods and procedures. It also provides measures against which the system management's effectiveness can be evaluated.

Basic Security Considerations

Managing the development of a new data processing system is one of the most crucial operations in maintaining good security. Locking the barn door after the horse has been stolen is easy but ineffective. It is equally true that it is easier to install good locks while you are building a door than it is to add them afterward. The development of data processing systems should consider system security as a fundamental element of the design from its inception. If the importance of security is kept to the forefront during the formulation of system concepts, it is relatively easy to build into the system controls that can greatly reduce the chances of security violations.

It is also possible to build in modules that will monitor the operation of the system and provide solid auditing trails. It is far more difficult, and less effective, to add such controls to an existing system than to build those controls as part of the basic system.

A concept that may also be useful here is that of building into the system software certain devices that correspond to locks. It is then possible to change the combination of these locks at will by very simple changes in program parameters. This directly corresponds to the electronically operated combination locks used to control access to the physical facilities. It is also possible to build into the software safeguards that are operable at will. These safeguards can be turned on or off by a simple operation, such as the date or other parameter. This type of safeguard provides more detailed checking or monitoring to look for a particular type of infringer while avoiding the cost of such checks every time the program is run.

The consideration of security at the time of system design is particularly important in systems involving remote terminals and data communications links. As discussed in an earlier chapter these communications use transmission lines subject to tapping or bugging. It is possible to build into the system safeguards of many kinds, extending from simple coding of the data to scramblers to make the intercepted information extremely difficult to reconstruct. Only in very specialized cases is this justified. However, only the user knows the real sensitivity of the information, thus he should determine the level of protection required.

In addition to the possibility of intercepting information on the phone line, there is always the possibility of loss or destruction of information due to poor line quality. Any good communication system design will take this into account and provide for a sufficient level of checking of transmitted information. As with any other aspect of overall system security, the greater the security against loss by theft or mistake in information, the higher the cost. As in any of the various aspects of system security we discussed, a trade-off analysis is necessary to determine the level of security reasonable for a particular operation.

Checks and Balances, or, How to Avoid Turning the Company Over to the Programmer

The computer mystique is generated by the efforts of computer professionals who, deliberately or not, have contributed to the lack of proper understanding of computer system by management. Given the opportunity, data processing staff, programmers, computer operators and their managers build their systems in such a manner as to keep management as far from adequate control of data processing operations as possible. They endeavor to maintain the air of mystery around what goes on within and around the computer and attempt to convince management that the understanding of these operations is an esoteric art requiring years of specialized training. This is nonsense.

To ensure that management maintains control of the company, clearly defined rules of operation must be placed into effect in all aspects of the data processing function. These rules must be recorded in procedure manuals that have the approval of data processing management and that lie within a framework of overall data processing operating regulations approved by general management.

While these controls have been discussed in some detail in Chapters 8 and 10, it appears desirable to recapitulate in a somewhat more abbreviated format at this point. This short review is intended not to serve the data processing manager setting up a system of controls, but for the purposes of the general manager interested in checking upon his data processing operation.

An executive or general manager must know what kinds of controls he should insist upon and the purpose of each of these controls. This knowledge will provide him with the ability to spot-check at will, to examine the procedures manuals and to quiz individual data processing system personnel if desired. It will enable him to monitor the overall operations from a top-management viewpoint.

As part of an overall management audit of internal controls, such checking must be done by some responsible individual in the managerial structure on a periodic basis, and this checking should not always be done by the same individual. The responsibility for such reviews should be circulated like the responsibilities for auditing functions, so that the possibility of internal collusion is minimized. If an operator or programmer knows that he is held responsible by a certain individual, he may learn how to fool that individual, or they may get to know each other so well that they join forces. To avoid such possibilities, it is necessary for all critical operations that give the individual an opportunity for establishing patterns of carelessness or dishonesty to be circulated periodically. The people responsible for sensitive areas must be changed from time to time, and the checks and audits must appear at wholly unpredictable intervals.

Computer Room Management

The computer room is a production facility and it should be managed so as to maximize throughput and control quality. The product developed in the computer room is information. The raw material that goes into the computer room is data. The computer room processes the data and turns out information just as a machine shop accepts metal and turns out parts. The management of the computer room should be so constituted as to expedite effective production, eliminate any interference with such production and minimize the operating costs while maintaining the best possible quality control.

The computer room has one peculiarity in comparing it to a production machine shop. In general, company management understands reasonably well what a production machine shop does and how it does it. They know what the processes are and may even have mastered the operation of these machines. Most important, they have learned what to expect from the machines and how to measure their effectiveness. This level of understanding is generally not present when considering the computer operations. The average individual in company management may understand only in a general way what the computer is supposed to do. In a great majority of cases, he has little or no understanding of how the computer operates and how it carries out its assigned tasks. He has probably had little or no formal training in any aspect of computers nor management of a data processing operation.

Once the decision is taken to study the feasibility of an in-house computer system, management learns certain things quickly. First, they learn that a separate physical facility is required for climate control. Then they find that a program development activity is required to translate user needs into computer language. They realize quickly that operations personnel are required to operate and maintain the system. Unfortunately, they may not recognize the risks to which they will be exposed or how to manage the overall system.

We have discussed these risks and presented some actions that can be taken to reduce risks and losses (Chapters 6 and 7.) We will now pull these together into an organized plan of managerial action. First, we will review briefly the physical considerations. Next, we will discuss the program development function and discuss the responsibilities of the individuals within this function. Finally, we will present the operations unit and the individuals of this group with their responsibilities.

Physical Facilities

The computing facility is a key nerve center in your organization. Within this facility should be the computer room itself, a separate data preparation area and the primary tape storage library. There must also be a control area from which general operations can be observed. Requests for service accompanied by the necessary input data ready for preparation should be presented to this control and outputs should be distributed through this contol area.

Proper control of the operation of this room is vital to your company's health. The rules for the management of the room have been described in some detail in Chapter 10. It is important to emphasize that only those whose business requires them to be in the computer room should be permitted in that room. Admit only the operating staff themselves and those maintenance and cleaning personnel whose admission is absolutely necessary. Even these people should wear badges to identify them, and these badges should be color coded so that the nature of their business can be determined by merely looking at the badge.

The cleaning staff and the maintenance people should be admitted only with either a member of the operating staff or a member of the security staff present. Systems design and programming personnel must not be admitted to the computer room. They should deal only with computer operators.

There may be a window through which work to be done may be passed into the computer room. The window should be of a size and in a location such that it will not permit physical entrance into the room. The passage of materials in or out should be accompanied by documentation which has the appropriate approval and indicates what the material is, what action is to be taken with it and to whom it is to be returned when completed. A history sufficient to retrace its handling should be recorded in case any questions arise later.

Program Development

The program development unit is responsible for three basic functions: system design, programming and program validation. (These represent the three people in the task assignment strategy discussed in Chapter 9.) Following is an explanation of the duties of the people in each of these groups.

The system designer is responsible for examining a problem or a desired process for the computer. He must look at the input data that will be available to the computer and the output information that the computer is expected to produce. He then must decide how to get from one to the other. If additional information is required to produce the needed output, he must determine the nature of this information and its source. He must decide how the various required information is to be brought to the computer. He must define the processing that is to go on within the system and determine the nature and format of the inputs and the outputs. He should decide what controls, checks and balances are necessary in the system to insure the accuracy of the results produced and to provide auditing trails and other security controls. He should develop a detailed breakdown of the flow of information through the system to be used by the programmers.

Before transmitting the design to the programming group it must be reviewed by the ultimate user. He is the one requesting service, he will eventually pay for service rendered, and he is responsible for insuring that the service he receives satisfies his needs. He should look at the computing system as an employee and program development as the employee training period.

In addition to user approval, the design must also have the approval of the internal auditor before it is released for implementation. The auditor must be satisfied with the auditing trail and control provisions and must indicate his approval before release for programming.

The programmer must take the system designer's information flow plan and translate this into detailed processing steps. He must check his work by having the computer instructions which he has developed run through the machine to see that the machine responds the way he expected. He must ensure that the results of the processing will produce exactly the output specified by the system designer. The programmer is also required to document what he has done just as the system designer did. He must prepare written descriptions of his programs, what they are intended to do and how they operate.

One part of the programming organization must be a group whose function in life is to check and validate all programs. When the programmer who is responsible for the implementation of a particular system feels he has finished his work, his programs should be turned over to this validation group. This group must check what has been done and compare it with the documentation, the system designer's indicated intentions and the user's stated objectives, to be sure that in all respects the program carries out the operations intended of it and produces the desired results.

Once the validation group has completed its work, the system designer should review and affirm that the system design is the same as that submitted for implementation. The user should then review all outputs to insure that they are accurate and that they in fact satisfy his needs both in processing achievement and auditing or monitoring controls. The auditor should also be given an opportunity for final review. Only after all four approvals have been given should a program be released for use.

Operations

The operations section includes four basic functions: control, input preparation, tape library and computer operation. The control function is the nerve center of operations. All inputs to the center and outputs from the center should be processed through the control group. The control group should verify that the request is proper and that all necessary resources are available. It must then schedule both input preparation and processing time. When the processing is complete, the control group should ensure that outputs are processed properly and delivered only in accordance with established procedures and to the designated recipients.

The input preparation group is responsible for the accurate transcription of input data into computer-readable form unless optical or magnetic-character reading equipment is used. In the latter case, the input preparation group may have no responsibility except to review the input to ensure that all documents are in fact machine readable.

In the course of running the computing room, data files on computer readable media such as magnetic tapes and magnetic disk units have to be supplied to the computer operators. These files are stored in a library (the organization of this library has been discussed in Chapter 10.)

In order to maintain proper management controls, logs must be maintained showing what files were issued, by what authority and for what purpose. Management must periodically spot-check the procedures being followed. The logs should be submitted daily and retained for reference. Periodic review of the logs should be performed to insure that issuance of files and storage media is being done only after receipt of appropriate approval.

The management of the data library has been discussed in some detail in Chapter 10. However, it is important to emphasize that this library houses on permanent machine-readable files every bit of information stored in your data processing system as well as all of the programs used to process that information. Without the contents of this one room your data processing operation is, and without adequate backup your whole company may be out of business.

The physical protection of this room from unauthorized access and fire, flood or other calamitous damage as well as the rules for removing and replacing individual items in that library must be rigidly enforced. The librarian must be carefully selected, must be of unquestionably impeccable character and must be kept a loyal employee by proper treatment.

The computer operators run the computer. They receive a schedule of programs to be run. Each program's operating instructions carries a statement of the input files needed and the outputs to be prepared. The operator obtains the required program, data and working files from the tape library. He obtains the required input from the input preparation section where information is transferred from human-readable to machine-readable form. He runs the program through the machine with the appropriate input and data files, carries out the operations built into the program, makes sure that the right tapes are mounted on the tape servos, makes sure that the right disk packs are placed on disk pack drive units, sees to it that the output printer has paper appropriately loaded and pushes the buttons to see that the system runs properly.

If the system stops, the operator must carefully record all details available at the time the stop occurred. He must review his operating procedures and the tape or disk file mountings to insure that stoppage is not the result of operating error. Any and all procedures that the operator should follow beyond this point must be part of the operating procedures for the specific programs. Routine calling of maintenance personnel or taking of memory dumps (printouts of memory contents) at program stops should be strictly forbidden.

The operator must also maintain a detailed log of programs run, their running time (on system times), and the final disposition of the job. He should be made to account for all downtime and for his activities during unutilized periods. These logs should be retained for future reference and periodically reviewed to ensure the proper use of computer time.

Summary

We have described the general operations and activities that must go on within a data processing operation. What are the problems from management's point of view in maintaining the security of these operations? How do we ensure that the computer personnel cannot manipulate information? How do we prevent these people from taking over the company by virtue of their complete control of all critical information within the company? Some general principles must be applied here for handling all aspects of management of the data processing function.

One rule is that we must use what security experts call compartmentalization. No one individual and no one part of the organization must be in a position to have available all of the pieces that can be put together to make a whole. This means that no one person should have access to computer programs and the operation of the computer and the design of systems. It means that the individuals who input data into the system should not be those that have access to software. It means that computer programmers who are concerned with applications programs should not have the ability to manipulate the operating system software and vice versa.

We must also develop specific standards to be enforced in each area of operations. Even though programming standards are not intended primarily for security purposes, they are extremely important to effective security. The inclusion of the appropriate controls within a program should be a portion of the programming standards, but not all of these controls can be sufficiently defined on a standardized basis; some of these controls must be defined in the system design. Only with adequate thought to programming standards and adequate enforcement of those standards can we hope to have a measure of security in this particular area. Any departure from established standards by data processing staff, system designers, programmers, keypunchers or librarians gives the individuals involved the opportunity to manipulate the data processing system, either through acts of carelessness or deliberate sabotage or with fraud as their intent.

An important means for management to insure the proper management of the data processing function is the surprise check test, audit or emergency drill. Any situation in which audits or checks of the operation occur only on prearranged schedules plays directly into the hands of the unscrupulous. The internal auditing staff must check data processing operations at will on an irregular schedule. Management should visit the computer room unannounced at random intervals reasonably often. To further check, it may well be worthwhile to hire outside data processing consultants to check the state of the data processing function from time to time. These audits are also sometimes carried out by sophisticated internal auditing groups, but many companies feel they cannot justify the costs of such groups on a full-time basis. Independent experts can prevent the use of the computer mystique as a camouflage behind which the data processing organization may hide.

Management must establish a strategy for security protection through the performance of a risk analysis, the performance of a trade-off analysis and the issuance of a specific policy on the matter. Methods, procedures and an organization must then be established consistent with the policy statement. The methods and procedures must be documented and then communicated to all personnel responsible for their implementation. Management must then perform periodic audits to ensure that methods and procedures are being properly and consistently implemented. They must also review the policy statement and the methods and procedures to ensure their currency and adequacy.

Remember: the function of data processing is to serve the company. If the data processing organization does not fill this requirement, it should be changed.

Chapter 14
Needed Legal and Accounting Controls
The Lawmakers' and Rulemakers' Roles

External Controls

External controls are necessary and are developed for two basic purposes: they afford controls and protection to third parties who are not in a position to protect themselves and they define the bounds of acceptable, responsible activity and provide for the punishment of offending parties if these bounds are violated. If all businesses were operated by owners who used computers in their internal company affairs only, there would be little need for the first type of external controls, but this is the exception rather than the rule. The second type of external controls would be necessary in any event.

We discussed in Chapter 11 the detection aspect of auditing upon computer operations and in Chapter 12 the legal aspects of computer operations have also been discussed. This chapter suggests some other external controls that should be developed to provide additional detection and protection capabilities necessary to provide adequate safeguards.

Privacy

The largest third-party group with an interest to be protected is the general public. Governments at all levels have turned to computers to collect and process data relative to the census, taxation, licensing, public assistance and many other projects. Hardly an individual lives who does not have a file in the government's data bank, if only the registration of his birth certificate or notation of being recognized as a tax deduction on his parents' income tax returns.

In the private sector, one need only apply for credit to have a file established with much of his most personal data recorded. In fact, one need only miss a payment or two on monthly bills, such as for telephone or electric service, or to have overdrawn his bank account a few times to virtually guarantee a file with the local credit bureau.

Once these files exist, all manner of people find all kinds of reasons why they should have access to the files. If a legitimate reason cannot be found to gain access to these files, a friend having such a reason may be willing to cooperate. If all else fails, anyone may resort to subterfuge.

The threat of abusive use of these data files and the failure of organizations handling the data to do so in a responsible manner has given rise to the privacy issue in data processing. As we are seeing currently, some protection against such misuse of data has been obtained through governmental action and further study has been instituted but only after an extensive and loud hew and cry on the part of the public.

Sweden had been the first nation to pass an extensive law regulating data banks. Australia is considering similar action as a result of political pressure through the Australian Medical Association. In the United States, Representative Barry Goldwater, Jr. (R-California) has introduced a bill on Fair Personal Information Practice similar to the Swedish law but without the licensing provisions. In essence, the Swedish law contains six main provisions.

1. Except for governmental records, authorization of a nine-man data inspection board is required before a data bank may be kept. The board will determine how each data bank may be used and what methods it may employ. The board will have free access to all data banks. Governmental agencies must consult with the board.
2. No data bank may list criminal records, psychiatric treatment, alcoholism or other sensitive matters except with the permission of the board.
3. No data bank may report political or religious affiliations, although political parties and churches may computerize their membership lists.
4. The board may order the operator of a data bank to notify everyone in it of his inclusion, and each of those listed is entitled to a free readable form printout of his file. Individuals may petition the board to order corrections in a file and may sue for damages if the misinformation damaged them.
5. Files may not be transmitted abroad without special permission.
6. Penalties for violations include fines and jail terms of up to a year.

The effectiveness of this law depends almost entirely upon the integrity and effectiveness of the data inspection board. Although the board has little control over governmental data banks, it has discretionary control over all other data banks. It is empowered to determine how each data bank may be used and the methods it may employ. Thus, at least indirectly, it can control who may operate a data base and for what purposes the data base may be used.

Even though one should have confidence in his government—and certainly the Swedes must, for the moment at least, take an optimistic view of the integrity of the board—this type of law offers only limited protection. In general, laws that impose a significant degree of self-control are far superior to laws that attempt direct control.

The essence of a good law is found in point four of the Swedish law—disclosure. In the financial field, disclosure has been the primary control mechanism for years and has worked well. The U.S. Postal Service requires the disclosure of ownership and circulation to prevent abuses of second-class mailing privileges. Disclosure affords protection by keeping all interested parties informed of what is going on and enabling them to make informed judgments as to whether they wish to participate and whether action is required to protect their interests.

The first task in developing a disclosure law will be to define the data bases to which the law applies. Obviously, if such a law were applied to all files that contain personal data, it would impose undue hardships on companies maintaining payroll or other files strictly for the convenience and processing efficiency of other companies developing and using these files. It is suggested that such a law should apply to all data bases that are released, even partially, for use by other than the organization collecting the data and maintaining the files.

The means of disclosure should parallel financial disclosure practices. An annual disclosure statement should be required that would be published in an Annual Report format and mailed to all who have had an active file in the data base since the last report whether or not such a file is active at "year end." Such disclosure statements should be available to prospects through salesmen and agents and new entrants should receive a copy at the time their file is established.

The disclosure statement should define in detail why the data are being collected, the primary sources of information, what data are collected, what they are used for or to whom (generically) they are sold (or given) and the procedures an entrant should follow to verify his file and to have misinformation corrected.

Obviously, privacy and data base regulations are on the way in this country. The effect of such laws will depend heavily upon whether they attempt direct governmental control and allow the data base managers to retain a high degree of secrecy or whether disclosure is required that enables reasonable decision-making on the part of the general public.

Fair Credit Reporting Act

At present the primary legislation in the United States applying to privacy of data base information is the Fair Credit Reporting Act

(P.L. 91-508, 84 Stat. 1127–1136, 15 U.S.C. 1601 et seq.). The basic purpose of the law, according to the Federal Trade Commission, is to protect consumers from inaccurate or obsolete information in a report that is used as a factor in determining an individual's eligibility for credit, insurance, or employment.

It does not apply to reports utilized for business, commercial or professional purposes. It does not limit the kind of information that can be gathered or require reporting of "relevant" information, and it does not give consumers the right to physically possess their file or to receive a copy of it. In fact, the Act gives the FTC control over the consumer-reporting industry and provides consumer protection only to the extent that the FTC can and does administer the Act effectively.

The law provides criminal penalties for obtaining information on a consumer from consumer-reporting agencies under false pretenses and for providing information to someone unauthorized to receive it. Further, consumer-reporting agencies employing automatic data processing equipment, particularly agencies that transmit information over distance by any mechanical means, must exercise special care to ensure that the data are accurately converted into a machine-readable format and that they are not distorted as a result of machine malfunction or transmission failure. Procedures should also be adopted that will provide security for such systems in order to reduce the possibility that computerized consumer information will be stolen or altered, by either authorized or unauthorized users of the information system.

The consumer is given the right to be told the name and address of the consumer-reporting agency when he is rejected for credit, insurance or employment at the time of such denial. In this manner, he will be made aware of the existence of any adverse information and can avail himself of the right to correct any erroneous information in his file.

Additionally, the consumer has the right to gain access to his file to learn the nature and substance of the information in the file at the consumer-reporting agency, whether or not adverse action has been taken. All information in the file is available to him with the exception of medical information and the sources of investigative information, which can only be obtained through discovery procedures of a court.

Compliance is enforced by the Federal Trade Commission with respect to consumer reporting agencies, users of reports and all others involved who are not regulated by another federal agency. The Federal Trade Commission can use its cease-and-desist power and any other procedural, investigative, and enforcement powers which it has under the FTC Act to secure compliance.

The private enforcement provisions of the Fair Credit Reporting Act permit the consumer to bring civil suit for willful noncompliance with the Act, with no ceiling on the amount of punitive damages. The consumer may also sue for negligent noncompliance for actual damages sustained by him. Attorney's fees, as determined by the court, will be allowed for both forms of action.

The woeful inadequacies of this law, particularly as regards computerized data bases are obvious. It provides no restrictions on who may collect data, what data may be collected or how the data may be used. Its scope is extremely limited and it provides for disclosure only after certain adverse actions result from the use of the data. The Act requires that procedures be adopted that will provide security of transmitted data, but it provides the individual with the right to take legal action only in the event of *willful* noncompliance with the Act.

The individual is left with the burden of discovering the existence of a file concerning himself. He may determine what information is in the file and have inaccuracies corrected but cannot in any way eliminate highly personal information, even if such information is irrelevant to the purpose of the data base. Finally, no matter how much harm may be done an individual, he may sue only if he can show *willful* noncompliance. This law smacks both of a guarantee that limits a manufacturer's responsibilities to less than would otherwise be the case and of the government's intent to control (an industry) rather than to protect the public.

In an October 6, 1973 *Business Week* article, a spokesman for the Retail Credit Company of Atlanta was quoted as saying "our position is that the Fair Credit Report Act is all we need." Retail Credit is a major investigative reporting company. According to the FTC the firm has files on 45 million Americans. A Retail Credit company spokesman claims they have more than 8500 investigators in about 1800 offices throughout the United States.

A recent Associated Press report noted that on December 18, 1973, the Federal Trade Commission issued a proposed complaint against Retail Credit, alleging failure to provide consumers with information required by law, circumventing the legal ban on the reporting of obsolete derogatory information and misrepresenting that some information was collected through personal interviews and observations when it was not.

It should be understood that the commission issues such complaints when it feels it has reason to believe there is a law violation. Such action does not imply adjudication. On February 21, 1974 the FTC issued a formal complaint against Retail Credit and the matter has been scheduled for trial.

Whether these accusations have any real basis is still to be determined. But what of the smaller consumer reporting companies? Can the FTC really administer this law effectively? How many individuals actually realize their rights under this law?

Certainly much additional legislation is required to provide decent protecion to the general public. Such legislation should first enable the public to protect itself, then it should define adequate penalties for offenders, and finally it should provide for governmental assistance to the public in protecting itself.

Financial Controls

The next largest third-party groups with an interest to protect are investors and creditors of a company or corporation. The investors actually own the company; the creditors hope they don't. In either case, both groups are looking to the executives to run a profitable operation so that they will eventually recover their initial investment with interest (or capital gains).

Securities and Exchange Commission regulations provide the basic controls in this area calling for the disclosure of financial status on a periodic basis. Tax regulations provide a second aspect of control by defining, to some extent, how certain aspects of the operations are to be handled for financial reporting purposes. Finally, these regulations together with the interests of management, have established the auditor as an independent reviewer who reviews practices and procedures to ensure that the disclosure statements are truthful and accurate.

Even here a problem exists, for Section 110.05 of the *Statements on Auditing Standards* holds that the independent auditor is responsible for failure to detect fraud "only when such failure clearly results from failure to comply with generally accepted auditing standards." Thus, the key point currently requiring attention is the definition of what constitutes "generally accepted auditing standards" and what constitutes the reasonable and adequate practices and procedures required for proper auditing in a computer-based operation.

Two groups are currently taking action in this area and vying for recognition of control authority. In the governmental sector, the Securities and Exchange Commission is attempting to seize control, and in the private sector, the newly instituted Financial Accounting Standards Board is attempting to establish its authority. One would hope that in the long run both groups will exist and have a sphere of influence. Self-control with an overseer is the preferred control mechanism.

In Chapter 10 we discussed the need for the compartmentalization of activities as a means of controlling abuses and criminal activities. The risk of such activities is significantly reduced if no one individual has complete knowledge of or control over an activity. A similar concept applies with regard to data processing techniques and financial information accuracy controls.

Although in general, the body that enforces must of necessity establish standards, it is most desirable to have industrial self-control. The establishment of adequate, enforceable standards is more likely to come from those with a vested interest to protect. These groups often need the tempering influence or an additional incentive to action that can be provided by a governmental organization. Further, they require support in the form of legislation that defines the bounds of honest activity and provides penalties for those who do not stay within these bounds.

Other Interests

Beyond the preceding groups, most other third parties with an interest to protect have adequate means for detecting malfunctions or criminal activity and thus for protecting themselves in a basic sense.

Employees can and should verify their weekly pay slips to ensure that they are receiving their proper pay. They should know what each deduction is for and ensure that it is in the proper amount. At year end when withholding tax notices are issued, the employee should have his pay stubs available and should double-check that reported totals agree with the total of the individual pay reports.

Likewise, if customers and suppliers verify their invoices and checks, they can protect themselves from inappropriate or inaccurate charges. Fraud or other criminal acts will seldom be attempted where the risk of detection and prosecution is known to be high. Accidents and malfunctions can occur at any time and it is necessary to be on constant alert for those events.

Prosecution

Prevention and detection are the first lines of defense against losses from criminal activities and mismanagement, but losses will occur. Part of the "price" for such activities should be damages for those who have been harmed and an accounting to society for illegal acts. It is in the latter area that the least progress has been made.

In one case, a programmer was accused of bigotry because he programmed a computer to eliminate black people in screening and selecting new employees. In another case, perpetrators were indicted under an obscene telephone call law. Reported and successfully prosecuted cases, however, have generally involved theft of funds through fraud or embezzlement or physical damage from vandalism. Prosecution in these cases revolved around the theft or vandalism with the computer involved only as an innocent bystander.

In one case a programmer programmed a withholding tax reporting program to reduce the amount reported for each employee and add the amount to his own withholding tax account. When caught, he was charged with stealing. But what if his act had been caught and corrected before any money had actually been stolen? Did the criminal act occur when the programmer put the offending steps into the program or only after actual loss occurred? Probably two levels of criminal act should be recognized in the same manner as the law recognizes breaking and entering versus burglary. But the author knows of no case to date in which an individual has been accused of a criminal act as a result of including such procedures in a program whether or not the procedures resulted in an actual loss.

And with what crimes would such an individual be charged? Attempted burglary? Malicious mischief? These and other alternatives pose significant problems in the interpretation of the law. In general, the law assumes an individual performs the act resulting in a loss. It provides for an individual enticing another individual as agent to perform the act and thus become an accomplice. In some cases conspiracy can be charged against an individual who helps plan but does not take part in the actual crime. Thus, by some legal interpretations the computer is an agent, a conspirator, an accomplice and the perpetrator. But how can a computer be prosecuted? One possible solution is to consider the computer as an extension of the programmer (or program manipulator) and in some cases as an actual physical part of the programmer. Thus, any crimes for which the computer would be held responsible if it were a person could be transferred to the programmer (or program manipulator) who would be prosecuted as though he has carried out all necessary physical activities to affect the crime in a noncomputer environment.

Certainly, changes will be required in the legal area. In some cases the interpretation of existing laws can be adapted to the computer environment. In other cases new laws will be required in order to appropriately cover the computer environment without adversely effecting noncomputer legal interpretations on similar crimes.

Of course, crimes resulting from the direct manipulation of input data or vandalism are not program-related problems. In fact, in these cases the computer's role is generally not considered in the crime. This class of crime forms the great bulk of crimes that have been perpetrated, discovered and prosecuted. They pose the fewest problems with respect to interpreting or applying existing statutes.

Finally, crimes involving the use of data communications pose interesting legal problems. Of particular concern are crimes involving manipulation or alteration of data files that does not result in financial loss, for example if communications lines were used to gain access to and alter criminal records or consumer reporting files. In this case there are none of the classic criminal activities such as physical breaking and entering or unauthorized search and seizure. In this area, significant changes are required in the law, probably including a complete new set of statutes specific to the computer industry.

Education

Another problem is illustrated by a recent case in which the complainant stated that, "The judge threw it out because it was too technical for a court to understand."

Judges are not generally counted among the less educated or less intelligent in our numbers. If a judge finds comprehension difficult, can the average juror be expected to understand? Additionally, the computer has frequently been made the goat when an individual has had difficulties, particularly with respect to errors in bills. Thus, many people distrust the computer and have little compassion for management when they experience difficulties with their computer.

The relationship between programmer and computer is analogous to that between animal trainer and his charge. Programming is the act of training or conditioning the beast to perform certain acts. Releasing the program for production usage is the equivalent of issuing the command for the beast to perform the acts taught him by the trainer. One significant difference is that the computer never acts, as a trained animal might, except on command, and it virtually never does anything it was not trained to do.

The same relationship exists between user and computer as exists between the user and any other piece of office equipment he utilizes to help him carry out his duties. If a bookkeeping machine or adding machine are being used to prepare paychecks and the checks are wrong, the payroll clerk is not allowed the excuse that the machine malfunctioned and is thus responsible for the errors. Why then should the computer be allowed to assume responsibility if it is substituted as the tool and an error arises?

The significant difference between a computer installation and the analogous situations given in the preceding discussions is that a multiplicity of people are involved with computers versus the individualized nature of the other situations. The computer installation in which a single programmer has written all the programs in use simply no longer exists—if in fact it ever did. The payroll clerk no longer collects the data, prepares the input, runs the machine and verifies the output as would occur if a bookkeeping machine or adding machine were used.

Thus, when erroneous output from a computer is detected a significant effort is required to determine which of the people involved actually caused the error or whether indeed the computer malfunctioned. Because this effort is often time-consuming and costly, so management finds it expedient to shed the problem with the simple comment that "the computer goofed."

The solution to this problem requires that the hardware-software system be designed with sufficient checks to catch and report hardware malfunctions before they result in erroneous output. Auditing trails and check data that will enable problems to be rapidly isolated and responsibility pinpointed must be included in the processing. Before this happens on a large scale, the public and the courts must decide that people control the machines and that people are, in fact, responsible for what the machine does and must therefore be held responsible. They must also realize that it is not necessary to know how a computer operates or how to write a program in order to know that the programmer is and should be held responsible for his product.

If a dog trainer trains attack dogs, and turns them loose on the public, neither the court nor the public needs to understand how to train an attack dog in order to realize that the real culprit is the trainer—not the dog. Why then is the computer seen as the culprit rather than the people behind it? The computer myth appears to be the answer. Computer professionals have planted and perpetuated the idea that the beast is difficult, if not impossible, to train and control. The layman has been snowed and is all too willing to blame the computer rather than the people who program it. Fortunately, the situation is changing rapidly. Losses and threats of loss are becoming too great and are touching too many people to be allowed to continue as an unsolvable, impersonal problem of the unruly computer.

Reasonable and responsible action in the future requires a concerted sincere effort on the part of computer system managers and computer users to educate the layman about the true character of computers. The layman must admit the role of people in the system and exercise his authority in establishing and upholding the responsibilities of people, if he is to exorcise the ghost that is the computer and expose the computer myth for what it is.

Appendix A
Data Processing Facility and Security Checklist

HAVING identified and presumably accepted the problem, how does one begin? Specifically, what are the ways in which a key manager, responsible for the security of a computer/communications system but himself no technical expert, can assess what's going on? One of the best ways is to ask appropriate questions of his EDP manager, his security people, and his consultants. This appendix provides a compendium, in the form of an abridged checklist, of computer security issues and concerns.

A word of warning is appropriate. This appendix, as the rest of the book, is not a do-it-yourself manual in computer security management. Since one is dealing with the unknown (in fact, a very intelligent and highly motivated unknown) a great deal of sheer experience and background is necessary to evaluate and upgrade the security of any computer or communications system. The best people to do this are those who:

1. Have experience in both the surveillance of computer systems and prevention of computer crime.
2. Know hardware, software, and "peopleware" equally well.
3. Are not selling a panacea
4. Have no axe to grind, meaning that they don't work for:
    a. The same organization
    b. The computer company
    c. The telephone company
    d. The regular software vendor

The purpose of this appendix is to provide you with a basis for starting investigation and action, a means for initiating a review and improvement plan for your company's data system security.

A. PHYSICAL FACILITIES

1. *Fire Exposure*
    a. Is the building housing the data processing facility constructed of fire resistant and noncombustible materials?
    b. Is the computer room enclosed by noncombustible fire resistant partitions, walls, and doors?

c. What provision is made for the storage of paper and other computer supplies?
d. What are the provisions for the storage of magnetic tapes and disks? Could a fireproof safe or vault be utilized to advantage?
e. Are there flammable materials in use, or other dangerous activities in spaces adjacent to the data processing facility?
f. Is the raised flooring in the computer room noncombustible?
g. Are false ceilings and their supports noncombustible?
h. Is training in fire-fighting techniques provided to any of the staff?
i. Are specific responsibilities assigned individuals in case of fire?
j. Are all furnishings noncombustible?
k. Is smoking permitted in the computer area?
l. Is the computer area protected by:
    1) Automatic carbon dioxide?
    2) Halon?
    3) Water?
        a) Wet pipe (releases water at a set temperature)?
        b) Dry pipe?
m. What types of portable extinguishers are provided and how are they distributed?
n. Are fire-extinguisher locations clearly marked?
o. Are emergency power shutdown controls accessible at all points of exit from the computer room?
p. Are ionization smoke detectors installed?
    1) In ceiling?
    2) Under false floor?
    3) In air return ducts?
    4) What action is triggered by smoke detection?
    5) When is the smoke detection system tested?
q. How often are "fire drills" held?
r. When is the space under the false floor cleaned?
s. What is the source of fire-fighting water?
t. Is battery-powered emergency lighting provided throughout the computer area?
u. Are fire alarm pull boxes easily accessible in all parts of the computer area?
v. Where does the alarm sound?
    1) Locally?
    2) At watchman station?
    3) At a central security station?
    4) At fire or police headquarters?
w. Is round-the-clock watchman coverage provided? If not, what coverage is provided during nonworking hours?
x. Are any flammable materials used in computer maintenance? If so, where are they stored?
y. What provisions are made for emergency access to the installation?

2. *Water Damage Exposure*

    a. Are all computers and data storage in areas above grade?
    b. Are there any overhead steam or water pipes other than sprinklers?
    c. Is there provision for adequate drainage under the raised floor?
    d. Is there adequate drainage to prevent water overflow from adjacent areas?
    e. Are all electrical junction boxes under the raised flooring mounted off slab to prevent water damage?
    f. Have pipe openings in walls been sealed to prevent water intrusion?
    g. Have protective covers been obtained and are they used?

3. *Air Conditioning Considerations*

    a. Is system exclusively for the computer area?
    b. How many independent cooling units cool the computer area?
    c. Are duct linings and filters noncombustible?
    d. Are there automatic duct closures operated by the fire control system?
    e. Where are the compressors located?
    f. Is there backup air conditioning capability?
    g. Are air intakes:
        1) Covered with protective screening?
        2) Located well above street level?
        3) Located so as to prevent the intake of pollutants or debris?

4. *Electrical Power*

    a. What provisions have been made for power failures?
    b. Have provisions been made for brownouts or voltage fluctuation?

5. *Natural Disaster Exposure*

    a. Is building structurally sound?
    b. Is location a flood, earthquake, or hurricane area?
    c. Have provisions been made for such natural problems?
    d. Are building and equipment properly grounded for lightning protection?

6. *Alternate Location*

    a. Are there arrangements for a backup computer facility?

7. *Access Control*

    a. Are guards stationed at all street entrances that might lead to the computer area?
    b. Is a photo badge system used for positive indentfication of employees?
    c. Who has access to the computer area?
    d. Who has access to file storage areas?
    e. What security devices are utilized to control access?
    f. What is the visitor control procedure?
    g. Are all exterior windows near street level covered by protective metal grilles?

h. What controls are used to limit off-shift access to the facility?
i. Is round-the-clock watchman service used?
j. Is the computer room visible from the street, the lobby, or any other public areas?
k. Is provision made for the operation of alarms and access control devices in the event of power failure?

8. *Housekeeping*

a. What provisions are made to ensure cleanliness of computer area?
b. Are provisions made for the disposal of waste carrying sensitive information?
c. Is eating permitted in the computer room?
d. Is smoking permitted in the computer room?
e. What type of waste containers are used?

9. *Other Facilities Considerations*

a. Have personnel been instructed on how to handle civil disturbances?
b. What is the liaison program with local law enforcement agencies?
c. Are there established methods for handling bomb threats?

B. PERSONNEL

1. Are background checks of new personnel used?
2. Are any checks of established employees used?
3. What provisions have been made for backup personnel in critical positions?
4. What is the state of employee morale?
5. What is the employee termination procedure?
6. Does personnel assignment strategy prevent single-person access and control to any part of the system?

C. HARDWARE

1. *Utilization*

a. Are all computer operations scheduled?
b. How are operations monitored for compliance with schedules?
c. Are complete operational logs maintained?
d. Are equipment meter hours checked against utilization hours?
e. How are scheduled maintenance activities monitored?
f. How are periods of downtime verified?
g. When are equipment meters checked and readings recorded?

2. *Magnetic Tapes and Disks*

a. Does the tape and disk control procedure record:
   1) When used?
   2) By whom used?
   3) Maintenance (cleaning and testing)?
b. How are magnetic tapes and disks stored?

c. What maintenance procedures are used for tapes and disk packs?
d. Are tapes kept in containers when not in use?
e. Are complete tape history records maintained?
f. When are tape drive heads cleaned?
g. How often are tape leaders replaced?
h. Where is the tape and disk pack library located?
i. What kind of storage vault is provided for tapes and disks?
j. Where are backup tapes and disks stored?

D. SOFTWARE SECURITY

1. *Physical Security*

a. Where are the essential programs and associated documentation located?
b. Are backup files for both the programs and the associated documentation kept at a secondary location?
c. How is access to essential programs and software systems controlled?
d. Is multilevel access control to data files employed and does it control access by:
    1) Need to know?
    2) Breakdown within a file, i.e., by block, record, field?
    3) Type of access: read only, write only, etc.?
e. How are software updates and changes controlled?
f. In the management of data bases, how is more than one user prevented from updating a file at any given time?

2. *Remote Terminals*

a. Is password protection used and, if so, how often are passwords changed?
b. What measures are used to limit access to system software from remote terminals?
c. Are techniques employed to protect data that are being transmitted by communication lines?

3. *Operating System*

a. Does the operating system provide a system activity log?
b. Can the operating system effectively handle multiple interrupts?
c. Is the memory partitioning scheme consistent with the memory protection features?
d. How much will be automatically dumped for programmer review:
    1) In event of program bug or hardware malfunction?
    2) By internal request of application program during debugging activities?
e. Are the file access restrictions sufficient to prevent unauthorized access to programs and data?
f. What rerun capabilities are provided?

g. Are memory, rerun data, scratch files, etc., erased or otherwise properly protected after job termination?

4. *Application Programs*

a. How are changes and maintenance of programs controlled and documented?
b. What tests are used to validate outputs from critical reporting systems?
c. Do programs store rerun data or other information in unsecured areas or by other means that could compromise security?

5. *Threat Monitoring*

a. Is a log of accesses to sensitive files maintained? How or who does it? What information is included? Who verifies?
b. Are attempted unauthorized accesses to sensitive files monitored? How?
c. Does the security program in the operating systems record and print out all such attempts?
d. How is the information on unauthorized access attempts used?

E. SERVICE PERSONNEL

1. *In-House*

a. How is access to vital areas by maintenance personnel controlled?
b. How are his tools and those supplies which are removed from the computer room controlled to prevent the loss of vital programs or data?

2. *Vendor*

a. Who keeps the list of each vendor's authorized service and support personnel? Who checks authorizations?
b. Does the list include telephone, air conditioning, and other non-computer-related service personnel requiring access?
c. Are vendor service personnel supervised? By whom?

F. FILES

1. *Program Files*

a. Are there duplicate files stored off-site?
b. How are program files protected at the off-site storage facility?
c. How are operational programs stored on-site?
d. What controls are used in the management of stored files?
e. How is the file backup system tested? By whom? How often?
f. How are program changes recorded and controlled?
g. What is the program change routine?
h. What controls are used for the protection of program files after withdrawal from the production library?
i. What controls of documentation are used to assure compliance with operational standards?

j. What backup of source data is maintained for programs under development?

2. *Documentation*

   a. *Do the documentation stardards call for:*
      1) Logic diagrams or flow charts?
      2) Current listing?
      3) Input and output formats?
      4) Output samples?
      5) User instructions?
      6) Test data?
      7) Explanation of error messages?
      8) Rejected record procedures?
      9) Explanation of halts?
      10) File description?
      11) Control instructions?
      12) Other explanations as needed?

   b. Are duplicates of all documentation maintained?
      1) Where are these duplicates kept?
      2) What controls are applied to this file?

   c. How is currency of documentation assured?

   d. What levels of approval are required for changes in programs and documentation?

   e. Are program changes reviewed by an internal auditor?

3. *Data Files*

   a. Who controls and maintains user data files?
   b. Is there a sensitivity classification for files?
   c. Where are files (tape, disk, or card) kept?
   d. How is the file storage area protected from fire?
   e. How is access to this area controlled?
   f. How are critical files stored?
   g. Are the legal requirements for record retention complied with?

G. ORGANIZATION

1. Is a single individual responsible for all systems security activities?
2. Has a policy for the maintenance of computer security been established?
3. Are there in-house service groups, local agencies, or outside consultants available to provide help in each of the following areas:

   a. Power systems, site preparation, facilities engineering, air conditioning, etc?
   b. Plant security (fire protection, guards, intrusion alarms, etc.)?
   c. Safety?
   d. Control of vital records?
   e. Personnel?
   f. Insurance?
   g. Auditing considerations?

H. INTERNAL AUDIT CONTROLS

1. Is there an explicitly stated audit control policy relating to computer systems?
2. What controls are imposed upon computer equipment utilization and production?
3. What controls exist to assure the receipt of full and correct data from user?
4. What is the error-reporting and follow-up procedure?
5. Where is responsibility for quality control assigned?
6. How are program changes controlled?
7. What are the established policies for program testing?
8. How is the installation protected against intrusion?
9. What provisions are there for backup of:
   a. Programs?
   b. Files?
   c. Equipment?
10. Against what types of loss does the company carry insurance?
11. What part does the internal or external auditor play in system design?

I. TIME-RESOURCE SHARING*

1. Are there any remote terminals on the system?
2. How is access to terminals controlled?
3. Are portable terminals used?
4. Are "passwords" used to indentify a specific terminal and a specific user?
5. How does the password system work?
6. What controls are imposed that limit access to read or modify specific data files?
7. Who has access to the password files?
8. What data file activity records are maintained in the installation?
9. Are scramblers or other cryptographic techniques utilized?
10. How is program debugging of the security features of the software controlled?
11. How is the on-line operating system protected from terminal users?
12. What means are used for protection of applications programs from remote terminal users?

J. INSURANCE

1. *Does the insurance program cover losses by:*
   a. Fire?
   b. Water damage?
   c. Criminal acts?
   d. Business interruption?
   e. Natural disasters?
   f. Fraud?
   g. Power failure?
   h. Performance warranty (for service bureau operations)?

*The concurrent use of any system by multiple users—including time-sharing, multiprocessing, and multiprogramming.

2. *Does the insurance cover loss of accounts receivable due to a computer system error?*

K. CONTINGENCY PLAN

1. *Backup Facilities*
   a. Is there a backup computer available?
   b. Has a formal plan for the use of a backup installation been developed?
   c. How often are the backup arrangements tested?
2. *Is there a contingency plan?*
   a. How are contingency responsibilities assigned?
   b. What are the emergency notification procedures?
   c. What are the emergency provisions for source document and data file protection?
   d. What is the emergency procedure for:
      1) Fire?
      2) Intrusion?
      3) Riot or civil disturbance?
      4) Power failure?
   e. What is the policy for emergency drills?

L. USE OF SERVICE BUREAUS

1. What use is made of an outside computer service bureau?
2. In selection of that facility, what consideration was given to:
   a. Location?
   b. Control of access to computer and file storage areas?
   c. Security of customer work area?
   d. Fire protection?
   e. General housekeeping?
   f. Competence and morale of their personnel?
   g. Adequacy of operating and control procedures?
   h. Contractual provisions for recovery of losses due to:
      1) Error?
      2) Loss of data?
      3) Inadvertent or deliberate release of your data?
      4) Failure to perform?
   i. Their ability to meet obligations:
      1) Are they financially sound?
      2) Have they adequate liability insurance coverage?
   j. Sensitivity of work being contracted?

Appendix B
Equity Funding Indictment Count One

UNITED STATES DISTRICT COURT
FOR THE CENTRAL DISTRICT OF CALIFORNIA
MARCH 1973 GRAND JURY

UNITED STATES OF AMERICA *Plaintiff,* v. STANLEY GOLDBLUM, SAMUEL B. LOWELL, JEROME H. EVANS, FRED LEVIN, MICHAEL E. SULTAN, JAMES CYRUS SMITH, JR., ARTHUR STANLEY LEWIS, DAVID JACK CAPO, LLOYD DOUGLAS EDENS, LAWRENCE GREY COLLINS, JAMES HOWARD BANKS, WILLIAM MERCADO, DONALD MCCLELLAN, WILLIAM EDWARD SYMONDS, LESTER MICHAEL KELLER, ALAN LEWIS GREEN, JULIAN S. H. WEINER, MARVIN AL LICHTIG, SOLOMON BLOCK, GARY STANLEY BECKERMAN, MARK CHARLES LEWIS, RICHARD GARDENIER, *Defendants.*	*No. CD* INDICTMENT [18 U.S.C. §371: Conspiracy; 15 U.S.C. §§77q(a), 77x: Fraud in Sale of Securities, False Statement in Registration Statement; 15 U.S.C. §§78j(b), 781, 78m, 78ff; 17 CFR §240.10b-5, Regs. 12B, 13A: Fraud in Sale of Securities, False Statement in Documents Required to be Filed with Securities and Exchange Commission; 18 U.S.C. §1341: Mail Fraud; 18 U.S.C. §1014: False Statement to Bank; 18 U.S.C. §2314: Interstate Transportation of Securities Taken by Fraud; 18 U.S.C. §2511: Interception of Communications]

The Grand Jury charges:

COUNT ONE

[18 U.S.C. §371]

1. Beginning on or about January 15, 1965, and continuing to on or about April 1, 1973, in the Central District of California and elsewhere, defendants STANLEY GOLDBLUM, SAMUEL B. LOWELL, JEROME H. EVANS, FRED LEVIN, MICHAEL E. SULTAN, JAMES CYRUS SMITH, JR., ARTHUR STANLEY LEWIS, DAVID JACK CAPO, LLOYD DOUGLAS EDENS, LAWRENCE GREY COLLINS, JAMES HOWARD BANKS, WILLIAM MERCADO, DONALD MC CLELLAN, WILLIAM EDWARD SYMONDS, LESTER MICHAEL KELLER, ALAN LEWIS GREEN, MARVIN AL LICHTIG, JULIAN S. H. WEINER, SOLOMON BLOCK, GARY STANLEY BECKERMAN, MARK CHARLES LEWIS, RICHARD GARDENIER and unindicted co-conspirators William Gootnick, Ronald Secrist, Francis D. Majerus, Aaron Venouziou and Wolfson Weiner Ratoff & Lapin, and divers other persons known and unknown to the Grand Jury, wilfully and knowingly agreed, confederated, combined and conspired together to commit offenses against the United States, to wit, to violate Title 15, United States Code, Sections 77g(a), 77x, 78j(b), 78l, 78m, 78ff, Title 17, Code of Federal Regulations, Section 240.10b-5, Regulation 12B and Regulation 13A, and Title 18, United States Code, Sections 1014, 1341, 2314, and 2511, all as further described below:

A. It was a part of said conspiracy that said defendants and co-conspirators wilfully and knowingly would, in the offer and sale of securities of Equity Funding Corporation of America (hereinafter in this Count the term "EFCA" is used, unless the context requires otherwise, to refer to Equity Funding Corporation of America and its subsidiaries), by the use of the means and instruments of transportation and communication in interstate commerce and by the use of the mails, directly and indirectly, (a) employ devices, schemes and artifices to defraud; (b) obtain money and property by means of untrue statements of material facts and omissions to state material facts necessary in order to make the statements made, in the light of the circumstances under which they were made, not misleading; and (c) engage in transactions, practices and courses of business which operated and would operate as a fraud and deceit upon the purchasers of said securities of EFCA, and upon any and all persons to whom the said defendants and unindicted co-conspirators would offer to sell said securities of EFCA, in violation of Title 15, United States Code, Sections 77q(a) and 77x.

B. It was a further part of said conspiracy that said defendants and unindicted co-conspirators wilfully and knowingly, directly and indirectly, by the use of the means and instrumentalities of interstate commerce, of the mails, and of the facilities of national securities exchanges would use and employ manipulative and deceptive devices and contrivances in connection with the sale of securities of EFCA as defined in Rule 10b-5 (17 CFR 240.10b-5), prescribed by the Securities and Exchange Commission as necessary and appropriate in the public interest and for the protection of investors, in violation of Title 15, United States Code, Sections 78j(b) and 78ff.

C. It was a further part of said conspiracy that said defendants and unindicted co-conspirators wilfully would make untrue statements of material fact in registration statements filed with the Securities and Exchange Commission and would omit to state material facts required to be stated in registration statements filed with the Securities and Exchange Commission and necessary to make the statements therein not misleading, in violation of Title 15, United States Code, Section 77x.

D. It was a further part of said conspiracy that said defendants and unindicted co-conspirators wilfully and knowingly would make statements which were false and misleading with respect to material facts in applications, reports and other documents required to be filed and filed with the American Stock Exchange, the New York Stock Exchange, the Pacific Coast Stock Exchange and the Securities and Exchange Commission, in violation of Title 15, United States Code, Sections 78l, 78m, 78ff and Title 17, Code of Federal Regulations, Regulations 12B and 13A, promulgated under Title 15, United States Code, Chapter 2B.

E. It was further a part of said conspiracy that said defendants and unindicted co-conspirators, having wilfully and knowingly devised and intended to devise schemes and artifices to defraud, and for obtaining money and property by means of false and fraudulent pretenses, representations, and promises, would, for the purpose of executing said schemes and artifices and attempting to do so, knowingly cause to be delivered by mail by the United States Post Office, according to the direction thereon, certain letters, packages and other matter, in violation of Title 18, United States Code, Section 1341.

F. It was a further part of said conspiracy that said defendants and unindicted co-conspirators knowingly would make materially false statements and reports for the purpose of influencing the action of banks, the deposits of which were then insured by the Federal Deposit Insurance Corporation, upon commitments and loans and upon the change and extension of commitments and loans by renewal, deferment of action and otherwise, in violation of Title 18, United States Code, Section 1014.

G. It was a further part of said conspiracy that said defendants and unindicted co-conspirators with unlawful and fraudulent intent would transport and cause to be transported in interstate commerce falsely make, forged and counterfeited securities, knowing the securities to have been falsely made, forged and counterfeited, in violation of Title 18, United States Code, Section 2314.

H. It was a further part of said conspiracy that said defendants and unindicted co-conspirators would cause to be transported in interstate commerce securities of a value in excess of $5,000, knowing the securities to have been stolen, converted and taken by fraud, in violation of Title 18, United States Code, Section 2314.

I. It was a further part of said conspiracy that said defendants and unindicted co-conspirators wilfully would endeavor to intercept, and procure others to intercept and endeavor to intercept wire communications, and wilfully would use and endeavor to use, and procure others to use and endeavor to use an electronic device to intercept oral communications made and had on the premises of a business the operations of which then affected interstate commerce, in violation of Title 18, United States Code, Section 2511.

2. The foregoing objects of the conspiracy were to be accomplished, in substance, through acts, transactions and practices which would, directly and indirectly, fraudulently overstate the income and assets and misrepresent the growth and general business and financial condition of EFCA. Said acts, transactions and practices would enable the defendants to continue EFCA's normal business operations, to fraudulently increase the market price of EFCA stock, to acquire assets and companies of EFCA with falsely valued EFCA stock and other consideration, to borrow money on behalf of EFCA, to realize incomes from EFCA salaries, commissions, bonuses, fees and expense allowances and to sell fraudulently valued EFCA stock owned by them, all the while concealing from other EFCA shareholders, the general business community, regulatory agencies and the public the true business and financial condition of EFCA. More specifically:

A. Defendant STANLEY GOLDBLUM, President of EFCA, would set periodic standards for growth in income, assets and earnings of EFCA, which growth he did not expect to be achieved, and which growth was not achieved, through the conduct of legitimate business operations, and he would direct defendants JEROME H. EVANS, SAMUEL B. LOWELL and FRED LEVIN, officers of EFCA and of its subsidiaries, to ensure that the books, records and financial reports of EFCA and its subsidiaries, including, but not limited to, Equity Funding Life Insurance Company (EFLIC), would reflect the growth in income assets and earnings set forth in the standards. Upon receiving defendant STANLEY GOLDBLUM's directions, defendants JEROME H. EVANS, SAMUEL B. LOWELL and FRED LEVIN would make and would arrange with other employees of EFCA and of its subsidiaries, including, but not limited to, defendants MICHAEL E. SULTAN, JAMES CYRUS SMITH, JR., DAVID JACK CAPO, ARTHUR STANLEY LEWIS and LLOYD DOUGLAS EDENS, to make false and fictitious entries to various types of accounts, including, but not limited to, receivables from purchasers of Equity Funding programs, notes receivable, receivables on the residual right to receive commissions on the sale of contractual plans, investments, insurance premium income, insurance commission income and securities commission income.

B. In order to conceal the true condition of EFCA's business operations and to obtain funds necessary to continue EFCA's operations defendants STANLEY GOLDBLUM, SAMUEL B. LOWELL and FRED LEVIN would arrange for advances and loans of money, including, but not limited to, bank loans negotiated and maintained through the submission to banks of false financial information, and defendants STANLEY GOLDBLUM and SAMUEL B. LOWELL would further arrange for certain of those obligations not to be properly recognized and reflected on the books, records and financial statements of EFCA.

C. In order to promote and to conceal the activities of EFCA, including, but not limited to, the insertion of fictitious and inflated assets and the nondisclosure of certain liabilities on the books, records and financial statements of EFCA and in order to conceal the activities of defendants STANLEY GOLDBLUM and SAMUEL B. LOWELL, defendants STANLEY GOLDBLUM and SAMUEL B. LOWELL would arrange for the use of corporations registered in jurisdictions outside the United States, including, but not limited to, Equity Funding Capital

Corporation, N. V., a Netherlands Antilles Corporation; Bishops Bank and Trust Company, a Bahamian Corporation; Equity Immobilaire Industriale, S.p.A., an Italian Corporation; Compania de Estudios y Asuntos, a Panamanian Corporation; and Etablissement Grandson, a Liechtenstein Corporation; which corporations directly and indirectly entered into various transactions at the direction of said defendants STANLEY GOLDBLUM and SAMUEL B. LOWELL.

D. In order to follow the directions and meet the standards concerning the income, assets and earnings which EFLIC was expected to have, and to contribute to the income, assets and earnings of EFCA, defendant FRED LEVIN would give directions to defendants JAMES CYRUS SMITH, JR., ARTHUR STANLEY LEWIS and LLOYD DOUGLAS EDENS to insert on the books and records of EFLIC the necessary amounts of fictitious business. Defendants ARTHUR STANLEY LEWIS and LLOYD DOUGLAS EDENS would arrange with defendants LESTER MICHAEL KELLER and ALAN LEWIS GREEN and unindicted co-conspirator Aaron Venouziou to write computer programs for the creation of fictitious insurance policies and related fictitious fiancial information, and to have said policies and fiancial information generated in the form of computer print-out and tape listings. Defendant LLOYD DOUGLAS EDENS would arrange with defendant WILLIAM EDWARD SYMONDS to make entries on computer records in order that genuine policies which had lapsed would appear to be in force. Defendant LLOYD DOUGLAS EDENS would further prepare false financial statements purporting to reflect the financial condition of EFLIC and would arrange for false financial statements and other financial information to be sent in interstate commerce and through the mails to persons and corporations with whom EFLIC did business and to various state agencies responsible for regulating insurance companies.

E. For the purpose of generating income and providing operating capital through the use of fictitious insurance policies, defendants FRED LEVIN, JAMES CYRUS SMITH, JR., and ARTHUR STANLEY LEWIS would negotiate and enter into reinsurance agreements with other insurance companies who would thereby agree to pay commissions for the privilege of reinsuring portions of EFLIC's insurance business, not knowing that such business, or any portion thereof, was fictitious. Defendants LESTER MICHAEL KELLER and ALAN LEWIS GREEN would arrange for computer print-out and tape listings containing fictitious insurance policies to be sent in interstate commerce and through the mails to various reinsuring companies. Defendants JAMES CYRUS SMITH, JR., ARTHUR STANLEY LEWIS, WILLIAM EDWARD SYMONDS, LESTER MICHAEL KELLER, and ALAN LEWIS GREEN would arrange for the reinsuring companies to send in interstate commerce and through the mails checks and money to EFLIC representing commissions on insurance policies sent by EFLIC to the reinsuring companies. In order to fulfill the terms of the reinsurance agreements, to maintain the confidence and goodwill of the reinsuring companies and thereby to guarantee the continued reinsurance of fictitious insurance and reduce the danger of its disclosure, defendants ARTHUR STANLEY LEWIS, WILLIAM EDWARD SYMONDS and LESTER MICHAEL KELLER would arrange for lists of insurance reserve rates and values to be sent in interstate commerce and through the mails to the reinsuring companies; and defendants FRED LEVIN, JAMES

CYRUS SMITH, JR., and LAWRENCE GREY COLLINS would arrange for correspondence regarding questions arising out of the interpretation and administration of the reinsurance agreements to be sent in interstate commerce and through the mails to the reinsuring companies.

F. In order to conceal the fact that monies were not being received on genuine business, and in order to provide further operating capital:

(1) Defendants FRED LEVIN and JAMES CYRUS SMITH, JR., would arrange with defendant JAMES HOWARD BANKS for the submission of death claims on fictitious insurance policies to be sent in interstate commerce and through the mails to the reinsuring companies and for the reinsuring companies to send in interstate commerce and through the mails checks and money to EFLIC representing death benefit payments on the basis of death claims.

(2) Defendants STANLEY GOLDBLUM, FRED LEVIN, MICHAEL E. SULTAN, JAMES CYRUS SMITH, JR., ARTHUR STANLEY LEWIS and LLOYD DOUGLAS EDENS would arrange for the development and sale, through use of the mails, of single premium annuities bearing the letterheads of Equity Funding Life Insurance Company, Bankers National Life Insurance Company, Equity Funding Life Insurance Company of New York and Northern Life Insurance Company all of which were subsidiaries of EFCA; and said defendants would further arrange that the sale of said annuities and the liabilities attributable thereto would not be properly reflected on the books, records and financial statements of the respective life insurance companies, or of EFCA.

G. In order to conceal the fictitious nature of the life insurance policies and to assist in the submission of fictitious death claims, defendant LAWRENCE GREY COLLINS would establish procedures for, and, with the aid of defendants WILLIAM EDWARD SYMONDS, MARK CHARLES LEWIS and RICHARD GARDENIER, oversee the manufacturing of fictitious insurance files and of fictitious death claim files which would correspond with the fictitious insurance policies placed on EFLIC's books and reinsured with reinsuring companies. Defendants MICHAEL E. SULTAN, JAMES CYRUS SMITH, JR., ARTHUR STANLEY LEWIS, DAVID JACK CAPO, LLOYD DOUGLAS EDENS, JAMES HOWARD BANKS, LESTER MICHAEL KELLER and ALAN LEWIS GREEN and unindicted co-conspirators Ronald Secrist and Francis D. Majerus would participate in the creation of the fictitious files.

H. In order to support EFLIC's assertions concerning its assets and to conceal its true business and financial condition from auditors and state examiners, defendants STANLEY GOLDBLUM, FRED LEVIN, JAMES CYRUS SMITH, JR., MICHAEL E. SULTAN, ARTHUR STANLEY LEWIS and LLOYD DOUGLAS EDENS would arrange through defendant GARY STANLEY BECKERMAN for the printing of counterfeit bonds which were to be listed as assets of EFLIC and which would be sent in interstate commerce to Chicago, Illinois. Said defendants would also arrange through defendant GARY STANLEY BECKERMAN for the printing of counterfeit bank documents and stationery to lend support to the purported genuineness of the counterfeit bonds. Defendant STANLEY GOLDBLUM, with the assistance of defendant MICHAEL E. SULTAN, would arrange to purchase certificates of deposit with EFCA funds, which certificates of deposit would be shown to auditors and state examiners and falsely represented to them to be assets of EFLIC and to have been purchased with funds of EFLIC. Defendants JAMES CYRUS SMITH, JR., ARTHUR STANLEY LEWIS and LLOYD DOUGLAS EDENS would arrange with unindicted co-conspirator William Gootnick to make alterations in computer records. To further guard against the disclosure of true business and financial information, and for the purpose of determining the course and direction of examinations conducted by certain state insurance examiners who were on EFCA's business premises, defendants STANLEY GOLDBLUM, FRED LEVIN, JAMES HOWARD BANKS and LAWRENCE GREY COLLINS would make arrangements to install, and defendants JAMES HOWARD BANKS and LAWRENCE GREY COLLINS would assist in installing, electronic surveillance equipment designed to intercept the private wire and oral conversation of said examiners.

I. In order to conceal the false and fictitious nature of various entries on the books and records of EFCA, defendant MICHAEL E. SULTAN would arrange through defendant GARY STANLEY BECKERMAN for the printing of certain counterfeit bank documents, including counterfeit confirmations of purchase and counterfeit debit memoranda. Defendants STANLEY GOLDBLUM, SAMUEL B. LOWELL and MICHAEL E. SULTAN would sign confirmations, contracts and letters falsely authenticating the amounts of various assets and accounts. Defendant SAMUEL B. LOWELL would give instructions, and adhering to those instructions, defendants WILLIAM MERCADO, DAVID JACK CAPO, ARTHUR STANLEY LEWIS and ALAN LEWIS GREEN would arrange to manipulate computer records containing detailed listings of the items in the account relating to receivables from purchases of Equity Funding programs so as to make the size of the account appear greater than it was; defendants DAVID JACK CAPO and DONALD MCCLELLAN would, with the cooperation of various employees of EFCA, including, among others, defendants FRED LEVIN, MICHAEL E. SULTAN, JAMES CYRUS SMITH, JR., ARTHUR STANLEY LEWIS, LLOYD DOUGLAS EDENS, LAWRENCE GREY COLLINS, JAMES HOWARD BANKS, WILLIAM EDWARD SYMONDS, ALAN LEWIS GREEN, GARY STANLEY BECKERMAN and RICHARD GARDENIER and unindicted co-conspirators Ronald Secrist and William Gootnick, obtain and devise names and addresses of individuals to whom fictitious investor confirmations, related to fictitious items in the said asset account could be sent; defendants DAVID JACK CAPO and DONALD MCCLELLAN would then arrange with the aforesaid defendants and unindicted co-conspirators to have the confirmations mailed to the addresses provided, to have them executed, and to have them returned via the mails to certain auditors in accordance with customary audit procedures, thereby making it appear as though the said fictitious items were genuine and reducing the possibility that the fraudulent nature of EFCA's books, records and financial statements would be exposed.

J. In order to facilitate EFCA's use of false and fraudulent financial data, defendants JULIAN S. H. WEINER, MARVIN AL LICHTIG and SOLOMON BLOCK and unindicted co-conspirator Wolfson Weiner Ratoff & Lapin, an independent certified public accounting firm whose responsibility it was to audit the books and records of EFCA, would conduct and cause to be conducted incomplete and insufficient audits and would accept and cause to be accepted substantial portions or all of the fictitious and inflated entries to asset and income accounts; said defendants and said unindicted co-conspirator would aid and assist in the preparation of false EFCA financial statements, and would cause said statements to be certified to have been audited in accordance with generally accepted auditing standards and to be an accurate representation of EFCA's financial position in accordance with generally accepted accounting principles.

K. For use in connection with the sale of EFCA securities and for the purpose of maintaining investor confidence in EFCA so as to induce both institutions and the general investing public to purchase and retain shares of EFCA common stock, thereby keeping the price of the stock at artifically inflated levels, defendants STANLEY GOLDBLUM, JEROME H. EVANS, SAMUEL B. LOWELL, FRED LEVIN, MICHAEL E. SULTAN, JAMES CYRUS SMITH, JR., DAVID JACK CAPO, LLOYD DOUGLAS EDENS, LAWRENCE GREY COLLINS, JAMES HOWARD BANKS, WILLIAM MERCADO, DONALD McCLELLAN, WILLIAM EDWARD SYMONDS, LESTER MICHAEL KELLER, ALAN LEWIS GREEN, JULIAN S. H. WEINER, MARVIN AL LICHTIG, SOLOMON BLOCK, GARY STANLEY BECKERMAN, MARK CARLES LEWIS and RICHARD GARDENIER would knowingly make and cause to be made false and fraudulent oral representations and statements and would arrange for the preparation, the filing with the Securities and Exchange Commission, and the distribution by mail and by other means to, among others, the American Stock Exchange, the New York Stock Exchange, the Pacific Coast Stock Exchange, banks and other financial institutions, financial analysts, stock brokerage houses, stockholders, prospective stockholders and other prospective investors in EFCA securities, of annual, semi-annual and quarterly reports, registration statements, prospectuses, proxy statements and other financial statements, some of which bore certifications of unindicted co-conspirator Wolfson Weiner Ratoff and Lapin, as well as press releases, which materials, as the defendants then and there well knew, would contain false, fraudulent and misleading promises, representations and statements of material fact, and would omit and conceal material facts.

(1) Among the false statements which the said defendants would knowingly make were the following:

(a) That on December 31, 1964, EFCA had an asset, Loans Receivable from Clients for Premium Loans, in the amount of $6,682,075.61.

(b) That on December 31, 1965, EFCA had an asset, Loans Receivable from Clients for Premium Loans, in the amount of $9,210,597.

(c) That on December 31, 1966, EFCA had an asset, Loans Receivable from Clients for Premium Loans, in the amount of $13,776,971.

(d) That on December 31, 1967, EFCA had an asset, Loans Receivable from Clients for Premium Loans, in the amount of $19,512,475.

(e) That on December 31, 1968, EFCA had an asset, Funded Loans and Accounts Receivable, in the amount of $35,476,037.

(f) That on December 31, 1968, approximately $19,911,408 in funded loans and accounts receivable were held by EFCA itself or one of its subsidiaries while the remainder of the asset was pledged in connection with loans.

(g) That on December 31, 1969, EFCA had an asset, Funded Loans and Accounts Receivable, in the amount of $51,188,119.

(h) That during 1969 EFCA had a total gross income from consolidated operations of $45,571,643, of which $19,954,887 was attributable to securities sales commissions and $15,247,569 was attributable to insurance sales commission; and that during the same year EFCA had earnings from consolidated operations before income tax of approximately $12,590,278.

(i) That on December 31, 1970, EFCA had an asset, Funded Loans and Accounts Receivable, in the amount of $63,324,413.

(j) That during 1970 EFCA had a total gross income from consolidated operations of $60,912,874 of which $15,931,895 was attributable to securities sales commissions and $17,638,207 was attributable to insurance sales commissions; and that during the same year, EFCA had earnings from consolidated operations before income taxes of $10,751,366.

(k) That during 1970, 11,139 Equity Funding Programs had been sold, and that on December 31, 1970, 31, 892 Equity Funding Programs were in effect.

(l) That during 1970, EFLIC placed in force $834,102,704 in face value of direct, paid-for new life insurance policies.

(m) That on December 31, 1971, EFCA had an asset, Funded Loans and Accounts Receivable, in the amount of $88,616,000.

(n) That during 1971, EFCA had total revenues of $130,951,000, of which $14,824,000 was attributable to securities sales commissions and $62,482,000 was attributable to insurance premiums and commissions; and that during the same year EFCA had earnings before income taxes of $26,636,000.

(o) That on December 31, 1971, EFCA had an asset, Contracts, Notes and Loans Receivable, of $34,162,000.

(p) That on December 31, 1971, approximately $61,682,000 in funded loans and accounts receivable were held by EFCA while the remainder of the asset was pledged in connection with loans.

(q) That during 1971, 13,813 Equity Funding Programs had been sold, and that on December 31, 1971, 41,121 Equity Funding Programs were in effect.

(r) That during 1971, the insurance subsidiaries of EFCA placed in force $1,780,270,704 in face value of paid-for new life insurance policies.

(s) That during the calendar year 1971, EFLIC acquired and sold a total of approximately $78,700,000 worth of debentures and collected a total of approximately $372,109.42 interest thereon.

(t) That as of June 30, 1972, EFCA had notes receivable from Equity Funding program participants of approximately $103,525,000.

(2) Among the material facts which the said defendants would knowingly conceal and omit to disclose and would knowingly cause to be concealed and to be omitted from disclosure were:

(a) That during the calendar year 1968, EFCA incurred liabilities in the form of short-term notes and commercial paper placed through Dishy, Easton & Co., with various lenders in the amount of approximately $4,600,000 (some of which were payable in Swiss Francs) which remained outstanding at the end of 1968 and which were not disclosed on the books or financial statements of EFCA for 1968.

(b) That during the calendar year 1969, EFCA incurred liabilities in the form of short-term notes and commercial paper placed through Dishy, Easton & Co., with various lenders in the amount of approximately $15,000,000 (all of which were payable in Swiss Francs) which remained outstanding at the end of 1969 and which were not disclosed on the books and financial statements of EFCA for 1969.

(c) That during the calendar year 1970, there was inserted in the books and accounts of EFCA, and included in the financial statements of EFCA as part of Contracts and Notes Receivable, a note receivable from Etablissement Grandson, and that Etablissement Grandson was a shell corporation which did not owe EFCA the amount stated, and was without the ability or the intention to make any payments on the note.

(d) That during the calendar year 1970, certain rights to receive future commissions were purportedly sold by EFCA to Compania de Estudios y Asuntos in return for the promise of Compania de Estudios y Asuntos to pay $13,500,000, and that Compania de Estudios y Asuntos was a shell corporation which was without the ability or the intention to guarantee the payment of any sum of money.

(e) That of the $39,593,000 purportedly held by EFCA as Cash and Short-Term Investment, on December 31, 1971, approximately $20,000,000 was fictitious and that documents purporting to support the existence of the $20,000,000 had been counterfeited.

(f) That of the $24,566,791.46 of bonds purportedly owned as assets by EFLIC on December 31, 1972, more than $23,000,000 were fictitious and that both bonds and certain documents purporting to support the legitimate existence of the bonds has been counterfeited.

(3) In making use of the aforesaid false and fraudulent financial information, defendant STANLEY GOLDBLUM, through the use of the mails and by other means, would contact and would cause to be contacted various financial institutions, including Bache & Co., New York Securities Company and Smith, Barney & Co., for the purpose of arranging groups of underwriters who would be used as conduits for the sale pursuant to prospectus, through use of the mails and by other means, of EFCA securities to the investing public, and the distribution, through the use of the mails and by other means, of prospectuses containing false and fraudulent financial information concerning EFCA.

(4) In making further use of the aforesaid false and fraudulent financial information, defendants STANLEY GOLDBLUM and FRED LEVIN, through the use of the mails and by other means, would contact and would cause to be contacted representatives of various corporations for the purpose of selling and exchanging stock of EFCA in return for the stock and assets of said corporations, and, for the purpose of inducing agreement to said sales and exchanges, said defendants would arrange for the distribution, by mail and other means, of false and fraudulent financial information concerning EFCA to the officers, directors and stockholders of said corporations. Defendants STANLEY

GOLDBLUM and FRED LEVIN would conclude acquisition arrangements with various corporations and would, through the use of the mails and by other means, cause stockholders of said corporations to exchange, by mail and other means, certificates of stock representing their ownership of the acquired corporations in return for certificates of stock in EFCA.

(5) In making further use of the aforesaid false and fraudulent financial information, various of the defendants, including STANLEY GOLDBLUM, SAMUEL B. LOWELL, JEROME H. EVANS, FRED LEVIN, MICHAEL E. SULTAN, JAMES CYRUS SMITH, JR., ARTHUR STANLEY LEWIS, DAVID JACK CAPO, LLOYD DOUGLAS EDENS, LAWRENCE GREY COLLINS, JAMES HOWARD BANKS, WILLIAM MERCADO, DONALD MCCLELLAN, WILLIAM EDWARD SYMONDS, MARVIN AL LICHTIG and GARY STANLEY BECKERMAN, would sell EFCA securities which they owned and held for their own benefit, well knowing of the false and fraudulent financial information concerning EFCA which had been publicly circulated and which they had assisted in generating and circulating, and without making public disclosure of what they knew to be the false and fictitious nature of said financial information.

3. To effect the objects of said conspiracy, the defendants and unindicted co-conspirators committed divers overt acts among which are the following:

(1) On or about January 15, 1965, in the Central District of California, defendant STANLEY GOLDBLUM had the first of several conversations with defendant JEROME H. EVANS in which he told defendant JEROME H. EVANS to make fictitious entries in certain receivable and income accounts of EFCA.

(2) On or about March 8, 1965, in the Central District of California, defendant STANLEY GOLDBLUM signed one in a series of Annual Reports of EFCA, which were to be distributed to EFCA stockholders and others and which contained inflated figures for certain receivable and income accounts and for earnings per share.

(3) On or about September 30, 1966, in the Central District of California, defendants STANLEY GOLDBLUM and JEROME H. EVANS signed an application to list shares of EFCA common stock for trading on the American Stock Exchange.

(4) On or about March 15, 1968, in the Central District of California, defendants JULIAN S. H. WEINER and MARVIN AL LICHTIG, of the accounting firm of Wolfson, Weiner and Company, issued an unqualified CPA certification of the 1967 EFCA financial statements.

(5) On or about January 16, 1969, defendant STANLEY GOLDBLUM sold approximately five thousand (5,000) shares of EFCA common stock owned by him, which was one of many sales of shares of EFCA common stock owned by him.

(6) On or about January 20, 1969, defendant JEROME H. EVANS sold approximately two thousand two hundred (2,200) shares of EFCA common stock owned by him.

(7) On or about January 27, 1969, in the Central District of California, defendant JEROME H. EVANS sent a letter concerning Custodial Collateral Notes to Charles L. Hamilton at New England Merchants National Bank.

(8) On or about February 10, 1969, in the Central District of California,

defendant STANLEY GOLDBLUM signed on behalf of EFCA a note for $4,535,195, which was one of a series of notes place for EFCA through Dishy, Easton, & Company.

(9) On or about February 22, 1969, in the Central District of California, defendant STANLEY GOLDBLUM had a conversation with defendant FRED LEVIN, in which he instructed defendant FRED LEVIN that publicly held companies do not lose money.

(10) On or about March 13, 1969, in the Central District of California, defendants, STANELY GOLDBLUM, JULIAN S. H. WEINER and MARVIN AL LICHTIG had a conversation in which defendant STANLEY GOLDBLUM explained that he wanted to have certain items which he called "reciprocals" included within the EFCA account known as Funded Loans and Accounts Receivable.

(11) On or about March 21, 1969, in the Central District of California, defendants JULIAN S. H. WEINER and MARVIN AL LICHTIG and unindicted co-conspirator Wolfson Weiner Ratoff and Lapin issued an unqualified CPA certification of the 1968 EFCA financial statements.

(12) On or about September 19, 1969, in the Central District of California, defendant SAMUEL B. LOWELL had a conversation with defendant FRED LEVIN in which defendant SAMUEL B. LOWELL explained that the funded loans and accounts receivable asset account was inflated and that certain liabilities which should have been disclosed on EFCA's financial statements had not been disclosed.

(13) On or about November 30, 1969, in the Central District of California, defendant DAVID JACK CAPO, at the instruction of defendant SAMUEL B. LOWELL, made the first in a series of journal entries to an EFCA account known as Client Contractual Receivable.

(14) On or about December 15, 1969, in the Central District of California, defendants FRED LEVIN, JAMES CYRUS SMITH, JR., ARTHUR STANLEY LEWIS, LLOYD DOUGLAS EDENS and LAWRENCE GREY COLLINS had a conversation in which they discussed placing in force, and reinsuring, life insurance policies which were not in force.

(15) On or about December 15, 1969, in the Central District of California, defendant WILLIAM MERCADO supervised the preparation of a computer print-out of funded loan receivable accounts containing a total for the accounts which was intentionally inflated.

(16) On or about February 12, 1970, in the Central District of California, defendant JULIAN S. H. WEINER had a conversation with defendant SOLOMON BLOCK in which they discussed the accounting treatment which was to be given EFCA's client contractual receivable account.

(17) On or about March 24, 1970, in the Central District of California, defendants JULIAN S. H. WEINER and SOLOMON BLOCK, and unindicted co-conspirator Wolfson Weiner Ratoff and Lapin issued an unqualified CPA certification of the 1969 EFCA financial statements.

(18) On or about March 31, 1970, in the Central District of California, defendant SAMUEL B. LOWELL had a conversation with defendant MICHAEL E. SULTAN in which defendant SAMUEL B. LOWELL explained that because

EFCA's legitimate earnings for the first quarter of 1970 were insufficient, defendant MICHAEL E. SULTAN would be required to make certain journal entries to increase the income reflected on EFCA's books.

(19) On or about May 5, 1970, in the Central District of California, defendant STANLEY GOLDBLUM had a conversation with Herbert Glaser, H. O. Van Petten, Norman Sanoff and Julius Lefkowitz in which they discussed the purchase by EFCA of Liberty Savings and Loan Association.

(20) On or about May 19, 1970, defendant STANLEY GOLDBLUM signed an agreement for the purported sale to Compania de Estudios y Asuntos of the rights to certain net trail commissions.

(21) On or about June 18, 1970, in the Central District of California, defendant MICHAEL E. SULTAN made a journal entry recording notes payable to Loeb, Rhoades & Company and a note receivable from Etablissement Grandson.

(22) On or about June 29, 1970, in the Central District of California, defendants STANLEY GOLDBLUM and FRED LEVIN had a conversation with Rodney Loeb, Ronald Cameron and James Mc Elvany in which they discussed the purchase by EFCA of Independent Securities Corporation.

(23) On or about August 10, 1970, in the Central District of California, defendants FRED LEVIN, JAMES CYRUS SMITH, JR., ARTHUR STANLEY LEWIS, LLOYD DOUGLAS EDENS and LAWRENCE GREY COLLINS had a meeting in which they discussed the manner and method of creating and reinsuring fictitious insurance policies.

(24) On or about August 20, 1970, defendants STANLEY GOLDBLUM and MARVIN AL LICHTIG signed an application to list shares of EFCA common stock for trading on the New York Stock Exchange.

(25) On or about September 15, 1970, in the Central District of California, defendants STANLEY GOLDBLUM and FRED LEVIN had a conversation in which they discussed the creation and reinsurance of fictitious insurance policies.

(26) On or about October 14, 1970, defendants STANLEY GOLDBLUM and SAMUEL B. LOWELL gave instructions for two million dollars to be sent to Account Number 001-1-821-774 at Banque Cifico-Leumi in Geveva, Switzerland for the account of Etablissement Grandson.

(27) On or about November 2, 1970, in the Central district of California, defendant LESTER MICHAEL KELLER, at the direction of defendant ARTHUR STANLEY LEWIS, wrote a computer program for the creation of fictitious insurance policies having a total face amount of approximately $430,000,000 and a total yearly premium of approximately $5,500,000.

(28) On or about December 4, 1970, in the Central District of California, defendant ARTHUR STANLEY LEWIS sent a memorandum to defendants LESTER MICHAEL KELLER and JAMES CYRUS SMITH, JR., concerning the relationship between EFLIC's fictitious insurance business and its reinsurance commitment.

(29) On or about December 16, 1970, in the Central District of California, defendant SAMUEL B. LOWELL had a conversation with defendant WILLIAM MERCADO during which they discussed the preparation of a computer

print-out of funded loan receivable accounts which would contain an intentionally inflated total.

(30) On or about January 20, 1971, in the Central District of California, defendants JAMES CYRUS SMITH, JR., ARTHUR STANLEY LEWIS, LLOYD DOUGLAS EDENS and LAWRENCE GREY COLLINS and unindicted co-conspirators Francis D. Majerus and Ronald Secrist filled out and signed forms and used the forms to create fictitious insurance policy files.

(31) On or about March 1, 1971, in the Central District of California, defendants SAMUEL B. LOWELL, FRED LEVIN, JAMES CYRUS SMITH, JR., ARTHUR STANLEY LEWIS, and LLOYD DOUGLAS EDENS signed a 1970 Annual Statement of EFLIC which was to be filed and was filed with the Department of Insurance of the State of California.

(32) On or about March 15, 1971, in the Central District of California, defendants STANLEY GOLDBLUM and FRED LEVIN had a meeting with John Brundage of Bankers National Life Insurance Company in which they discussed the purchase by EFCA of Bankers National Life Insurance Company.

(33) On or about March 24, 1971, in the Central District of California, defendant JAMES CYRUS SMITH, JR., had a conversation with defendant JAMES HOWARD BANKS in which he explained that fictitious insurance policies had been reinsured and that defendant JAMES HOWARD BANKS would be expected to make death claims on various of the fictitious insurance policies.

(34) On or about April 1, 1971, in the Central District of California, defendant SAMUEL B. LOWELL had a conversation with Roger Coe, manager of Bishops Bank and Trust Company, Ltd., in which defendant SAMUEL B. LOWELL said that defendant STANLEY GOLDBLUM had given instructions for Roger Coe to cease attempting to confirm a certain $2,000,000 receivable which was on the books of Bishops Bank.

(35) On or about May 19, 1971, in the Central District of California, defendant JAMES HOWARD BANKS made the first in a series of death claims on fictitious EFLIC insurance policies by mailing to Phoenix Mutual Life Insurance Company a letter enclosing documents relating to the death of Fenton Taylor, insured under fictitious EFLIC policy number 7101481.

(36) On or about July 20, 1971, in the Central District of California, defendant RICHARD GARDENIER supervised and helped to prepare fictitious insurance files and defendants JAMES CYRUS SMITH, JR., ARTHUR STANLEY LEWIS, DANIEL JACK CAPO, LLOYD DOUGLAS EDENS, and LAWRENCE GREY COLLINS completed the documents in the fictitious files and forged signatures on them.

(37) On or about September 30, 1971, in the Central District of California, defendants SAMUEL B. LOWELL and FRED LEVIN had a conversation in which defendant SAMUEL LOWELL asked how much income EFLIC could reflect on its books in order to reduce the amount of fictitious business which would need to be inserted on EFCA's books.

(38) On or about November 30, 1971, in the Central District of California, defendants FRED LEVIN, MICHAEL E. SULTAN, JAMES CYRUS SMITH, JR., ARTHUR STANLEY LEWIS and LLOYD DOUGLAS EDENS had a meeting during which they discussed the transfer of funds from EFCA to EFLIC and the

counterfeiting of various documents reflecting fictitious purchases of commercial paper.

(39) On or about December 6, 1971, in the Central District of California, defendants STANLEY GOLDBLUM, SAMUEL B. LOWELL, FRED LEVIN and MARVIN AL LICHTIG signed a registration statement for the sale of $38,500,000 in EFCA convertible debentures, which registration statement was to be filed and was filed with the Securities and Exchange Commission.

(40) On or about December 9, 1971, in the Central District of California, defendant SAMUEL B. LOWELL had a telephone conversation with Hugh C. Brewer of First National City Bank concerning a proposed $75,000,000 loan to EFCA.

(41) On or about December 10, 1971, in the Central District of California, defendant STANLEY GOLDBLUM had a conversation with defendant MICHAEL E. SULTAN in which he told defendant MICHAEL E. SULTAN to proceed with the counterfeiting of documents relating to fictitious purchases of commercial paper.

(42) On or about December 18, 1971, in the Central District of California, defendants SAMUEL B. LOWELL and MICHAEL E. SULTAN had a conversation concerning the absence of assets in EFLIC and the necessity to transfer funds to EFLIC to conceal the absence of assets.

(43) On or about December 21, 1971, in the Central District of California, defendants ARTHUR STANLEY LEWIS and DAVID JACK CAPO had a conversation in which they discussed creation of a computer print-out listing which would contain fictitious funded loan accounts.

(44) On or about December 23, 1971, in the Central District of California, defendants MICHAEL E. SULTAN, LLOYD DOUGLAS EDENS and GARY STANLEY BECKERMAN had a conversation in which they discussed the counterfeiting of documents relating to fictitious purchases of commercial paper.

(45) On or about December 23, 1971, in the Central District of California, defendants ARTHUR STANLEY LEWIS and ALAN LEWIS GREEN had a conversation in which they discussed creating a computer print-out listing which would contain fictitious funded loan accounts.

(46) On or about January 3, 1972, in the Central District of California, defendant LESTER MICHAEL KELLER arranged to be sent through the mails to Kentucky Central Life Insurance Company, a letter enclosing a computer tape listing of EFLIC's 1971 reinsurance cession for Kentucky Central.

(47) On or about January 14, 1972, in the Central District of California, defendant WILLIAM EDWARD SYMONDS, upon instructions of defendants ARTHUR STANLEY LEWIS and LLOYD DOUGLAS EDENS, began manipulating computer records so as falsely to show five thousand lapsed policies to be in force.

(48) On or about February 15, 1972, in the Central District of California, defendants FRED LEVIN and JAMES CYRUS SMITH, JR., had the first in a series of conversations during which they discussed the amount of fictitious insurance business which would have to be created in 1972.

(49) On or about March 1, 1972, in the Central District of California, defendants MICHAEL E. SULTAN and SOLOMON BLOCK had a conversation

during which they discussed the making of an intentional mistake in the calculation of EFCA's 1971 earnings per share.

(50) On or about March 10, 1972, in the Central District of California, defendants WILLIAM EDWARD SYMONDS and RICHARD GARDENIER had a conversation during which they discussed the creation of fictitious insurance files.

(51) On or about March 15, 1972, in the Central District of California, defendants STANLEY GOLDBLUM, SAMUEL B. LOWELL and MICHAEL E. SULTAN had a conversation during which they discussed the making of fictitious entries to EFCA's Funded Loans and Accounts Receivable account and commission income accounts.

(52) On or about April 4, 1972, in the Central District of California, defendant MARVIN AL LICHTIG signed an EFCA annual report on Form 10-K which was to be filed and was filed with the Securities and Exchange Commission and which contained EFCA's 1971 financial statements.

(53) On or about April 11, 1972, in the Central District of California, defendant SAMUEL B. LOWELL had a meeting with L. E. Holloway of Wells Fargo Bank during which they discussed a $75,000,000 credit agreement and defendant SAMUEL B. LOWELL delivered to the said L. E. Holloway various EFCA Annual Reports.

(54) On or about June 15, 1972, in the Central District of California, defendants SAMUEL B. LOWELL, MICHAEL E. SULTAN and JULIAN S. H. WEINER had a conversation during which they discussed the making of a payment on a note receivable from Etablissement Grandson.

(55) On or about June 29, 1972, in the Central District of California, defendant JAMES CYRUS SMITH, JR., sent a letter to Dan Di Sipio which set forth the terms of a reinsurance agreement between EFCA and Pennsylvania Life Insurance Company and which gave instructions on the manner in which certain checks were to be made out.

(56) On or about July 14, 1972, in the Central District of California, defendants JAMES CYRUS SMITH, JR., ARTHUR STANLEY LEWIS, DAVID JACK CAPO, LAWRENCE GREY COLLINS, LLOYD DOUGLAS EDENS, JAMES HOWARD BANKS, MARK CHARLES LEWIS and RICHARD GARDENIER helped to prepare fictitious hard copy insurance documents and forged signatures on the documents.

(57) On or about July 28, 1972, in the Central District of California, defendant ALAN LEWIS GREEN sent a computer tape listing of EFLIC's second quarter 1972 reinsurance cession to Ranger National Life Insurance Company.

(58) On or about September 1, 1972, in the Central District of California, defendants STANLEY GOLDBLUM and FRED LEVIN had a conversation in which they discussed the sale of single premium annuities.

(59) On or about October 26, 1972, in the Central District of California, defendants STANLEY GOLDBLUM, FRED LEVIN, MICHAEL E. SULTAN, JAMES CYRUS SMITH, JR., ARTHUR S. LEWIS and LLOYD DOUGLAS EDENS had a conversation in which they discussed the printing of counterfeit bonds.

(60) On or about December 18, 1972, in the Central District of California, defendant STANLEY GOLDBLUM had a telephone conversation with defen-

dant FRED LEVIN in which they discussed the renting of an office in Chicago, Illinois, to be used as a mail drop in connection with the use of counterfeit bank documents.

(61) On or about December 20, 1972, in the Central District of California, on the instructions of defendant STANLEY GOLDBLUM, defendant GARY STANLEY BECKERMAN ordered stationery bearing the letterhead of the American National Bank and Trust Company of Chicago.

(62) On or about December 27, 1972, in the Central District of California, defendants DAVID JACK CAPO and DONALD MCCLELLAN compiled addresses of various persons to whom funded loan confirmations could be sent.

(63) On or about January 5, 1973, in the Central District of California, defendant SAMUEL B. LOWELL had a conversation with unindicted coconspirator William Gootnick concerning the company's fictitious life insurance business.

(64) On or about January 8, 1973, in the Central District of California, defendant JAMES HOWARD BANKS had a conversation with defendant JAMES CYRUS SMITH, JR., in which they discussed the amount of money to be derived in 1973 from making death claims on fictitious life insurance policies.

(65) On or about January 15, 1973, in the Central District of California, defendant MICHAEL E. SULTAN made entries on counterfeit bank documents relating to fictitious purchases of commercial paper.

(66) On or about January 15, 1973, in the Central District of California, defendants FRED LEVIN, JAMES CYRUS SMITH, JR., MICHAEL E. SULTAN, LLOYD DOUGLAS EDENS and GARY STANLEY BECKERMAN met at EFCA's printing plant and commenced the printing of counterfeit bonds.

(67) On or about February 27, 1973, in the Central District of California, defendants LESTER MICHAEL KELLER and ALAN LEWIS GREEN instructed unindicted co-conspirator Aaron Venouziou on writing computer programs for fictitious insurance business.

(68) On or about March 12, 1973, in the Central District of California, defendants STANLEY GOLDBLUM, FRED LEVIN, MICHAEL E. SULTAN, JAMES CYRUS SMITH, JR., ARTHUR STANLEY LEWIS, LLOYD DOUGLAS EDENS and JAMES HOWARD BANKS had a conversation in which they discussed disposition of the counterfeit bonds.

(69) On or about March 14, 1973, in the Central District of California, defendant WILLIAM EDWARD SYMONDS set computer print-out listings of insurance reserve rates and values to Kentucky Central Life Insurance Company and Great Southern Life Insurance Company.

(70) On or about March 14, 1973, in the Central District of California, defendant STANLEY GOLDBLUM had a conversation with defendant JAMES HOWARD BANKS in which they discussed the electronic surveillance of state insurance examiners who were working on EFCA's business premises.

(71) On or about March 14, 1973, in the Central District of California, defendants LAWRENCE GREY COLLINS and JAMES HOWARD BANKS together with Steven Michael Goodman and Lorn Aiken made the first of a series of installations of electronic surveillance equipment in an office where state insurance examiners were working on EFCA's business premises.

(72) On or about March 22, 1973, in the Central District of California, unindicted co-conspirator William Gootnick on the instructions of defendants JAMES CYRUS SMITH, JR., ARTHUR STANLEY LEWIS, LLOYD DOUGLAS EDENS, LAWRENCE GREY COLLINS and JAMES HOWARD BANKS, supervised the writing of computer programs designed to conceal the existence of EFLIC's fictitious insurance business from auditors and state insurance examiners.

(73) On or about March 23, 1973, in the Central District of California, defendants LAWRENCE GREY COLLINS, WILLIAM EDWARD SYMONDS and MARK CHARLES LEWIS, at the instructions of the defendant JAMES CYRUS SMITH, JR., removed all documents relating to the creation of insurance files from 341 North Maple Drive, Beverly Hills, California.

(74) On or about March 26, 1973, defendants STANLEY GOLDBLUM, SAMUEL B. LOWELL, FRED LEVIN, MICHAEL E. SULTAN, JAMES CYRUS SMITH, JR., ARTHUR STANLEY LEWIS, LLOYD DOUGLAS EDENS, LAWRENCE GREY COLLINS, JAMES HOWARD BANKS and DONALD MC CLELLAN sold shares of EFCA stock which they owned.

(75) On or about March 27, 1973, in the Central District of California, defendants LAWRENCE GREY COLLINS and JAMES HOWARD BANKS, together with Steven Michael Goodman and Lorn Aiken, tried to install electronic surveillance equipment designed to intercept telephone conversations of state insurance examiners.

(76) On or about March 30, 1973, in the Central District of California, defendant MARVIN AL LICHTIG had a conversation with defendant FRED LEVIN during which defendant MARVIN AL LICHTIG asked whether defendant FRED LEVIN wanted any documents destroyed.

Appendix C
A Brief Survey of Programmer Ethics and Honesty

THIS appendix appeared as Appendix B to the final report *COMPUTER ABUSE* prepared by Donn B. Parker, Susan Nycum and S. Stephen Oüra of Stanford Research Institute, for The National Science Foundation, RANN NSF/RA/S-73-017. It is presented here to acquaint management with the attitudes and ethics prevailing within the computer profession.

Donn B. Parker of SRI talked on Computer-Related Crime at a dinner meeting on April 12, 1973, of the San Francisco Peninsula Chapter, ACM. The results of a questionnaire he distributed there are presented below.

The respondents were told in answering the questions to assume that malicious intent was present which could result in losses, injuries, or damage to innocent victims. Definitions of what constitutes unethical, dishonest, and illegal behavior were purposely left for each respondent to decide.

The results are presented in four groups based on programming, management, and service company employment, as follows:

Group	*Number of Respondents*
1. Managers of programmers (all with programming experience) in noncomputer service organizations	14
2. Managers of programmers (all with time-sharing terminal experience) in computer service organizations	4
3. Programmers in computer service organizations.	12
4. Programmers in noncomputer service organizations.	24
One claiming none of these categories and not counted in total below	1
Total	55

QUESTIONNAIRE

Suppose you have signed a standard contract to use and pay for time-sharing services. The contract does not include any limitations about what you can and cannot do through your terminal.

Please indicate below your opinion about each of the described actions.

1. Request a listing of a program from the on-line program library and use it in another computer.

Group	Okay	Unethical	Dishonest	Illegal	Can't Decide	Have done it
1	7	2	2	0	2	4
2	3	1	0	0	0	2
3	7	1	1	1	0	2
4	15	8	3	3	1	1
	32	12	6	4	3	9

2. Request of listing of a program from the computer, discover a comment statement in the program stating that the program is the property of the time-sharing service, but use it in another computer in spite of that.

Group	Okay	Unethical	Dishonest	Illegal	Can't Decide	Have done it
1	2	8	2	2	0	0
2	0	2	1	1	1	0
2	3	4	2	2	0	0
4	4	9	6	8	1	0
	9	23	11	13	2	0

3. Attempt to discover unpublished system commands by trial and error for the purpose of using them in your work.

Group	Okay	Unethical	Dishonest	Illegal	Can't Decide	Have done it
1	8	4	2	1	0	4
2	4	0	0	0	0	3
3	7	0	0	0	1	2
4	15	5	2	3	1	3
	34	9	4	4	2	12

4. Attempt to discover another user's LOGON identification to use one of his programs.

Group	Okay	Unethical	Dishonest	Illegal	Can't Decide	Have done it
1	2	6	7	1	1	4
2	0	4	1	0	0	0
3	2	4	3	2	0	1
4	1	12	8	5	1	4
	5	26	19	8	2	9

5. Use a time-sharing salesman's LOGON identification to obtain unauthorized service usage.

Group	Okay	Unethical	Dishonest	Illegal	Can't Decide	Have done it
1	1	3	8	5	0	1
2	0	3	2	0	0	1
3	1	1	7	1	0	0
4	1	5	11	12	1	1
	3	12	28	18	1	3

6. Use a LOGON identification that you accidentally discovered by making a mistake in using your own LOGON identification.

Group	*Okay*	*Unethical*	*Dishonest*	*Illegal*	*Can't Decide*	*Have done it*
1	1	2	11	1	1	0
2	0	3	2	0	0	0
3	2	2	3	2	2	0
4	1	7	12	10	1	1
	4	14	28	13	4	1

7. Attempt to LOGON to a time-sharing service for which you are not an authorized user.

Group	*Okay*	*Unethical*	*Dishonest*	*Illegal*	*Can't Decide*	*Have done it*
1	2	5	3	5	0	3
2	2	2	1	0	0	1
3	3	2	3	1	0	3
4	6	3	5	11	2	3
	13	12	12	17	2	10

8. Offer the use of a program you have written at your employer's expense to an employee of a different employer without permission.

Group	*Okay*	*Unethical*	*Dishonest*	*Illegal*	*Can't Decide*	*Have done it*
1	2	6	1	6	0	2
2	1	4	2	0	0	2
3	5	4	2	1	2	1
4	5	12	4	7	2	2
	13	26	9	14	4	7

9. Accept and use a program given to you by a friend working for another company.

Group	*Okay*	*Unethical*	*Dishonest*	*Illegal*	*Can't Decide*	*Have done it*
1	7	5	2	0	0	2
2	4	1	0	0	0	2
3	7	2	2	1	0	3
4	15	6	5	1	2	2
	33	14	9	2	2	9

10. Exchange programs with others without written agreements.

Group	*Okay*	*Unethical*	*Dishonest*	*Illegal*	*Can't Decide*	*Have done it*
1	7	2	1	1	3	2
2	4	0	0	0	0	3
3	5	2	2	1	0	2
4	14	4	3	3	4	3
	30	8	6	5	7	10

11. For amusement, attempt to do things through a terminal not described in the user's manuals.

Group	*Okay*	*Unethical*	*Dishonest*	*Illegal*	*Can't Decide*	*Have done it*
1	12	0	1	0	1	4
2	4	0	0	0	0	3
3	8	1	0	0	0	3
4	23	0	0	0	0	4
	47	1	1	0	1	14

12. Accept the challenge offered by a time-sharing service to penetrate the security of a system.

Group	*Okay*	*Unethical*	*Dishonest*	*Illegal*	*Can't Decide*	*Have done it*
1	10	2	1	1	1	3
2	3	0	0	0	1	0
3	9	0	0	0	0	1
4	13	4	3	2	5	5
	35	6	4	3	7	9

Even a brief examination of the above results uncovers a significant lack of agreement over what constitutes accepted practices among the respondents. Question 7 shows an almost even distribution of reaction to attempted unauthorized use of a time-sharing service, and ten respondents said it is okay to offer the use of a program to another organization without permission, and half said it is only unethical. This may indicate that programmers feel that they have at least some rights to programs they have written for their employers. Answers to Questions 1 and 2 indicate considerable support to the "Peninsula Ethic" that a program is a period in the public domain unless demonstrated otherwise by elaborate precautions. (This ethic relates to a 1971 criminal case in the San Francisco Bay Area over the theft of a program "trade secret.")

Listed below are comments submitted by respondents when asked to "Indicate any other practice you believe is questionable but is in use." (Two comments have not been repeated here because of their potentially libelous nature.)

Using computer communication systems for personal use, conversations.

Using computer access for program testing to obtain data base information (driver's license and vehicle registration).

Using computer time for game playing and other recreation.

Computer programs are the written embodiment of a stream of logic or thought. Although I believe in protecting wordings—for example, copyright—I do not believe in "protecting thoughts "—for example, patent. Mathematical formulas and program ideas should not be protected.

Use employer's computer facilities to develop programs for one's own benefit or usage.

I believe the dishonest imposition of finance charges by banks, loan companies, etc., fits the category of computer crime.

Unwarranted prosecution and unwarranted designation of programs as proprietary or as trade secrets.

Let us develop standards for program testing to create substantive definition of programming malpractice.

Billing and dunning systems must take special precautions against error and should probably have ancillary human systems with adequate notice available as to how to get to the people. This is probably the most serious (i.e., widespread) offense concerned with unethical behavior. Unfortunately, it usually can't be traced back to one individual.

Use a known proprietary program in a way which avoids proprietary charge.

Use a computer to send out phony bills (either totally false, or adding, say 5–10% additional quantity of standard items) could also be done as a company policy.

Use proprietary data to predict stock market changes (de facto insider info).

Receiving info whose source believes you still hold a former job.

Using employer's computer after hours for running a personal program.

Taking listings and internal documentation when changing jobs.

Cruel and inhuman working time, hours and conditions, especially of systems personnel (Not my current company, or much of previous company, but it is an illegal, unethical and dishonest use of human beings—I have been severely subjected to it in the past.) I suspect a very prevalent case of "theft" is the use of computer resources for personal use by employees of service bureaus, manufacturers or any other computer installation.

Computer matching or dating services for which nobody can generally describe the matching algorithm. By generally, I mean four or more statements. (Most use high-pressure tactics.)

I believe the following is particularly prevalent in universities. Use of legitimately acquired computer funds for classwork used for either personal use or for classwork in other courses. Also, use of funds and LOGONS acquired through working for a department at the university or for a company in town using the university's computer system for purposes other than intended (like for classwork). These acts were prevalent at the university I attended.

Unauthorized copying of load modules onto tape for personal or public use at another location (batch system).

Unauthorized access of documentation on certain proprietary programs (i.e., HASP, IBM's confidential information, etc.).

Appendix D
The Fair Credit Reporting Act
Public Law 91-508

SECTION 601. The Consumer Credit Protection Act is amended by adding at the end thereof the following new title:

TITLE VI—CONSUMER CREDIT REPORTING

§601. *Short title*

This title may be cited as the Fair Credit Reporting Act.

§602. *Findings and purpose*

(a) The Congress makes the following findings:

(1) The banking system is dependent upon fair and accurate credit reporting. Inaccurate credit reports directly impair the efficiency of the banking system, and unfair credit reporting methods undermine the public confidence which is essential to the continued functioning of the banking system.

(2) An elaborate mechanism has been developed for investigating and evaluating the credit worthiness, credit standing, credit capacity, character, and general reputation of consumers.

(3) Consumer reporting agencies have assumed a vital role in assembling and evaluating consumer credit and other information on consumers.

(4) There is a need to ensure that consumer reporting agencies exercise their grave responsibilities with fairness, impartiality, and a respect for the consumer's right to privacy.

(b) It is the purpose of this title to require that consumer reporting agencies adopt reasonable procedures for meeting the needs of commerce for consumer credit, personnel, insurance, and other information in a manner which is fair and equitable to the consumer, with regard to the confidentiality, accuracy, relevancy, and proper utilization of such information in accordance with the requirements of this title.

§603. *Definitions and rules and construction*

(a) Definitions and rules of construction set forth in this section are applicable for the purposes of this title.

(b) The term 'person' means any individual, partnership, corporation, trust, estate, cooperative, association, government or governmental subdivision or agency, or other entity.

(c) The term 'consumer' means an individual.

(d) The term 'consumer report' means any written, oral, or other communication of any information by a consumer reporting agency bearing on a consumer's credit worthiness, credit standing, credit capacity, character, general reputation, personal characteristics, or mode of living which is used or expected to be used or collected in whole or in part for the purpose of serving as a factor in establishing the consumer's eligibility for (1) credit or insurance to be used primarily for personal, family, or household purposes, or (2) employment purposes, or (3) other purposes authorized under section 604. The term does not include (A) any report containing information solely as to transactions or experiences between the consumer and the person making the report; (B) any authorization or approval of a specific extension of credit directly or indirectly by the issuer of a credit card or similar device; or (C) any report in which a person who has been requested by a third party to make a specific extension of credit directly or indirectly to a consumer conveys his decision with respect to such request, if the third party advises the consumer of the name and address of the person to whom the request was made and such person makes the disclosures to the consumer required under section 615.

(c) The term 'investigative consumer report' means a consumer report or portion thereof in which information on a consumer's character, general reputation, personal characteristics, or mode of living is obtained through personal interviews with neighbors, friends, or associates of the consumer reported on or with others with whom he is acquainted or who may have knowledge concerning any such items of information. However, such information shall not include specific factual information on a consumer's credit record obtained directly from a creditor of the consumer or from a consumer reporting agency when such information was obtained directly from a creditor of the consumer or from the consumer.

(f) The term 'consumer reporting agency' means any person which, for monetary fees, dues, or on a cooperative nonprofit basis, regularly engages in whole or in part in the practice of assembling or evaluating consumer credit information or other information on consumers for the purpose of furnishing consumer reports to third parties, and which uses any means or facility of interstate commerce for the purpose of preparing or furnishing consumer reports.

(g) The term 'file', when used in connection with information on any consumer, means all of the information on that consumer recorded and retained by a consumer reporting agency regardless of how the information is stored.

(h) The term 'employment purposes' when used in connection with a consumer report means a report used for the purpose of evaluating a consumer for employment, promotion, reassignment or retention as an employee.

(i) The term 'medical information' means information or records obtained, with the consent of the individual to whom it relates, from licensed physicians or medical practitioners, hospitals, clinics, or other medical or medically related facilities.

§604. *Permissible purposes of reports*

A consumer reporting agency may furnish a consumer report under the following circumstances and no other:

(1) In response to the order of a court having jurisdiction to issue such an order.

(2) In accordance with the written instructions of the consumer to whom it relates.

(3) To a person which it has reason to believe——

(A) intends to use the information in connection with a credit transaction involving the consumer on whom the information is to be furnished and involving the extension of credit to, or review or collection of an account of, the consumer; or

(B) intends to use the information for employment purposes; or

(C) intends to use the information in connection with the underwriting of insurance involving the consumer; or

(D) intends to use the information in connection with a determination of the consumer's eligibility for a license or other benefit granted by a governmental instrumentality required by law to consider an applicant's financial responsibility or status; or

(E) otherwise has a legitimate business need for the information in connection with a business transaction involving the consumer.

§605. *Obsolete Information*

(a) Except as authorized under subsection (b), no consumer reporting agency may make any consumer report containing any of the following items of information:

(1) Bankruptcies which, from date of adjudication of the most recent bankruptcy, antedate the report by more than fourteen years.

(2) Suits and judgments which, from date of entry, antedate the report by more than seven years or until the governing statute of limitations has expired, whichever is the longer period.

(3) Paid tax liens which, from date of payment, antedate the report by more than seven years.

(4) Accounts placed for collection or charged to profit and loss which antedate the report by more than seven years.

(5) Records of arrest, indictment or conviction of crime which, from date of disposition, release or parole, antedate the report by more than seven years.

(6) Any other adverse item of information which antedates the report by more than seven years.

(b) The provisions of subsection (a) are not applicable in the case of any consumer credit report to be used in connection with —

(1) a credit transaction involving, or which may reasonably be expected to involve, a principal amount of $50,000 or more;

(2) the underwriting of life insurance involving, or which may reasonably be expected to involve, a principal amount of $50,000 or more; or

(3) the employment of any individual at an annual salary which equals, or which may reasonably be expected to equal, $20,000 or more.

§606. *Disclosure of investigative consumer reports*

(a) a person may not procure or cause to be prepared an investigative consumer report on any consumer unless—

(1) it is clearly and accurately disclosed to the consumer that an investigative consumer report including information as to his character, general reputation, personal characteristics, and mode of living, whichever are applicable, may be made, and such disclosure (A) is made in a writing mailed, or otherwise delivered to the consumer, not later than three days after the date on which the report was first requested, and (B) includes a statement informing the consumer of his right to request the additional disclosures provided for under subsection (b) of this section; or

(2) the report is to be used for employment purposes for which the consumer has not specifically applied.

(b) Any person who procures or causes to be prepared an investigative consumer report on any consumer shall, upon written request by the consumer within a reasonable period of time after the receipt by him of the disclosure required by subsection (a) (1), shall make a complete and accurate disclosure of the nature and scope of the investigation requested. This disclosure shall be made in a writing mailed, or otherwise delivered, to the consumer not later than five days after the date on which the request for such disclosures was received from the consumer or such report was first requested, whichever is the later.

(c) No person may be held liable for any violation of subsection (a) or (b) of this section if he shows by a preponderance of the evidence that at the time of the violation he maintained reasonable procedures to assure compliance with subsection (a) or (b).

§607. *Compliance procedures*

(a) Every consumer reporting agency shall maintain reasonable procedures designed to avoid violations of section 605 and to limit the furnishing of consumer reports to the purposes listed under section 604. These procedures shall require that prospective users of the information identify themselves, certify the purposes for which the information is sought, and certify that the information will be used for no other purpose. Every consumer reporting agency shall make a reasonable effort to verify the identify of a new prospective user and the uses certified by such prospective user prior to furnishing such user a consumer report. No consumer reporting agency may furnish a consumer report to any person if it has reasonable grounds for believing that the consumer report will not be used for a purpose listed in section 604.

(b) Whenever a consumer reporting agency prepares a consumer report it shall follow reasonable procedures to assure maximum possible accuracy of the information concerning the individual about whom the report relates.

§608. *Disclosures to governmental agencies*

Notwithstanding the provisions of section 604, a consumer reporting agency may furnish identifying information respecting any consumer, limited to his name, address, former address, places of employment, or former places of employment, to a governmental agency.

§609. *Disclosures to consumers*

(a) Every consumer reporting agency shall, upon request and proper identification of any consumer, clearly and accurately disclose to the consumer:

(1) The nature and substance of all information (except medical information) in its files on the consumer at the time of the request.

(2) The sources of the information except that the sources of information acquired solely for use in preparing an investigative consumer report and actually used for no other purpose need not be disclosed PROVIDED: That in the event an action is brought under this title, such sources shall be available to the plantiff under appropriate discovery procedures in the court in which the action is brought.

(3) The recipients of any consumer report on the consumer which it has furnished——

(A) for employment purposes within the two-year period preceding the request, and

(B) for any other purpose within the six-month period preceding the request.

(b) The requirements of subsection (a) respecting the disclosure of sources of information and the recipients of consumer reports do not apply to information received or consumer reports furnished prior to the effective date of this title except to the extent that the matter involved is contained in the files of the consumer reporting agency on that date.

§610. *Conditions of disclosure to consumers*

(a) A consumer reporting agency shall make the disclosures required under section 609 during normal business hours and on reasonable notice.

(b) the disclosures required under section 609 shall be made to the consumer——

(1) in person if he appears in person and furnishes proper identification; or

(2) by telephone if he has made a written request, with proper identification, for telephone disclosure and the toll charge, if any, for the telephone call is prepaid by or charged directly to the consumer.

(c) Any consumer reporting agency shall provide trained personnel to explain to the consumer any information furnished to him pursuant to section 609.

(d) The consumer shall be permitted to be accompanied by one other person of his choosing, who shall furnish reasonable identification. A consumer reporting agency may require the consumer to furnish a written statement granting permission to the consumer reporting agency to discuss the consumer's file in such person's presence.

(e) Except as noted in sections 616 and 617, no consumer may bring any action or proceeding in the nature of defamation, invasion of privacy, or negligence with respect to the reporting of information against any consumer, reporting agency, any user of information, or any person who furnishes information to a consumer reporting agency, based on information disclosed pursuant to section 609, 610, or 615, except as to false information furnished with malice or willful intent to injure such consumer.

§611. *Procedure in case of disputed accuracy*

(a) If the completeness or accuracy of any item of information contained in his file is disputed by a consumer, and such dispute is directly conveyed to the consumer reporting agency by the consumer, the consumer reporting agency shall within a reasonable period of time reinvestigate and record the current status of that information unless it has reasonable grounds to believe that the dispute by the consumer is frivolous or irrelevant. If after such reinvestigation such information is found to be inaccurate or can no longer be verified, the consumer reporting agency shall promptly delete such information. The presence of contradictory information in the consumer's file does not in and of itself constitute reasonable grounds for believing the dispute is frivolous or irrelevant.

(b) If the reinvestigation does not resolve the dispute, the consumer may file a brief statement setting forth the nature of the dispute. The consumer reporting agency may limit such statements to not more than one hundred words if it provides the consumer with assistance in writing a clear summary of the dispute.

(c) Whenever a statement of a dispute is filed, unless there is reasonable ground to believe that it is frivolous or irrelevant, the consumer reporting agency shall, in any subsequent consumer report containing the information in question, clearly note that it is disputed by the consumer and provide either the consumer's statement or a clear and accurate codification or summary thereof.

(d) Following any deletion of information which is found to be inaccurate or whose accuracy can no longer be verified or any notation as to disputed information, the consumer reporting agency shall, at the request of the consumer, furnish notification that the item has been deleted or the statement, codification or summary pursuant to subsection (b) or (c) to any person specifically designed by the consumer who has within two years prior thereto received a consumer report for employment purposes, or within six months prior thereto received a consumer report for any other purpose, which contained the deleted or disputed information. The consumer reporting agency shall clearly and conspicuously disclose to the consumer his rights to make such a request. Such disclosure shall be made at or prior to the time the information is deleted or the consumer's statement regarding the disputed information is received.

§612. *Charges for certain disclosures*

A consumer reporting agency shall make all disclosures pursuant to section 609 and furnish all consumer reports pursuant to section 611(d) without charge to the consumer if, within thirty days after receipt by such consumer of a notification pursuant to section 615 or notification from a debt collection agency affiliated with such consumer reporting agency stating that the consumer's credit rating may be or has been adversely affected, the consumer makes a request under sections 609 or 611(d). Otherwise, the consumer reporting agency may impose a reasonable charge on the consumer for making disclosure to such consumer pursuant to section 609, the charge for which shall be indicated to the consumer prior to making disclosure; and for furnishing notifications, statements, summaries, or codifications, to persons designated by the consumer pursuant to section 611(d), the charge for which shall be indicated to the consumer prior to furnishing such information and shall not exceed the charge that the consumer reporting agency would impose on each designated recipient for a consumer report except that no charge may be made for notifying such persons of the deletion of information which is found to be inaccurate or which can no longer be verified.

§613. *Public record information for employment purposes*

A consumer reporting agency which furnishes a consumer report for employment purposes and which for that purpose compiles and reports items of information on consumers which are matters of public record and are likely to have an adverse effect upon a consumer's ability to obtain employment shall——

(1) at the time such public record information is reported to the user of such consumer report, notify the consumer of the fact that public record information is being reported by the consumer reporting agency, together with the name and address of the person to whom such information is being reported; or

(2) maintain strict procedures designed to insure that whenever public record information which is likely to have an adverse effect on a consumer's ability to obtain employment is reported it is complete and up to date. For purposes of this paragraph, items of public record relating to arrests, indictment, convictions, suits, tax liens, and outstanding judgments shall be considered up to date if the current public record status of the item at the time of the report is reported.

§ 614. *Restrictions on investigative consumer reports*

Whenever a consumer reporting agency prepares an investigative consumer report (other than information which is a matter of public record) may be included in a subsequent consumer report unless such adverse information has been verified in the process of making such subsequent consumer report, or the adverse information was received within the three-month period preceding the date the subsequent report is furnished.

§615. *Requirements on users of consumer reports*

(a) Whenever credit or insurance for personal, family or household purposes, or employment involving a consumer is denied or the charge for such credit or insurance is increased either wholly or partly because of information contained in a consumer report from a consumer reporting agency, the user of the consumer report shall so advise the consumer against whom such adverse action has been taken and supply the name and address of the consumer reporting agency making the report.

(b) Whenever credit for personal, family, or household purposes involving a consumer is denied or the charge for such credit is increased either wholly or partly because of information obtained from a person other than a consumer reporting agency bearing upon the consumer's credit worthiness, credit standing, credit capacity, character, general reputation, personal characteristics, or mode of living, the user of such information shall, within a reasonable period of time, upon the consumer's written request for the reasons for such adverse action received within sixty days after learning of such adverse action, disclose the nature of the information to the consumer. The user of such information shall clearly and accurately disclose to the consumer his right to make such written request at the time such adverse action is communicated to the consumer.

(c) No person shall be held liable for any violation of this section if he shows by a preponderance of the evidence that at the time of the alleged violation he maintained reasonable procedures to assure compliance with the provisions of subsections (a) and (b).

§616. *Civil liability for willful noncompliance*

Any consumer reporting agency or user of information which willfully fails to comply with any requirement imposed under this title with respect to any consumer is liable to that consumer in an amount equal to the sum of——

(1) any actual damages sustained by the consumer as a result of the failure;

(2) such amount of punitive damages as the court may allow, and

(3) in the case of any successful action to enforce any liability under this section, the costs of the action together with reasonable attorney's fees as determined by the court.

§617. *Civil liability for grossly negligent noncompliance*

Any consumer reporting agency or user of information which is negligent in failing to comply with any requirement imposed under this title with respect to any consumer is liable to that consumer in an amount equal to the sum of——

(1) any actual damages sustained by the consumer as a result of the failure;

(2) in the case of any successful action to enforce any liability under this section, the costs of the action together with reasonable attorney's fees as determined by the court.

§618. *Jurisdiction of courts; limitation of actions*

An action to enforce any liability created under this title may be brought in any appropriate United States district court without regard to the amount in controversy, or in any other court of competent jurisdiction, within two years from the date on which the liability arises, except that where a defendent has materially and willfully misrepresented any information required under this title to be disclosed to an individual and the information so misrepresented is material to the establishment of the defendent's liability to that individual under this title, the action may be brought at any time within two years after discovery by the individual of the misrepresentation.

§619. *Obtaining information under false pretenses*

Any person who knowingly and willfully obtains information on a consumer from a consumer reporting agency under false pretenses shall be fined not more than $5,000 or imprisoned not more than one year, or both.

§620. *Unauthorized disclosures by officers or employees*

Any officer or employee of a consumer reporting agency who knowingly and willfully provides information concerning an individual from the agency's files to a person not authorized to receive that information shall be fined not more than $5,000 or imprisoned not more than one year, or both.

§621. *Administrative enforcement*

(a) Compliance with the requirements imposed under this title shall be enforced under the Federal Trade Commission Act by the Federal Trade Commission with respect to consumer reporting agencies, and all other persons subject thereto except to the extent that enforcement of the requirements imposed under this title is specifically committed to some other government agency under subsection (b) hereof. For the purpose of the exercise by the Federal Trade Commission of its functions and powers under the Federal Trade Commission Act, a violation of any requirement or prohibition imposed under this title shall constitute an unfair or deceptive act or practice in commerce in violation of section 5(a) of the Federal Trade Commission Act and shall be subject to enforcement by the Federal Trade Commission under section 5(b) thereof with respect to any consumer reporting agency or person subject to enforcement by the Federal Trade Commission pursuant to this subsection, irrespective of whether that person is engaged in commerce or meets any other jurisdictional tests in the Federal Trade Commission Act. The Federal Trade Commission shall have such procedural, investigative, and enforcement powers, including the power to issue procedural rules in enforcing compliance with the requirements imposed under this title and to require the filing of reports, the production of documents, and the appearance of witnesses as though the applicable terms and conditions of the Federal Trade Commission Act were part of this title. Any person violating any of the provisions of this title shall be subject to the penalties and entitled to the privileges and immunities provided in the Federal Trade Commision Act as though the applicable terms and provisions thereof were part of this title.

(b) Compliance with the requirements imposed under this title with respect to consumer reporting agencies and persons who use consumer reports from such agencies shall be enforced under——

(1) section 8 of the Federal Deposit Insurance Act, in the case of:

(A) national banks, by the Comptroller of the Currency;

(B) member banks of the Federal Reserve System (other than national banks), by the Federal Reserve Board; and

(C) banks insured by the Federal Deposit Insurance Corporation (other than members of the Federal Reserve System), by the Board of Directors of the Federal Deposit Insurance Corporation.

(2) section 5(d) of the Home Owners Loan Act of 1933, section 407 of the National Housing Act, and sections 6(i) and 17 of the Federal Home Loan Act, by the Federal Home Loan Bank Board (acting directly or through the Federal Savings and Loan Insurance Corporation), in the case of any institution subject to any of those provisions;

(3) the Federal Credit Union Act, by the Administrator of the National Credit Union Administration with respect to any Federal credit union;

(4) the Acts to regulate commerce, by the Interstate Commerce Commission with respect to any common carrier subject to those Acts;

(5) the Federal Aviation Act of 1958, by the Civil Aeronautics Board with respect to any air carrier or foreign air carrier subject to that Act; and

(6) the Packers and Stockyards Act, 1921 (except as provided in section 406 of that Act), by the Secretary of Agriculture with respect to any activities subject to that Act.

(c) For the purpose of the exercise by an agency referred to in subsection (b) of its powers under any Act referred to in that subsection, a violation of any requirement imposed under this title shall be deemed to be a violation of a requirement imposed under that Act. In addition to its powers under any provision of law specifically referred to in subsection (b), each of the agencies referred to in the subsection may exercise, for the purpose of enforcing compliance with any requirement imposed under this title any other authority conferred on it by law.

§622. *Relation to State laws*

This title does not annul, alter, affect, or exempt any person subject to the provisions of this title from complying with the laws of any State with respect to the collection, distribution, or use of any information on consumers, except to the extent that those laws are inconsistent with any provision of this title, and then only to the extent of the inconsistency.

EFFECTIVE DATE

Sec. 602. Section 504 of the Consumer Credit Protection Act is amended by adding at the end thereof the following subsection:

(d) Title VI takes effect upon the expiration of one hundred and eighty days following the date of its enactment."

Index